SINGER

the new
STEP-BY-STEP
HOME DECORATING PROJECTS

CREATIVE
PUBLISHING
international

CHANHASSEN, MINNESOTA
www.creativepub.com

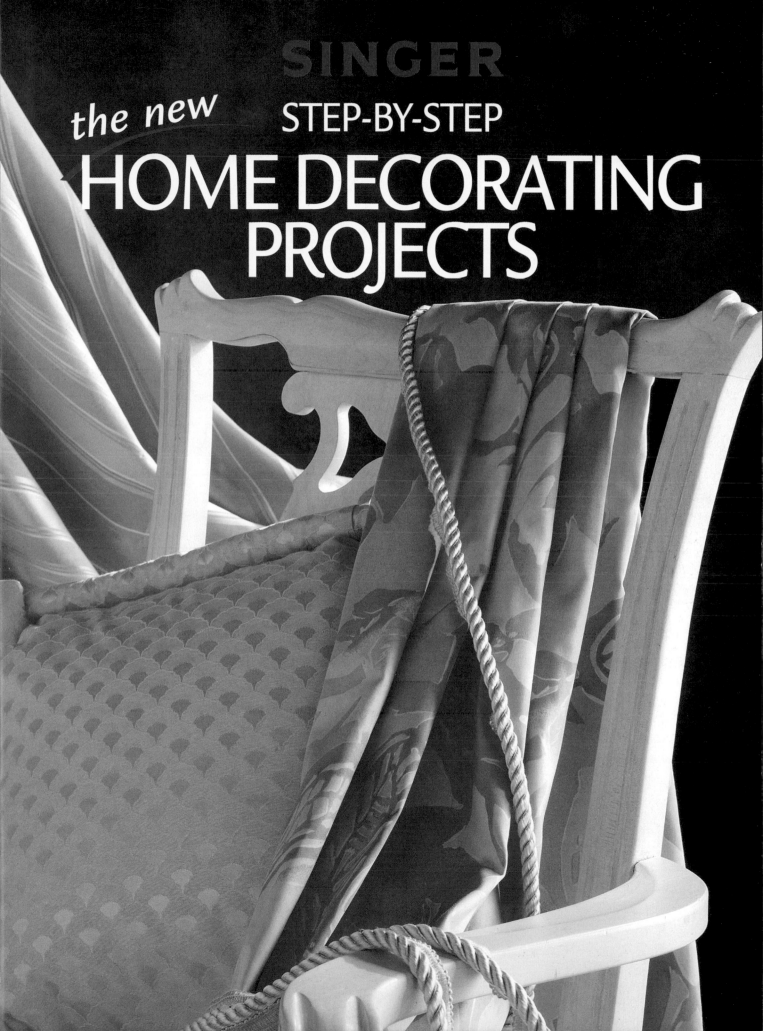

SINGER

the new STEP-BY-STEP

HOME DECORATING PROJECTS

Contents

CREATIVE PUBLISHING international

President/CEO: Michael Eleftheriou
Vice President/Publisher: Linda Ball
Vice President/Retail Sales & Marketing:
   Kevin Haas

Copyright © 1998,
Creative Publishing international, Inc.
18705 Lake Drive East
Chanhassen, Minnesota 55317
1-800-328-3895
www.creativepub.com
All rights reserved
ISBN 0-86573-179-9 (hardcover)

Created by: The Editors of Creative Publishing
   international, Inc., in cooperation with
   the Sewing Education Department, Singer
   Sewing Company. Singer is a trademark of
   The Singer Company Limited and is used
   under license.
Printed by:
   R. R. Donnelley
   10 9 8 7 6 5 4 3 2

How to Use This Book

Any successful sewing project for the home requires two things: a thorough understanding of basic sewing skills and the specific information needed to create projects from curtains to slipcovers. *The New Step-by-Step Home Decorating Projects* provides both. Now you can update or revitalize any room in your home, or simply add a finishing touch.

Getting Started

This section helps you plan your project. It gives basic information on colors, patterns, and fabrics, as well as on measuring, marking, and cutting. Basic seams and sewing techniques are also clearly explained and illustrated.

Home Sewing Projects

The sections of this book deal with general projects, such as curtains, pillows, slipcovers, and table linens, and projects for specific rooms, such as the bathroom and the bedroom.

The Windows section includes designer window treatments as well as basic information on hardware selection, covering and installing mounting boards, and sewing rod pockets and hems. Learn how to make shades and tent-flap curtains or curtain panels for a casual look. Or for a more formal look, choose from a variety of special curtains, rod-pocket swags and cascades, or pleated draperies. Swags, tiebacks, and an assortment of top treatments such as stagecoach valances, layered or handkerchief valances, and covered poles and finials complete this section.

The Pillows section begins with plain or welted pillows. It includes many with a designer flair, such as buttoned flaps, sash, knotted-corner, and reversible rosette pillows. The section ends with a no-sew fringed pillow and four quick ideas for pillow covers.

Sewing for the Bedroom features projects like comforter covers, pillow shams, and bed skirts that can be sewn for a coordinated look. Other projects include a reverse sham bed cover, a daybed dust skirt and tufted cover, and a padded headboard. The styles range from basic to very elegant.

Bathroom Decorating projects include shower curtains and valances, sink and vanity skirts, bath mats, and embellished towel ideas.

A variety of decorative ideas for table linens are presented in the Tables section. Placemats, table runners, and napkins utilize techniques such as mitering, fagoting, and satin stiching.

The Seating section will teach you to make reversible seat covers and easy slipcovers for folding chairs. A comprehensive guide to slipcovers for upholstered furniture takes you from pin-fitting to laying out, cutting, and sewing slipcovers and cushions. This section also includes easy reupholstery projects from slip seats and footstools to side chairs.

The final section of the book will inspire true creativity. Embellish projects with trims and tassels, fabric rosettes and bows. Learn how to add transparent appliqués, cutwork, and monograms for a special finishing touch.

Step-by-Step Guidance

From beginning to end, the step-by-step instructions make your sewing-for-the-home projects easy and understandable. Whether you are an experienced sewer or a beginner, you will find this book to be a help and an inspiration. Use it for many successful home decorating and sewing projects.

PS-15

PL-14

PL-15

PS-15

Planning Your Project

The first step in planning any project, no matter how large or small, is to analyze the room in which the project will be placed. Think about what you like in the room and what you want to change. If possible, collect samples of any carpeting, fabric, wallpaper, or paint that will remain in the room. Then bring the samples with you to the fabric store, to help you coordinate the old and the new.

You may want to look through recent decorating magazines for ideas to inspire you in updating your room. Pictures can help you decide on a style you like. Rooms with several print fabrics tend to appear cozier and smaller. Rooms with mostly solid colors tend to look restful and larger. The colors you select can also have an effect on the way you feel. Bright, strong colors are more cheerful; muted colors, more relaxing.

Keep in mind that there is no right or wrong way to coordinate the decor of a room. Some general guidelines can help you make good decisions, but your own feelings and preferences are the most important considcration. Salespeople or designers may give helpful suggestions, but be sure to follow your own instincts if you are not comfortable with their ideas.

Learn about the various types of decorating fabrics that are available (pages 16 and 17). Bring home samples of the fabrics you are considering before making your final decisions. Place the samples where they will be used in the room. If a fabric will be used for a valance, place it at the top of the window. Be sure to check the fabrics during daytime and evening hours, since natural and artificial light affect the way colors match or coordinate. Leave the samples in place for a few days to be sure you are comfortable with your decisions. Your initial reactions may change.

Planning the Colors & Patterns

When planning the style of a room, try to visualize the colors and patterns of your sewing projects and how they will be used in the room. Avoid using equal amounts of all the fabrics. Use the primary fabric for about two-thirds of the room furnishings, use a secondary fabric for about one-third, and use accent colors in small amounts. The size of the fabric samples should be in proportion to how they will be used, such as large samples for draperies, small samples for accent pillows.

Vary the textures in the room. Nubby or textured fabrics and surfaces, mixed with smooth ones, add interest. For example, textured sheers contrast with a shiny brass pole.

How to Plan a Coordinated Decor

1) **Select** the primary patterned fabric. This will be the main fabric and will be used for about two-thirds of the fabric in the room. Select a print that will coordinate with existing furnishings, such as carpeting.

2) Add a secondary patterned fabric that includes some of the colors from the primary fabric. The secondary pattern is used for about one-third of the fabric in the room. Striped fabric works well as a secondary pattern, but florals or plaids may be used, if desired. Vary the scale of the pattern so it is different from the primary print.

3) Add accent patterned fabrics to be used in small amounts. These fabrics can introduce another color from the primary fabric. Or you can add texture by selecting fabrics such as lace; some prints have a textural appearance, even though the fabric has a smooth surface.

4) Select solid-colored fabrics to unify the patterned fabrics and give visual relief. Choose colors you want to emphasize from the other fabrics.

Mixing Patterned Fabrics

Plaid fabric was selected as the primary pattern, because a tailored style was desired. A traditional paisley print was chosen as the secondary pattern to soften the look and repeat the colors in the plaid. The striped fabric adds a bright accent.

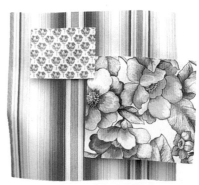

Floral patterns are traditionally the basis for a romantic look. A coordinated fabric group designed by the manufacturer was used for this decorating scheme. The soft colors of the prints are accented with a brighter solid color.

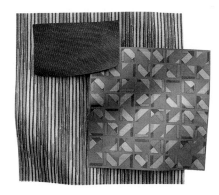

Geometric designs give a more active, contemporary look. These patterned fabrics have a rich textural appearance and an interesting mix of color. The solid-colored accent fabric emphasizes one of the colors in the prints, while its ribbed texture contrasts with the smooth finish of the patterned fabrics.

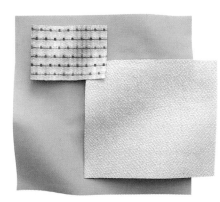

Solid-colored fabrics were selected as the primary and secondary fabrics, giving a more passive look to the room. The colors are compatible, yet offer contrast. Texture has been used to provide variety. For an accent fabric, a novelty weave was used to tie in the colors of the solid fabrics.

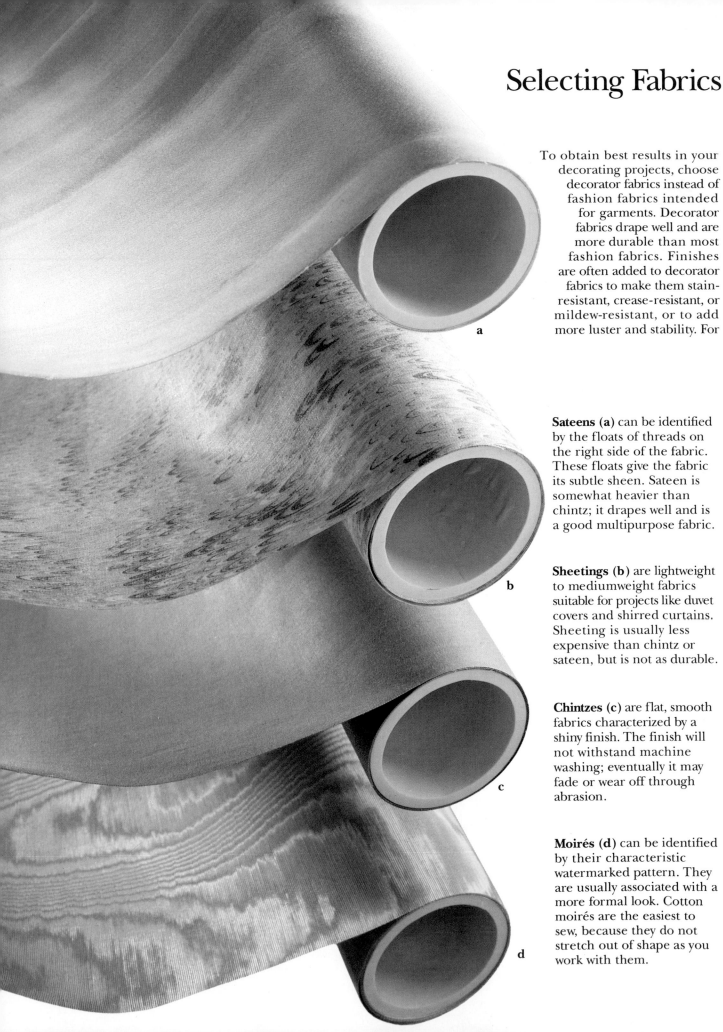

Selecting Fabrics

To obtain best results in your decorating projects, choose decorator fabrics instead of fashion fabrics intended for garments. Decorator fabrics drape well and are more durable than most fashion fabrics. Finishes are often added to decorator fabrics to make them stain-resistant, crease-resistant, or mildew-resistant, or to add more luster and stability. For

Sateens (a) can be identified by the floats of threads on the right side of the fabric. These floats give the fabric its subtle sheen. Sateen is somewhat heavier than chintz; it drapes well and is a good multipurpose fabric.

Sheetings (b) are lightweight to mediumweight fabrics suitable for projects like duvet covers and shirred curtains. Sheeting is usually less expensive than chintz or sateen, but is not as durable.

Chintzes (c) are flat, smooth fabrics characterized by a shiny finish. The finish will not withstand machine washing; eventually it may fade or wear off through abrasion.

Moirés (d) can be identified by their characteristic watermarked pattern. They are usually associated with a more formal look. Cotton moirés are the easiest to sew, because they do not stretch out of shape as you work with them.

best results, do not preshrink decorator fabrics. Washing may remove the finishes, change the fabric's hand, or fade the colors. Dry cleaning is recommended to keep the finished projects looking their best. Several types of fabric may be used in one room. When different fabric types are used, the various surface textures add interest and variety to the decor.

Sheers (a) are lightweight fabrics that add softness to a window treatment and allow light to filter into the room for a bright, airy look. They usually have plain weaves or linenlike textures.

Laces (b), available in many patterns and weights, add texture to the room decor. When used at the window, lace lets in light. Lace may also be used for room accessories, such as tablecloths and pillows.

Duck (c) and lightweight canvas are coarsely woven and have a flat finish. Medium to heavy in weight, they are durable fabrics suitable for casual decorating.

Novelty weaves (d) have woven-in patterns or designs. They add texture and interest to the decor of a room.

Timesaving Fabrics

Whether you are planning a large or small home decorating project, the choice of fabric can save you time in the long run. When looking for fabrics that are timesaving, use these general guidelines.

Prints bring style and the impression of detailing to quick sewing projects. They also provide a built-in color scheme for attractive room settings, hide any imperfect stitches, and show soil or wear less quickly than plain fabrics. Choose allover or small-scale prints rather than larger motifs that must be matched at the seams, centered, or balanced, and you will save fabric as well as time.

Coordinated prints give you a custom look quickly. These fabrics may have coordinated borders or a companion print, such as a stripe, that can be cut apart for trims, tiebacks, and ruffles. Specialty groups include decorative panels that look like handcrafted patchwork or appliqué for shortcut wall hangings and pillows. There are also preprints designed for easy-to-make home accessories, such as kitchen appliance covers, placemat and napkin sets, holiday accents, and nursery items.

Dull or matte finish fabrics absorb rather than reflect light; therefore, they do not require the perfection in sewing or draping needed for fabrics with luster or sheen.

Wide fabrics are best for large projects, such as window treatments, bed coverings, and tablecloths; the wider the fabric, the fewer the seams that are needed. Most home decorating fabrics are at least 54" (140 cm) wide to keep seams to the minimum, but some sheers are 110" (280 cm) or wider so you can eliminate seams entirely. For seamless window treatments, choose fabric wide enough to make headings and lower hems on the selvage edges so the lengthwise fabric grain runs across the window.

Flat bed sheets come in generous sizes that are often large enough for seamless projects. In addition, many sheet styles have borders or applied trims that can be used as prefinished project edges or cut apart to make small items, such as tiebacks.

Reversible fabric, which has no apparent right or wrong side, allows you to eliminate linings and backings. Both fabric faces are attractive on many sheers, jacquard weaves, synthetic suedes, and woven plaids. Create a reversible fabric by using two fabrics back to back. Glue, fuse, or machine-baste wrong sides together.

Lace is suitable for many decorating projects; it does not ravel or require hems or linings. Take advantage of lace border designs by using them as ready-made edges. For window treatments, choose lace that has one edge prefinished as a border and the other prefinished with openings for a curtain rod.

Plaids and stripes have built-in timesaving features. For cutting, measuring, and marking, the lines of a woven plaid or stripe are always on a straight grain. Check to be sure that a printed geometric is printed on-grain or it will be difficult to work with.

Notions & Equipment

Fusible web saves time when used to apply trim or make hems as well as to anchor seam allowances inside a rod pocket for easy curtain rod insertion.

Glue stick is a fast way to position trims, hems, backings, and linings for stitching.

Liquid fray preventer seals exposed ends and edges of fabrics and trims. It also protects buttonholes and slits cut into curtains or valances for inserting a rod or brackets.

Serger, or overlock machine, makes neat, fast hems and edge finishes on ruffles, shades, tablecloths, runners, placemats, and napkins. Also use the serger to sew sheer fabrics without puckers and to sew long, straight seams on curtains, draperies, or bed coverings in minutes.

Rotary cutter is ideal for cutting straight pieces, such as ties, ruffles, bindings, and trimming strips.

Bias tape maker uniformly folds the raw edges of fabric strips as you press. Use it for bias binding, curtain tabs, decorative tapes, and custom band trims. Tape makers come in four sizes to make folded strips ½", ¾", 1", or 2" (12, 18, 25, or 50 mm).

Fabric adhesive, such as craft or white glue, can be used to anchor a shade hem to a lining or to close an opening left for turning a project right side out.

Tapes with self-styling cords are stitched flat to fabric and pulled to shirr, smock, pleat, or fold fabric automatically. Tape is a fast, easy way to make decorative headings on curtains, draperies, valances, and dust ruffles. Ring tape and shade tape are other self-styling tapes. Ring tape has plastic rings sewn at 6" (15 cm) intervals; shade tape has cord tacked loosely at intervals. Both can be used to form swagged hems quickly.

Measuring for Home Fashions

Measuring for Window Fashions

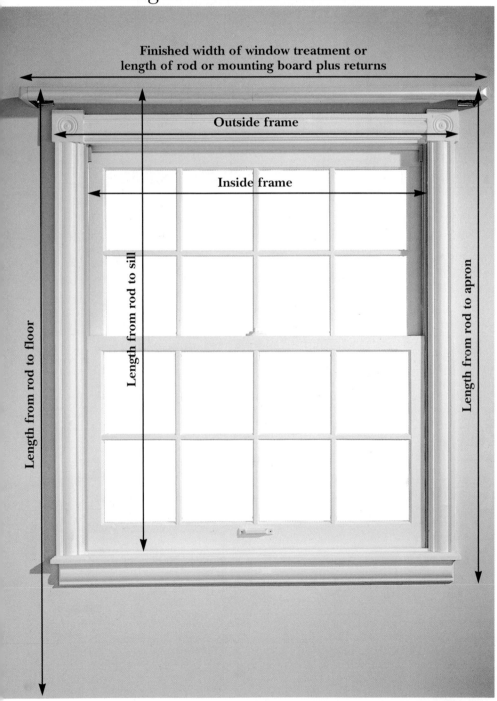

Finished width of window treatment or length of rod or mounting board plus returns

Outside frame

Inside frame

Length from rod to sill

Length from rod to floor

Length from rod to apron

Sketch the window treatment to scale on graph paper, to help you determine the most pleasing proportion for the treatment as well as the correct placement of any hardware. After installing the hardware, take all necessary measurements, using a steel tape measure for accuracy, and record the measurements on the sketch.

For each project, you will need to determine the finished length and width of the treatment. The finished length is measured from the top of the mounting board or rod, or from where you want the upper edge of a curtain, to where you want the lower edge of the window treatment. The finished width is determined by measuring the length of the rod or mounting board. For treatments with returns, the finished width includes twice the projection of the rod or mounting board.

Specific instructions for determining the cut lengths and widths of the fabric are given for each project in this book. In general, the cut width is determined by multiplying the finished width by the amount of fullness desired. Fullness describes the finished width of the curtain or valance in proportion to the length of the rod or mounting board. For example, two times fullness means that the width of the curtain measures two times the length of the rod.

Yardage requirements can be determined by multiplying the cut length by the number of fabric widths needed to obtain the cut width. Special considerations for determining yardage requirements for patterned fabrics are given on page 28.

Tips for Measuring

Plan the proportion of window treatment layers so the length of the top treatment is about one-fifth the length of the overall treatment. The top treatment may be installed higher than the window, to add visual height; it may start at the ceiling, provided the top of the window frame is not visible at its lower edge.

Plan for the shortest point of a top treatment to fall at least 4" to 6" (10 to 15 cm) below the top of the window glass.

Make a top treatment 4" (10 cm) wider and 2" to 3" (5 to 7.5 cm) deeper than an under-treatment.

Allow ½" (1.3 cm) clearance between the lower edge of the curtain and the floor when measuring for floor-length curtains.

Add 2" (5 cm) to the measurement for floor-length curtains for a window treatment that breaks on the floor (page 84).

Add 20" (51 cm) to the measurement for floor-length curtains for a window treatment that puddles on the floor (page 64).

Measure for all curtains in the room to the same height from the floor, for a uniform look. Use the highest window in the room as the standard for measuring the other windows.

Terms to Know

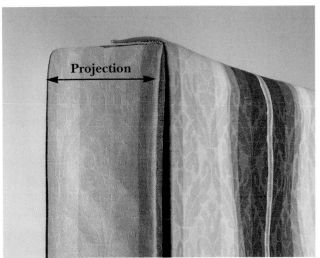

Projection is the distance the rod or mounting board stands out from the wall.

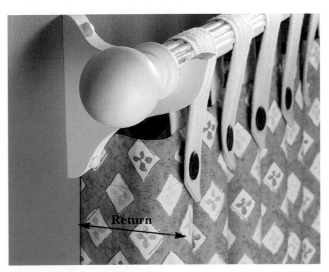

Return is the portion of the curtain or top treatment extending from the end of the rod or mounting board to the wall, blocking the side light and view.

The heading (a) is the portion at the top of a rod-pocket window treatment that forms a ruffle when the curtain is on the rod. The depth of the heading is the distance from the top of the finished curtain to the top stitching line of the rod pocket.

The rod pocket (b) is the portion of the curtain where the curtain rod or pole is inserted. Stitching lines at the top and bottom of the rod pocket keep the rod or pole in place. To determine the depth of the rod pocket, measure around the widest point of the rod or pole; add ½" (1.3 cm) for ease, and divide this amount by two.

Bed Fashions

Custom-made bed fashions such as comforter covers, pillow shams and dust ruffles can be ruffled or tailored to suit the decor. Chintzes, polished cottons and sateens are good choices for most bed coverings. Sheets are another practical fabric choice; their width makes seaming unnecessary on comforter covers. Permanent press fabrics with soil-resistant finishes are advisable in a child's room. Select fabrics that will launder well without fading.

Comforter covers, also known as *duvet covers,* are removable for easy care. They protect new comforters, salvage worn ones, and quickly change the look of a comforter. They also eliminate the need for a top sheet and blanket on the bed.

Pillow shams are removable, decorative pillow covers. Make pillow shams in matching or contrasting fabrics to complement the comforter and dust ruffle. Traditional pillowcases may also be trimmed with ruffles and used as pillow shams.

Dust ruffles or bed skirts are used with comforters. They may be gathered or tailored. Make them in one piece for beds that do not have a footboard. Make them in three pieces for beds that do have a footboard. Attach dust ruffles to a fitted sheet placed over the box spring or to a muslin *deck,* a piece of fabric which fits between the mattress and the box spring.

Fabrics for dust ruffles should be considered for their weight and draping quality, as well as suitability for the style of the dust ruffle or bed skirt.

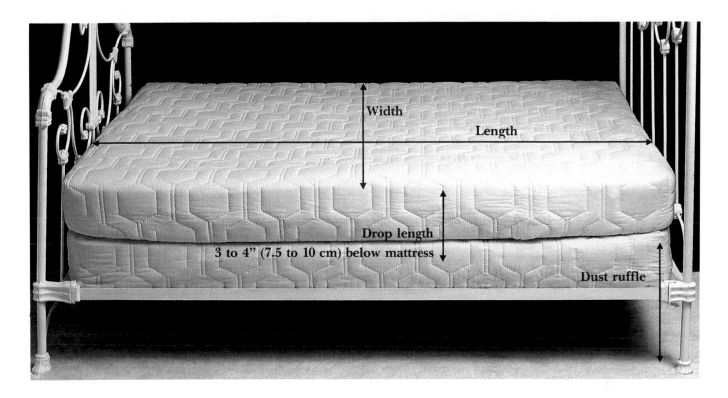

Measuring the Bed

Measure accurately to make bed fashions that fit the bed perfectly.

Comforters should reach 3" to 4" (7.5 to 10 cm) below the mattress line. They have a *drop length* (the distance from the upper edge of the mattress to the bottom of the comforter) of 9" to 14" (23 to 35.5 cm), depending on the depth of the mattress. To determine an appropriate comforter size, measure from side to side across the top of the mattress for width, and from the head to the foot of the bed for length. Add the desired drop length to the length of the bed, and twice the drop length to the width of the bed for finished measurements. Consider fabric stiffness which

may cause the comforter to stand away from the side of the bed.

Batting for comforters is available in standard widths for beds of standard sizes; select the proper size for your comforter.

For the finished dust ruffle length, measure from the top of the box spring to the floor; for the deck, measure the width and length of the box spring.

Pillow sizes are 20" × 26" (51 × 66 cm) standard; 20" × 30" (51 × 76 cm) queen; and 20" × 40" (51 × 102 cm) king. Pillow puffiness varies, however, so make the best-fitting shams by measuring the width and length of the pillow with a tape measure across the center of the pillow.

Tabletop Fashions

Home-sewn table fashions, unlike purchased ones, are not limited to a small selection of standard sizes. When you design a tablecloth yourself, you can scale it to the exact size and shape of your table. You can also choose from an abundant supply of fabric colors, patterns and textures that complement the decor of your room.

Customized tabletop fashions are a simple way to change the look of a room without spending too much time or money. These easy projects make good home sewing sense.

Because most tablecloths are wider than one fabric width, you must seam fabric widths together to make the tablecloth the width you need. Avoid a center seam by using a full fabric width in the center and stitching narrower side panels to it.

Use selvage edges in the seams to eliminate seam finishing. If the selvage tends to pucker, clip it at regular intervals of 1" to 6" (2.5 to 15 cm). If selvages are not used in seams, finish with French or overedge seams. Use plain seams for reversible tablecloths.

Placemats, napkins and table runners give you an opportunity to experiment with finishing techniques you may be reluctant to try on larger projects.

Selecting Fabrics

When you design tabletop fashions, look for durable, stain-resistant fabrics that have been treated to repel soil and water. Permanent press fabrics offer easy care. Drape the fabric over your arm to see how it hangs.

For everyday use, lightweight cotton is appropriate; use a lightweight tablecloth with a table pad to protect fine wood tables. For an elegant look, use a sheer lace or eyelet tablecloth over a heavier cloth.

Small random prints are easier to work with than prints that may need matching. Avoid heavily napped fabrics or fabrics with difficult-to-match design motifs such as printed plaids or stripes, diagonals or one-way patterns.

Measuring the Table

The length of the tablecloth from the edge of the table to the bottom of the cloth is called the *drop* (right). Be sure to include the drop length in your tablecloth measurements.

Round tablecloth. Measure the diameter of the table, then determine the drop length of the cloth. The size of the tablecloth is the diameter of the table plus twice the drop length plus 1" (2.5 cm) for a narrow hem allowance. A narrow hem is the easiest way to finish the curved edge of a round tablecloth.

Square tablecloth. Measure the width of the tabletop; then determine the drop length of the cloth. Add twice the drop length plus 1" (2.5 cm) for a narrow hem allowance or 2½" (6.5 cm) for a wide hem allowance.

Rectangular tablecloth. Measure the length and width of the tabletop, then determine the drop length of the cloth. The size of the finished tablecloth is the width of the tabletop plus twice the drop length, and the length of the tabletop plus twice the drop length. Add 1" (2.5 cm) for a narrow hem or 2½" (6.5 cm) for a wide hem.

Oval tablecloth. Measure the length and width of the tabletop, then determine the drop length of the cloth. Join fabric widths as necessary to make a rectangular cloth the length of the tabletop plus twice the drop length, and the width of the tabletop plus twice the drop length; add 1" (2.5 cm) to each dimension for a narrow hem allowance. Put a narrow hem in an oval tablecloth because it is the simplest way to finish the curved edge. Because oval tables vary in shape, mark the finished size with the fabric on the table. Place weights on the table to hold the fabric in place, then use a hem marker or cardboard gauge to mark the drop length evenly.

Three common drop lengths are: short, 10" to 12" (25.5 to 30.5 cm); mid-length, 16" to 24" (40.5 to 61 cm); and floor-length, 28" to 29" (71 to 73.5 cm). Short cloths end at about chair seat height and are good for everyday use. Mid-length cloths are more formal. Elegant floor-length coverings are used for buffet and decorator tables.

Estimating Yardage

Because fabric widths vary, the yardage requirements for decorating projects cannot be calculated until the fabric has been selected. After you have taken the necessary measurements and determined the finished size of the project, you will need to figure the cut length and cut width of the project.

To determine the cut length and cut width of a fabric that does not require matching, add the amounts needed for any hems, rod pockets, headings, ease, seam allowances, and fullness to the finished size of the project. For example, if you are sewing a gathered valance, add the amount needed for rod pockets, headings, and hems to the finished lengths; then add side hems, seam allowances, and fullness to the finished width. If the fabric requires matching, you will need to allow extra fabric (page 28).

Frequently a decorating project will require more than one width of fabric. To determine the number of fabric widths required, divide the cut width of the project by the width of the fabric.

To calculate the amount of fabric you will need, multiply the cut length of the project by the number of fabric widths required; this is the total fabric length in inches (centimeters). Divide this measurement by 36" (100 cm) to determine the number of yards (meters) required.

Shirred rod covers (page 62) are made from striped fabric that has been railroaded, changing the direction of the stripes. The stripes that run along the lengthwise grain of the fabric are turned horizontally on the railroaded valance. The curtains were not railroaded, so the lengthwise grain of the fabric runs lengthwise on the curtain.

Railroading Fabrics

Many fabrics can be railroaded, or cut so the lengthwise grain will run horizontally on the finished project. This is possible when the cut length is shorter than the fabric width. Railroading is often used for cutting fabric for valances, bed skirts, and short curtains to eliminate seams and save sewing time.

If the fabric is patterned, check to see that the design can be turned sideways. Flowers with stems, birds, and other one-way designs cannot be turned sideways. Striped fabrics may be railroaded, but stripes on the lengthwise grain will run horizontally if the fabric is railroaded.

Yardage requirements are calculated differently when fabric is railroaded. To determine how many yards (meters) of fabric you will need, divide the cut width by 36" (100 cm). Depending on the project, railroading may require more or less fabric.

Sunburst curtain (page 80) has been railroaded to prevent seams. Seams would be noticeable in the sheer fabric when light comes through the window.

Handkerchief valance (page 132) has been railroaded to prevent seams, which would detract from the overall appearance of the valance.

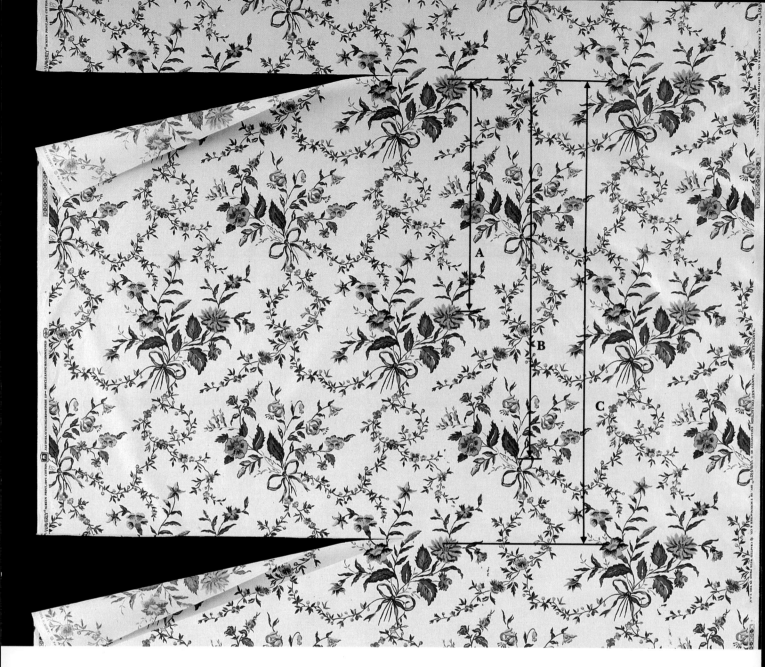

Cutting & Matching Patterned Fabrics

For professional results, always match the pattern of a fabric at the seamlines. Extra yardage is usually needed in order to match the pattern.

The pattern repeat (**A**) is the lengthwise distance from one distinctive point on the pattern, such as the tip of a particular petal in a floral pattern, to the same point in the next pattern design. Some patterned fabrics have pattern repeat markings (+) printed on the selvage. These markings mark the beginning of each pattern repeat, and they are especially helpful for fabrics that include several similar designs.

Add the amounts needed for any hems, rod pockets, headings, ease, seam allowances, and fullness to the finished length, to determine how long the lengths of fabric need to be (**B**). Then round this measurement

up to the next number divisible by the size of the pattern repeat. This is the cut length (**C**). For example, if the pattern repeat (**A**) is 19" (48.5 cm), and the finished length plus hems, rod pockets, and other allowances (**B**) is 30" (76 cm), the actual cut length (**C**) is 38" (96.5 cm). To have patterns match from one panel to the next, each panel must be cut at the same point on the pattern repeat.

To calculate the amount of fabric you will need, multiply the cut length by the number of fabric widths required for the project; add one additional pattern repeat so you can adjust the placement of the pattern on the cut lengths. This is the total fabric length in inches (centimeters); divide this measurement by 36" (100 cm) to determine the number of yards (meters) required.

How to Match a Patterned Fabric

1) **Position** the fabric widths, right sides together, matching the selvages.

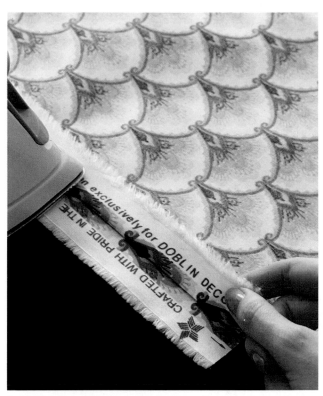

2) **Fold** selvage back at one end until pattern matches. Lightly press foldline.

3) **Unfold** selvage. Pin on foldline; check the match from right side.

4) **Reposition** pins perpendicular to foldline; stitch on foldline. Trim away selvages. Trim fabric to finished length plus hems, rod pockets, and other allowances, as calculated opposite.

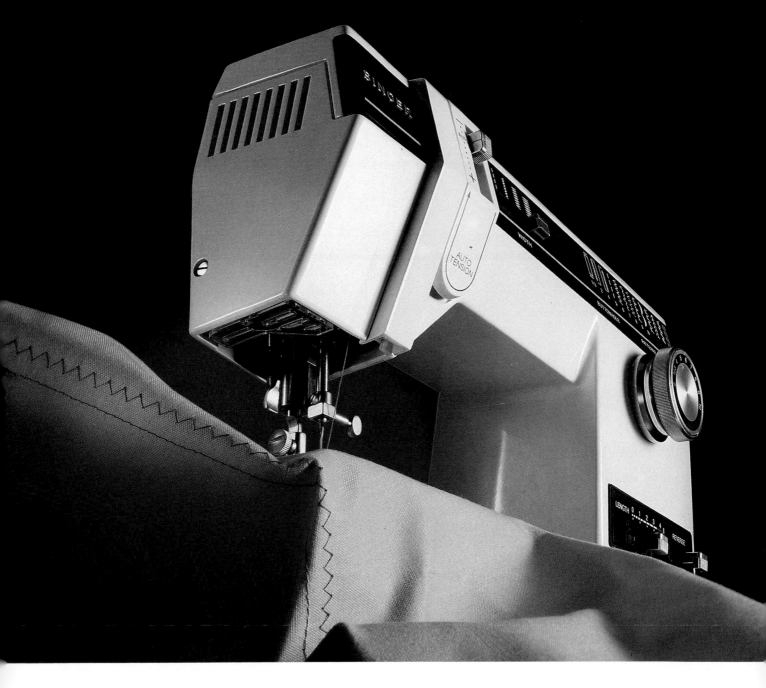

Machine Stitching

Most home decorator sewing can be done entirely by machine with a straight or zigzag stitch. Although machines vary in capabilities, each has the same basic parts and controls. Consult your machine manual to review the threading procedures and to locate the controls that operate the principal parts.

Tension, pressure and stitch length and width are the main adjustments that create perfect straight or zigzag stitching. Choosing the appropriate needle and thread for the sewing project and fabric also helps to create quality stitching.

Tension is the balance between the upper and bobbin threads as they pass through the machine.

When tension is perfectly balanced, the stitches look even on both sides of the fabric because they link midway between fabric layers. Tension that is too tight causes seams to pucker and stitches to break easily. Tension that is too loose results in weak seams.

Pressure regulates the even feeding of fabric layers. When pressure is too heavy, the bottom fabric layer gathers, forcing the upper layer ahead of the presser foot. This unevenness can make a difference of several inches at the end of a long seam, such as one on a curtain. Pressure that is too light may cause skipped stitches, crooked stitching lines and weak, loose stitches.

Stitch length is controlled with a regulator that is on an inch scale from 0 to 20, a metric scale from 0 to 4, or a numerical scale from 0 to 9. On the metric and numerical scales, higher numbers form a longer stitch, lower numbers a shorter stitch. For normal stitching, set the regulator at 10 to 12 stitches per inch (2.5 cm). This setting is equivalent to 2.5 to 3 on the metric scale, and 5 on the numerical scale.

Needle, size 80/14, is used for general-purpose sewing on mediumweight fabrics. Because the firm weave and glazed finish of many home decorator fabrics dull a needle quickly, change the needle often. A bent, blunt, or burred needle damages fabric. Prevent damage to the needle by removing pins from the seam as you come to them. Never sew over pins or let them get under the fabric where they may come in contact with the feed dogs.

Thread for general-purpose sewing is suitable for most home decorator projects. Use an all-purpose weight. Choose all-cotton, all-polyester, or cotton-wrapped polyester thread that matches the fiber content of the fabric. For balanced tension, use the same type of thread in the bobbin and the needle.

Thread the machine correctly; incorrect threading can cause a stitch to be too loose or too tight. To rethread the machine, remove the spool completely and begin again, in case the thread has tangled in the tension or over the spool pin.

Use a scrap of fabric to test the tension, pressure, and stitch length before starting to sew. To check the balance of the tension, you may want to thread the machine with different colors for upper and bobbin threads so the stitches are easier to see.

Perfect Straight & Zigzag Stitching

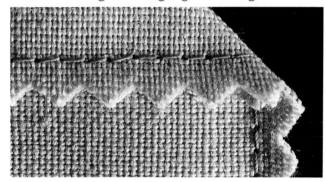

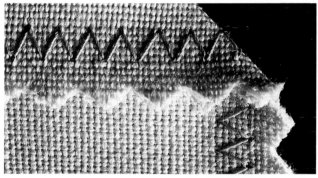

Straight stitches should link midway between fabric layers so stitches are the same length on both sides of fabric. Adjust tension and pressure so stitches do not break easily and the seam does not pucker.

Zigzag stitching is adjusted correctly when the links interlock at the corner of each stitch. Stitches should lie flat. Adjust the zigzag width and density with the stitch length and width regulators.

Machine Stitching Terms

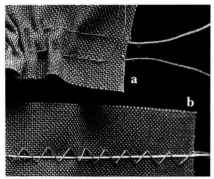

Bastestitching (a) is the longest straight stitch on the machine: 6 on the inch scale, 4 on the metric scale, and 9 on the numerical scale. Some sewing machines have a separate built-in bastestitch **(b)** that makes two stitches to the inch (2.5 cm). Use it for speed-basting straight seams.

Gathering stitch is done with two rows of bastestitching placed ½" (1.3 cm) and ¼" (6 mm) from the fabric edge. Loosen tension, use heavier bobbin thread, and pull up bobbin thread to form gathers **(a)**. For long areas of gathers, zigzag over cord, string, or dental floss without catching cord in the stitch **(b)**. Pull up cord to gather.

Edgestitching is placed on the edge of a hem or fold. The straight-stitch foot and straight-stitch needle plate aid in the close control needed for this stitching. The narrow foot rides on the folded edge, and the small hole of the needle plate keeps fragile fabric from being drawn into the feed dogs.

1   2   3   4   4   4

Basic Seams & Techniques

All seams in home decorator sewing are ½" (1.3 cm) unless otherwise specified. To secure seams, backstitch at each end of the seam by stitching in reverse for ½" (1.3 cm). Four seam techniques are used in home decorator sewing.

1) Plain seam is suitable for almost every fabric and sewing application when you plan to enclose the seam or cover it with a lining.

2) French seam eliminates raw edges in exposed seams. Use it whenever a seam is visible on the wrong side or is subjected to frequent laundering.

3) Interlocking fell or self-bound seam, like the French seam, completely encloses raw edges. For this seam, sew on the wrong side of the fabric. Use the narrow hemmer attachment as a timesaver.

4) Overedge or zigzag seams are plain seams with a zigzag finish to prevent raveling. Use them on heavy, textured fabrics that are too bulky for French or self-bound seams. Or use an overlock or serger seam, and allow ¼" (6 mm) seam allowances.

Long straight seams tend to pucker in some fabrics. To prevent this, use taut sewing, pulling equally on the fabric in front of and in back of the needle, and let fabric feed through the machine on its own. Do not stretch.

How to Sew a Plain Seam

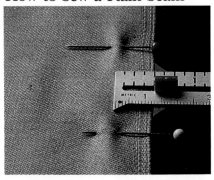

1) Pin right sides of fabric together, placing pins at right angles to seam line for easy removal. If using basting tape, place it at the raw edge and do not stitch through it.

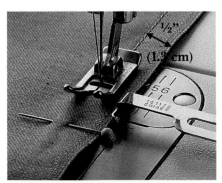

2) Use seam guide to sew even seams. Backstitch to secure; then stitch seam, removing pins as you come to them. Backstitch at end of seam. Lift presser foot and remove fabric by pulling 2" to 3" (5 to 7.5 cm) of thread to the left.

3) Clip threads close to the end of seam. Press seam open or to one side. If seam is on the selvage, clip selvage diagonally every 1" to 6" (2.5 to 15 cm) to prevent the seam from puckering.

How to Sew a French Seam

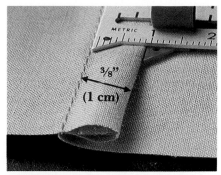

1) Pin fabric *wrong* sides together. Stitch a scant ¼" (6 mm) seam. Press seam allowance to one side. For narrower finished seam, trim seam allowance to ⅛" (3 mm).

2) Turn fabric panels right sides together to enclose the trimmed seam allowance. Stitching line should be exactly on fold.

3) Stitch ⅜" (1 cm) from folded edge, enclosing first seam. Press the seam to one side. If first seam was trimmed, stitch ¼" (6 mm) from the edge.

How to Sew an Interlocking Fell Seam

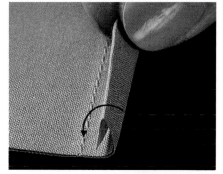

1) Pin fabric, right sides together, with edge of top layer ½" (1.3 cm) from edge of bottom layer. Stitch ¾" (2 cm) from edge of bottom fabric layer.

2) Fold and press ¼" (6 mm) on seam allowance of bottom layer so that it meets edge of top layer. Fold and press again, covering the stitching line.

3) Edgestitch close to fold. Press seam to one side, holding fabric taut to eliminate puckering. Or use narrow hemmer for final stitching (page 34).

Three Ways to Sew an Overedge Seam

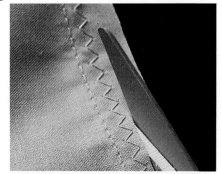

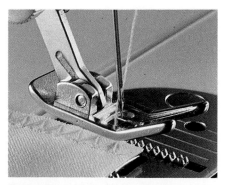

Zigzag plain seam. Stitch ½" (1.3 cm) plain seam. Zigzag seam allowances together close to raw edge. This eliminates trimming the seam, but results in a wider seam. Press seam to one side. This is the easiest overedge seam to sew and is suitable for most fabrics.

Zigzag narrow seam. Stitch ½" (1.3 cm) plain seam. Zigzag seam allowances together, stitching with wide zigzag close to stitching. Trim seam allowances close to zigzag stitching. This seam requires time for trimming. It can be used as an alternative to French seams.

Overedge seam. Trim seams to ¼" (6 mm) before stitching. Then stitch seam with built-in overedge stitch. This makes a straight seam and zigzags over cut edge in one step. Use this seam on medium to heavyweight fabrics which ravel.

Timesaving Accessories

Many home decorator sewing projects require long seams or hems. There are several machine attachments and special feet that speed hemming, binding, ruffling and straight stitching. Some of these accessories come with the machine; others are available from your machine dealer.

Before buying special-purpose attachments, find out if your machine has a high, low or slanted shank. Consult the machine manual if you are not sure what type of shank your machine has. Snap-on presser feet will fit any machine with a snap-on, all-purpose shank.

Special-purpose foot is used for decorative stitching and machine embroidery. The plastic foot lets you see the stitching easily, and a groove under the foot allows for a build-up of thread. Use the foot for general-purpose sewing and special tasks such as closely spaced satin stitching.

Zipper and cording foot is used for inserting zippers, applying snap tape and for making and applying cording. The needle pierces the fabric on either side of the foot, allowing stitching to be placed close to bulk on one side of the seam.

Even Feed® foot feeds top and bottom layers of fabric at the same rate, ensuring that seams start and end evenly. This foot helps keep plaids and other matched designs aligned in long seams. Use on heavy, bulky or quilted fabrics.

Narrow hemmer automatically double-folds the fabric edge and stitches a ⅛" (3 mm) hem without pressing or pinning. The foot is useful for hemming and for stitching interlocking fell seams.

Seam guide helps keep seam allowances even. It attaches to the bed of the machine (a) and adjusts for seam widths up to 1¼" (3.2 cm). A magnetic seam guide (b) attaches to any metal machine bed.

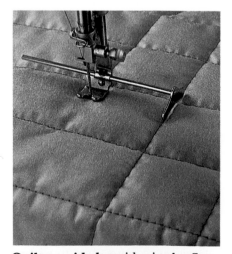

Quilter guide-bar rides in the first row of stitching to form perfectly parallel quilting lines. Use it for topstitching or channel quilting. The bar adjusts to widths up to 3" (7.5 cm) and can be used on either side of the needle.

Ruffler Attachment or Gathering Foot

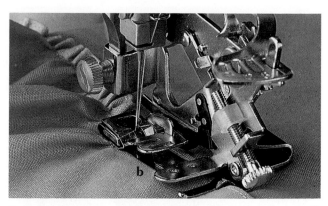

Ruffler attachment automatically gathers strips of light or mediumweight fabric. Stitch length affects fullness; short stitches give more fullness and longer stitches give less. Gather one layer of fabric (**a**).

Or gather one layer and attach it to another layer of fabric in one step (**b**). Insert fullness at every stitch, or at 6 or 12-stitch intervals. Use this attachment for ruffles on curtains, pillows or dust ruffles.

Blindstitch Hem Foot & Guide

Blindstitch hem foot is used with the built-in blind hemming stitch. The foot (**a**) positions the hem for sewing with straight and zigzag stitches which are

barely visible on the right side. Blindstitch hem guide (**b**) is used with the general-purpose foot to position the hem for blindstitching.

Binder Attachment

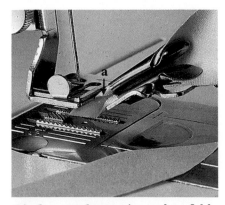

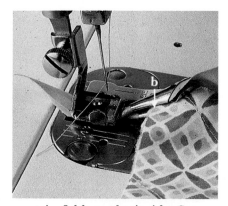

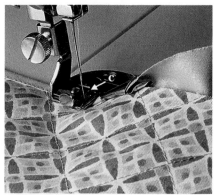

Binder attachment is used to fold and attach bias bindings in one step. First, cut a sharp point at end of bias strip. Feed the point through scroll on foot (**a**). Pull point through

so strip folds to the inside. Sew a few stitches to hold bias fold in place. Insert fabric to be bound into slot between scroll edges (**b**). Adjust position of foot so that

needle stitches on edge of fold (**c**). Guide fabric gently as you stitch. Use the binder attachment for finishing edges of any fabric.

How to Miter Corners on an Outside Edge

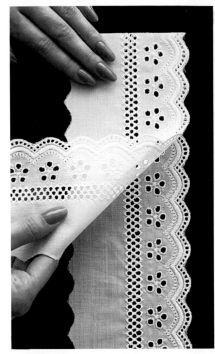

1) Place two lengths of trim, right sides together and edges even. Fold top trim at right angle to form diagonal at corner; press.

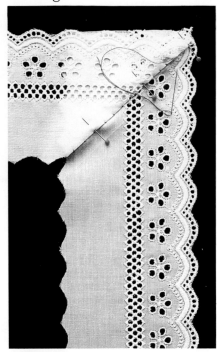

2) Slip-baste the two pieces together on the diagonal fold. Unfold trim.

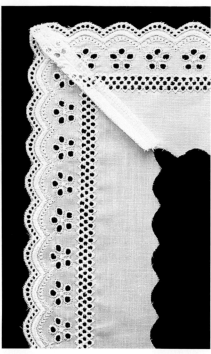

3) Stitch on the line of slip basting on the wrong side. Trim the seams, and finish the edges.

How to Use a Bias Tape Maker

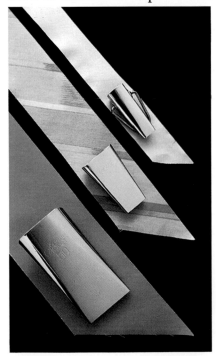

1) Cut bias strip scant 1" (2.5 cm) for ½" (1.3 cm) bias tape; cut 1⅞" (4.7 cm) for 1" (2.5 cm) tape; or 3¼" (8.2 cm) for 2" (5 cm) tape.

2) Trim one end of bias strip to a point. Thread point through wide end of tape maker, bringing point out at narrow end. Insert pin in slot to pull point through. Pin point to pressing surface.

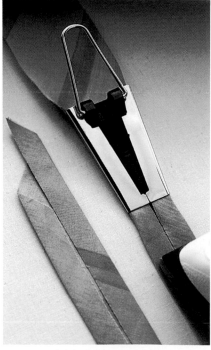

3) Press folded bias strip as you pull tape maker the length of strip. Tape maker automatically folds raw edges to center of strip to create uniform bias tape.

How to Apply Topstitched Banding

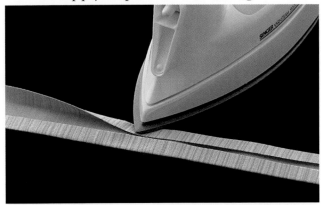

1) Cut strips 1" (2.5 cm) wider than desired band width; add ½" (1.3 cm) to length for each mitered corner. Press under ½" (1.3 cm) along both long edges of strips. Omit steps 2 and 3 for bands without mitered corners.

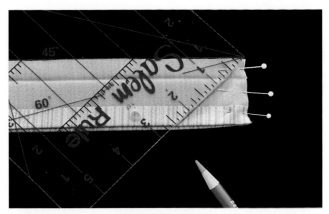

2) Unfold outer pressed edge at end. Mark a point ½" (1.3 cm) from end of strip on foldline. Pin ends of adjoining strips right sides together. Draw a line from marked point to pressed edge, at 45° angle.

3) Stitch along line to marked point; pivot, and stitch to edge at right angle from previous stitching line. Trim seam allowance to ¼" (6 mm); trim diagonally at pivot point. Press seam open; turn outer edge to back along pressed foldline.

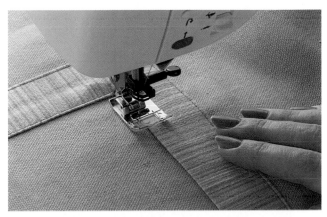

4) Repeat steps 2 and 3 for each mitered corner. Mark placement for banding on the fabric. Pin or glue-baste banding along marked lines. Topstitch in place close to pressed edges; stitch in same direction to prevent diagonal wrinkles.

How to Apply Faced Banding

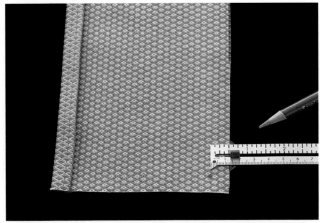

1) Cut strips as in step 1, above. Press under ½" (1.3 cm) along one long edge of each banding strip. Repeat for all facing strips. Mark a point ½" (1.3 cm) from end of strip, ½" (1.3 cm) from unpressed edge. Repeat for all strips.

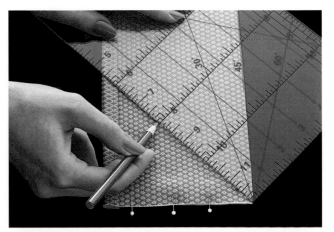

2) Pin ends of adjoining strips right sides together, matching pressed edges and raw edges. Draw a line from marked point to pressed edge, at 45° angle.

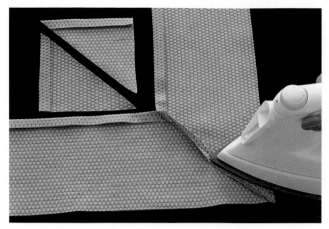

3) Stitch along line through marked point to outer corner. Trim seam allowance to ¼" (6 mm); press open. Repeat for each set of adjoining strips, mitering corners.

4) Pin banding strip faceup to right side of treatment, matching raw edges. Pin facing strip over banding strip, right sides together, matching raw edges and mitered seams.

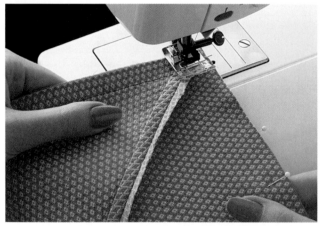

5) Stitch ½" (1.3 cm) from raw edges through all layers; pivot stitching at mitered seams.

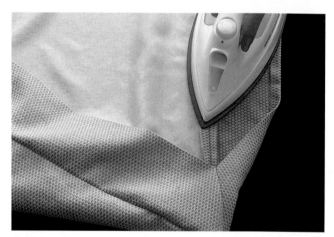

6) Trim the seam allowances diagonally across the corner. Fold out facing strip, and press seam open between band and facing, getting as close as possible to corners.

7) Turn the facing to back of treatment; press along seam. Glue-baste or pin banding and facing strips in place along inner pressed edges.

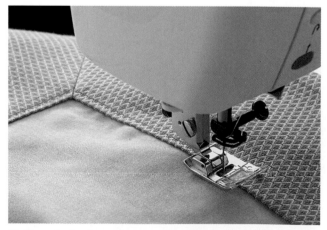

8) Topstitch along inner edge of band, catching inner edge of facing on back of treatment.

Decorative Welting

Just as piping is used in garments to outline a fashion detail, welting is used in home decorator sewing to define or finish seams. Welting is fabric-covered cording, sewn into a seam to provide extra strength and a decorative finishing touch. Welting is the term used in upholstery and home decorating, and piping is the fashion term; however, the two terms are often interchanged.

Fabric strips for welting may be cut on the bias or the straight grain. For more economical use of the fabric, they are cut on the straight grain. Straight-grain welting is preferred for fabrics that are not tightly woven because bias welting can stretch too much, resulting in an uneven, wavy appearance.

For firm fabrics that must be shaped around curves, bias welting works better than straight-grain welting because it does not wrinkle. Bias welting strips do not have to be cut on the true bias. Cutting the strips at an angle less than 45° gives the flexibility of bias grain but requires less yardage. For stripes and plaids, bias welting does not require matching.

To determine how wide to cut the fabric strips, wrap a piece of fabric or paper around the cording. Pin it together, encasing the cording. Cut ½" (1.3 cm) from the pin. Measure the width, and cut strips to match.

Cording, which comes on large spools, may have a tendency to curl or twist even after it is uncoiled from the spool. When sewing the welting, take care to smooth out the cording, removing any twists, to prevent the finished welting from appearing twisted.

Double welting is glued in place as a finishing treatment to cover seams and raw edges in nonsewn items, such as the edges where two fabrics meet on padded headboards or upholstered walls.

Cording Sizes

5/32" is the usual cording for pillows, cushions, and slipcover seams. Cut fabric strip 1½" (3.8 cm) wide.

8/32" is slightly larger for similar applications. This size is appropriate for gathered welting. Cut fabric strip 1¾" (4.5 cm) wide.

12/32" is jumbo cording that can be used for tiebacks and for decorative finishing. Cut the fabric strip 3¾" (9.5 cm) wide.

22/32" is used for pillows, tiebacks, and tablecloth edgings. It provides weight for a better hang at the bottom of bedspreads and comforters. Cut fabric strip 4½" (11.5 cm) wide.

How to Cut and Make Bias Strips

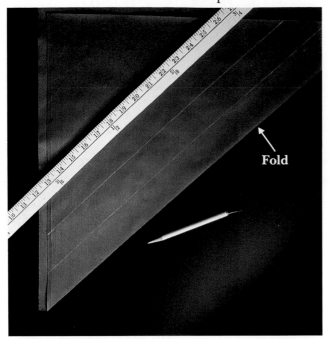

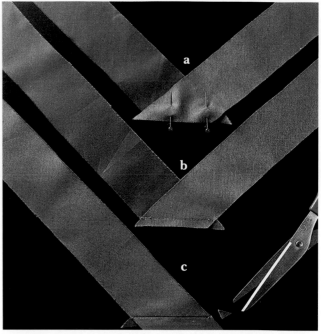

1) Cut bias strips. Determine bias grainline by folding fabric diagonally so selvage aligns with crosswise cut. For ¼" (6 mm) cord, mark and cut 1⅝" (4.2 cm) strips parallel to bias grainline. Cut wider strips for thicker cord.

2) Pin strips at right angles, right sides together, offset slightly **(a)**. Stitch ¼" (6 mm) seams **(b)**, and press open, making one continuous strip equal in length to perimeter of pillow plus 3" (7.5 cm). Trim seam allowances even with edges **(c)**.

How to Make and Apply Welting

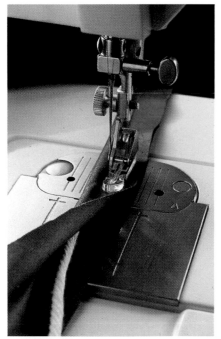

1) Center cord on wrong side of bias strip. Fold strip over cord, aligning raw edges. Using zipper foot on right side of needle, stitch close to cord, gently stretching bias to help welting lie smooth around curves and corners.

2) Pin the welting to the right side of the pillow or cushion front, with raw edges aligned. To ease corners, clip seam allowances to stitching at corners.

3) Begin stitching 2" (5 cm) from end of welting: stitch on bastestitching line. To ease at rounded corners, clip seam allowances to bastestitching.

How to Make Double Welting

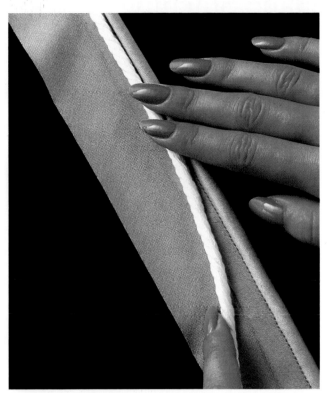

1) Place ⁵⁄₃₂" cording on wrong side of 3" (7.5 cm) fabric strip. Fold fabric over cording, with ½" (1.3 cm) seam allowance extending. Stitch with zipper foot next to cording.

2) Place second cording next to first welt. Bring fabric over second cording.

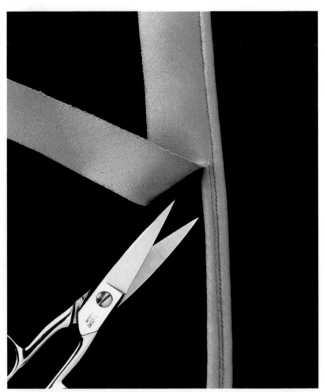

3) Stitch between the two cords on previous stitching line. Loosen tension and use zigzag foot riding on top of the welting.

4) Trim off excess fabric next to stitching for clean edge finish. Raw edge is on the back of the finished double welting.

Hand Stitching

Almost all sewing for home decorator projects can be done on the machine, but sometimes hand stitching is necessary. Closing seam openings on pillows, attaching trims and finishing hems are tasks which may require delicate hand sewing.

To make hand stitching easier, run the thread through beeswax to make it stronger and prevent it from snarling. Use a long needle for the running stitch. Hemming and tacking are usually easier with a short needle.

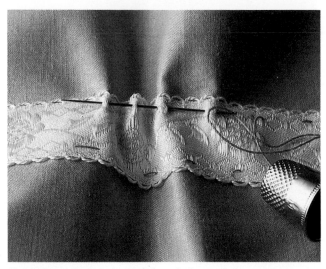

Running stitch is a straight stitch used for temporary basting, easing, gathering or stitching seams. Work from right to left, taking several stitches onto needle before pulling it through. For easing or gathering or for seams, make stitches ⅛" to ¼" (3 to 6 mm) long. For basting, make stitches ½" to ¾" (1.3 to 2 cm) long; use longer stitches for speed-basting.

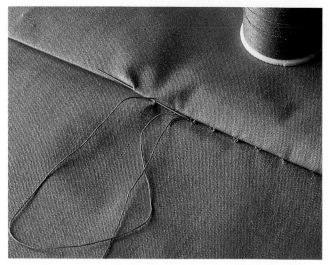

Slipstitch is a nearly invisible stitch for hems, seam openings, linings or trims. Work from right to left, holding folded edge in left hand. Bring needle up through fold and pull thread through. Then take a tiny stitch in body of fabric, directly opposite point where thread came out. Continue taking stitches every ¼" (6 mm).

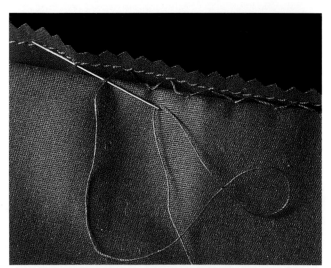

Blindstitch makes a hem that is inconspicuous from either side. Work from right to left with needle pointing left. Take a tiny stitch in body of fabric. Roll hem edge back slightly and take next stitch in underside of hem, ¼" to ½" (6 mm to 1.3 cm) to left of first stitch. Do not pull thread too tightly.

Tacking is used to attach rings and weights, secure linings or hold facings in place. Using double thread, take two or three stitches in the same place, one on top of the other. Secure with a backstitch. When tacking through more than one layer of fabric, do not sew through to outside layer.

Padded Work Surface

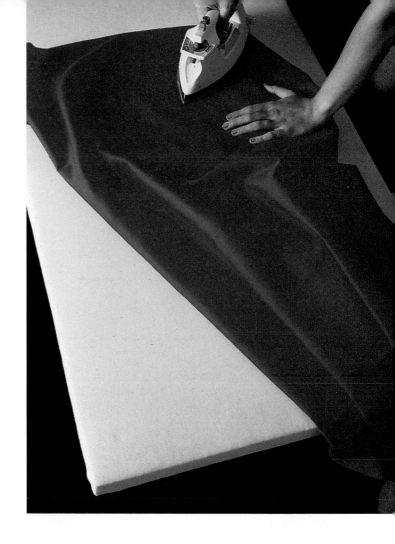

Make a padded work surface to lay out an entire panel for cutting, measuring, squaring off ends and pressing. The square corners and ample width make it easier to work with square and rectangular shapes. Fabric does not slide on the muslin-covered surface; you can also pin into it and press directly on it.

For small projects, use the *square* end of a regular ironing board as a work surface.

Use a steam-spray iron for all your pressing needs. To press fabric, lift and lower the iron in one place. This up-and-down motion prevents fabrics from stretching or distorting. Let the steam do the work. To make sharp creases or to smooth a stubborn wrinkle, spray the fabric with water or spray sizing.

YOU WILL NEED

Hollow door or ¾" (2 cm) plywood, approximately 3' × 7' (.95 × 2.16 m), set on saw horses.

Padding, cotton batting (not polyester), table pads or blankets, ¼" to ½" (6 mm to 1.3 cm) thick, enough to overlap door or plywood 6" (15 cm) on all sides.

Muslin or unpatterned sheet, approximately 6" (15 cm) larger than door or plywood on all sides.

How to Make a Padded Work Surface

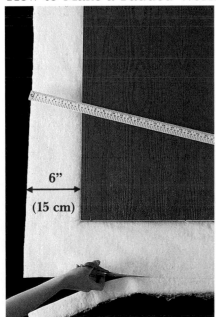

1) Place layers of padding on the floor or on a large, flat surface. Center the door on top of the padding; cut padding 6" (15 cm) larger than the door on all sides.

2) Fold padding over one long edge of the door and tack with 4 or 5 staples. Pull padding on opposite edge and tack. Repeat on both ends. Secure with staples 3" (7.5 cm) apart.

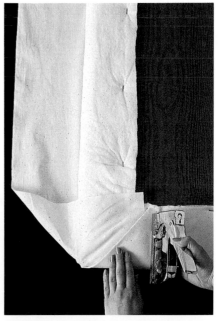

3) Center padded door on top of muslin. Wrap and fasten with staples 3" (7.5 cm) apart. Turn right side up and spray muslin with water. As it dries, muslin shrinks slightly so cover fits tightly.

Windows

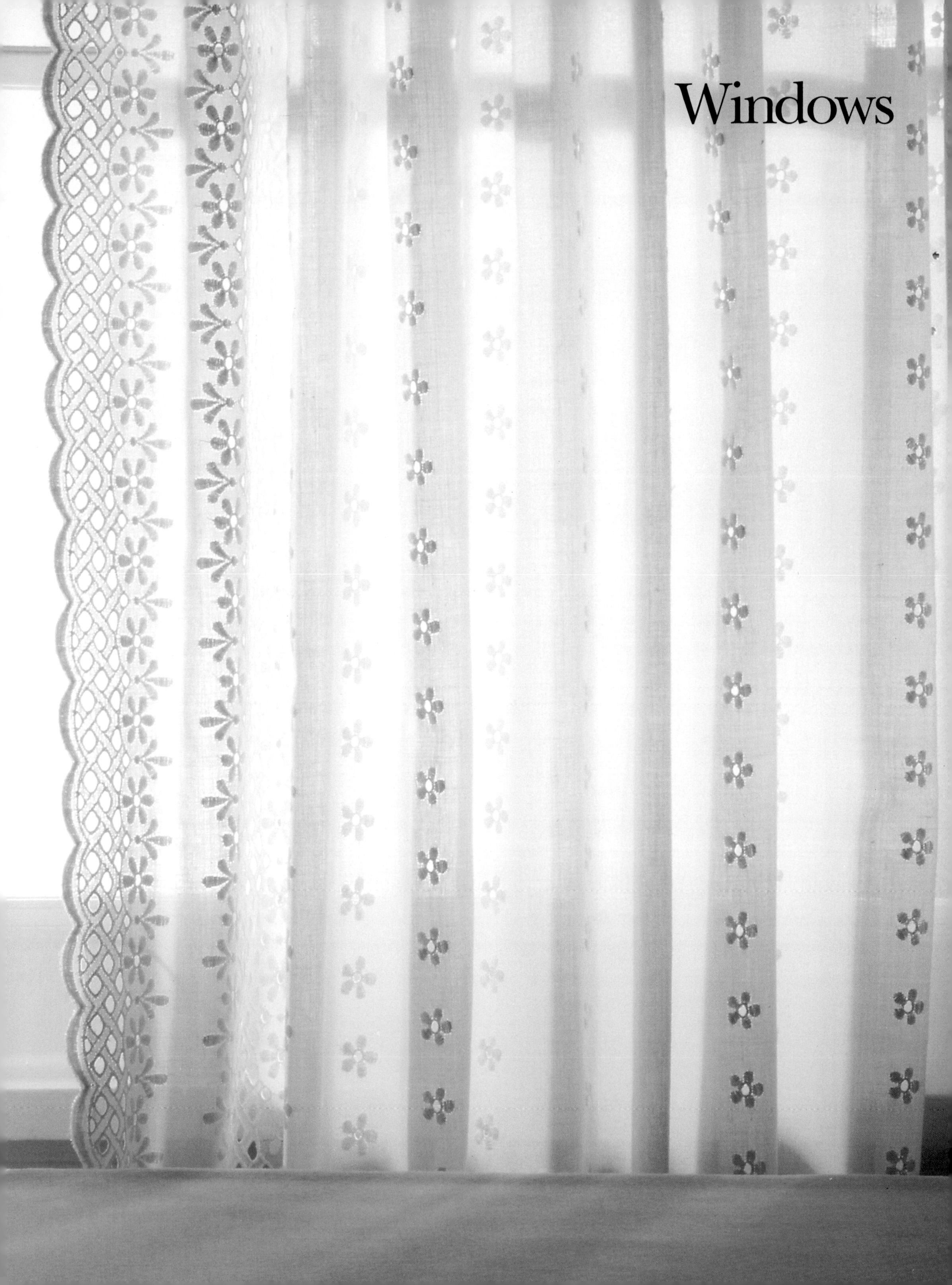

Hardware

Select the drapery hardware before measuring for the window treatment, because the cut length of the fabric will vary, depending on the drapery rods.

Support drapery rods with brackets to prevent the rods from bowing in the middle. The brackets are usually positioned at intervals of 45" (115 cm) or less, across the width of the window. Whenever possible, screw the brackets into wall studs. Use molly bolts if it is necessary to install brackets between wall studs into drywall or plaster.

How to Install a Drapery Rod Bracket Between Wall Studs Using Molly Bolts

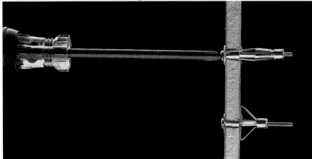

1) Hold drapery rod bracket at desired placement; mark hole locations. Drill ⁵⁄₁₆" (7.5 mm) holes into drywall or plaster; for heavy window treatments, use two molly bolts for each bracket. Tap long molly bolt into drilled hole. Tighten screw; molly bolt expands as it is tightened.

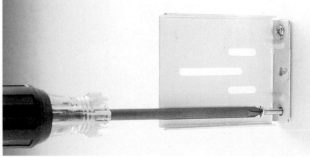

2) Remove screw from molly bolt; insert screw into drapery rod bracket. Align screw to installed molly bolt. Screw bracket securely in place.

Basic Rods

Curtain rods (**a**) are used for simple rod-pocket curtains and valances. When lace or sheer fabric is used, select a curtain rod of clear or opaque plastic to prevent it from showing through and detracting from the fabric.

Wide curtain rods (**b**), known as Continental® and Dauphine® rods, available in both 2½" (6.5 cm) and 4½" (11.5 cm) widths, add depth and interest to the rod pockets of shirred curtains and top treatments. Corner connectors are used to make these rods suitable for bay windows and corner windows. The connectors allow you to sew a continuous window treatment, without interruptions or breaks in the treatment at the corners.

Flexible ⅜" (1 cm) plastic tubing (**c**), found in the plumbing department of hardware stores, can be shaped to fit the curve of arch windows.

Decorative Pole Sets

Contemporary metal pole sets (**d**) can be used for tab curtains with returns, and for swags. These drapery rods, also available for traverse draperies, have metallic and pearlized finishes in several colors.

Traditional brass pole sets (**e**) come in various sizes and finial styles. Brass hardware is used for rod-pocket curtains and valances as well as with draped swags or pole swags. Brass rods in smaller diameters can be bent for use in bay windows.

Wood pole sets (**f**) with plain or fluted poles are available in finished or unfinished wood. Finials in various styles give the wood poles a decorator look. The poles and finials may be covered with fabric, or painted.

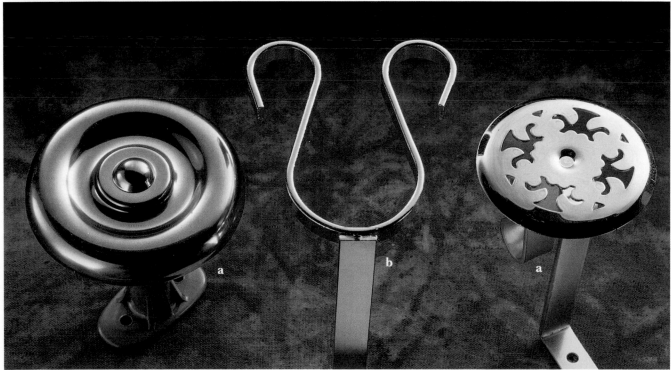

Drapery accessories are used to secure the draped fabric in swag window treatments and in tieback draperies. Tieback holders (**a**) with projection arms or stems are used instead of fabric tiebacks to hold curtains in place. They may also be used for scarf swag window treatments (page 109). Swag holders (**b**) are also used for scarf swags when rosettes are desired.

Covered Poles
& Finials

Fabric-covered drapery poles and ball finials add a designer touch to scarf swags and other window treatments. Use unfinished wood poles and finials. The poles may be covered with either shirred or flat fabric.

A smooth covered rod is used to support the scarf swag shown at right. Twisted welting, draped with the swag, is also used to embellish the coordinating covered finial. A shirred covered rod is featured with rod-pocket curtains and covered finials with ruffles (inset, right).

✄ Cutting Directions

The cut length of the rod sleeve is equal to the rod circumference plus 1½" (3.8 cm) for 1⅜" (3.5 cm) diameter wood poles, or the circumference plus 1¾" (4.5 cm) for 2" (5 cm) wood poles.

For a flat rod sleeve, the cut width of the rod sleeve is equal to the length of the wood pole. For a shirred rod sleeve, the cut width is two or three times the length of the wood pole.

Cut the fabric circles for the finials as on page 50 or 51.

YOU WILL NEED

Decorator fabric.

Wood pole set with ball finials.

Brackets designed to be used with Cirmosa® rods.

Cord, braid, or ribbon trim for finials.

Fabric glue.

Tacks; or heavy-duty stapler and staples.

How to Make a Smooth Covered Pole

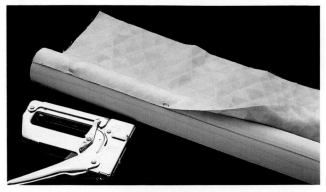

1) **Mark** line on wood pole, as in step 4, page 136. Staple or tack one edge of fabric to pole, aligning raw edge with marked line.

2) **Wrap** fabric snugly around pole. Fold under raw edge; staple or tack in place. Apply glue around end of pole so rod sleeve will adhere. Allow glue to dry.

How to Make a Shirred Covered Pole

Sew plain rod sleeve as on page 62, except do not stitch side hems. Insert drapery rod, gathering fabric evenly. Apply glue around end of wood pole, so rod sleeve will adhere. Allow glue to dry.

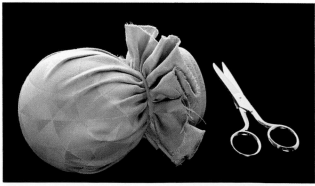

Alternate method for rod-pocket curtain. Sew plain rod sleeve for exposed portion of wood pole only, as on page 62, except do not stitch side hems. Insert drapery rod, gathering fabric evenly. Apply glue to pole at ends of rod sleeve; allow to dry. Curtain covers remainder of pole.

How to Make a Covered Finial

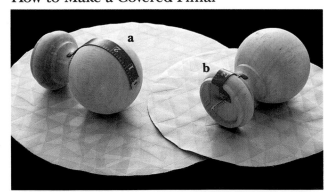

1) **Measure** ball portion of finial from top of finial to neck (**a**); cut one fabric circle for each finial, with a radius 1" (2.5 cm) longer than measurement. Measure the crown portion of finial from neck to base (**b**); cut one fabric circle for each finial, with radius 1" (2.5 cm) longer than measurement.

2) **Center** ball of finial on first fabric circle; wrap fabric around ball to neck of finial. Secure fabric at neck with rubber band, adjusting fullness evenly; trim to within ½" (1.3 cm) of rubber band.

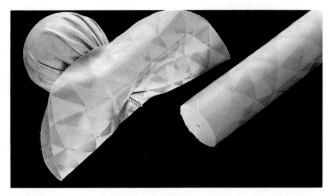

3) Pierce center of second fabric circle; twist fabric over screw. Attach finial to wood pole.

4) Apply bead of glue around neck. Wrap second circle to neck, securing with second rubber band and adjusting gathers evenly; allow glue to dry. Trim fabric close to rubber band. Cover rubber band with cord, braid, or ribbon trim.

How to Make a Covered Finial with a Ruffle

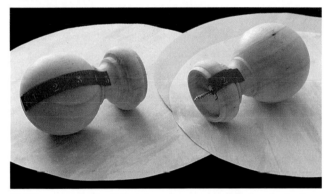

1) Measure ball of finial and cut one fabric circle for each finial, as in step 1 for covered finial, opposite. Measure crown of finial as in step 1; cut two fabric circles for each finial, with radius of each circle equal to measurement plus depth of ruffle plus ½" (1.3 cm).

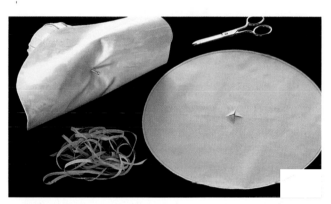

2) Place fabric circles for crown right sides together. Stitch in ¼" (6 mm) seam; trim to ⅛" (3 mm). Slash 1" (2.5 cm) "X" through one layer of fabric at center. Turn right side out through slash; press. Finish as in steps 2 to 4 for covered finial, opposite, but do not trim ruffle.

How to Install a Covered Pole with Finials

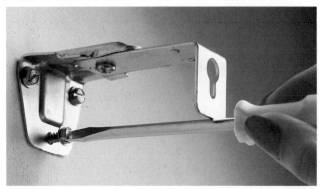

1) Attach brackets to the wall or window frame, using molly bolts (page 46) or pan-head screws (page 52).

2) Attach screws to covered rod, positioning them same distance apart as keyhole openings on brackets. Hang covered rod on brackets.

Covering & Installing Mounting Boards

Some window treatments are mounted on boards instead of being hung on drapery rods. For a professional look, cover the mounting board with fabric. This gives it a more finished appearance and protects the window treatment from being snagged by unfinished wood.

The mounting board is cut to the finished width of the window treatment and may be mounted inside or outside the window frame. For an inside mount, the board is attached inside the window frame, using #8 gauge 1½" (3.8 cm) pan-head screws. Predrill the holes for the screws, using a ⅛" (3 mm) drill bit.

For an outside mount, the board is installed at the top of the window frame or on the wall above the window. For clearance, the board is cut wider than the outside measurement of the window frame or undertreatment, and it projects out from the wall farther than the window frame or undertreatment. Angle irons are used to install the mounting board. The angle irons must be a little shorter than the width of the mounting board. Whenever possible, screw the angle irons into wall studs, using pan-head screws and predrilling the holes for the screws, using a ⅛" (3 mm) drill bit. If it is necessary to install angle irons between wall studs into drywall or plaster, use molly bolts to ensure a secure installation. To prevent the mounting board from bowing in the middle, position angle irons at 45" (115 cm) intervals or less.

Supplies include mounting board **(a)**, angle irons **(b)**, pan-head screws **(c)**, and molly bolts **(d)**.

How to Determine the Size of the Mounting Board

Inside mount. Cut 1" × 1" (2.5 × 2.5 cm) mounting board ½" (1.3 cm) shorter than inside measurement of window frame, to ensure that the board will fit inside the frame after it is covered with fabric.

Outside mount. Cut mounting board 2" (5 cm) longer than width of undertreatment or window frame and at least 2" (5 cm) wider than projection of undertreatment or window frame.

How to Cover the Mounting Board with Fabric

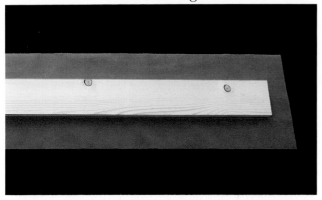

1) Cut fabric to cover mounting board, with width of fabric equal to distance around board plus 1" (2.5 cm) and length of fabric equal to length of board plus 4½" (11.5 cm). Center board on wrong side of fabric.

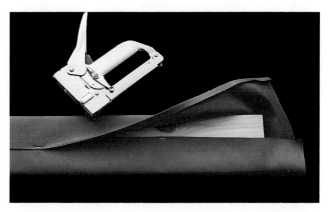

2) Staple one long edge of fabric to board, placing staples about 8" (20.5 cm) apart; do not staple within 6" (15 cm) of ends. Wrap fabric around board; fold under ⅜" (1 cm) on long edge, and staple to board, placing staples about 6" (15 cm) apart.

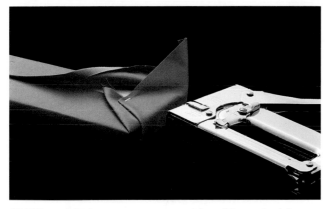

3) Miter fabric at corners on side of board with unfolded edge of fabric; finger-press. Staple miters in place near raw edge.

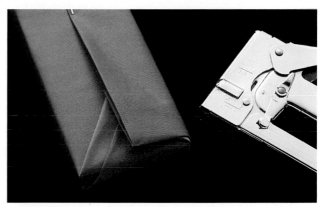

4) Miter fabric at corner on side of board with folded edge of fabric; finger-press. Fold excess fabric under at end of board; staple near fold.

How to Install a Mounting Board Using Angle Irons

1) Screw angle irons into covered mounting board, using #8 gauge ¾" (2 cm) pan-head screws. Hold board at desired placement, making sure that it is level; mark screw holes on wall or window frame, using pencil.

2) Remove angle irons from board. Secure angle irons to wall, using ⅛" (3 mm) L (long) molly bolts (page 46) or ¾" (2 cm) pan-head screws.

3) Mount window treatment onto mounting board, using staples. Place mounting board on installed angle irons. Screw angle irons into mounting board.

Lining Curtains

Linings add body and weight to curtains to help them hang better. A lining also adds opaqueness, prevents fading and sun damage to curtain fabric, and provides some insulation.

Curtains may be lined the traditional way or lined to the edge with coordinating fabric to create a custom look.

Select linings according to the weight of the curtain fabric. White or off-white sateen is the most often used lining fabric. Specially treated linings that resist staining and block out light are also available.

✄ Cutting Directions

For a lined curtain with a casing, cut the curtain as directed on page 26. For lining with 2" (5 cm) double-fold hem, cut lining the finished length of curtains plus 2½" (6.5 cm); cut lining 6" (15 cm) narrower than cut width of curtain. Seam and press widths, aligning curtain and lining seams if possible.

For curtains lined to the edge, cut curtain and lining the finished length plus amount for double-fold hem and ½" (1.3 cm) for seam at upper edge. Cut panels the finished width plus 1" (2.5 cm) for side seams.

How to Line Curtains

1) **Turn,** press and stitch 2" (5 cm) double-fold hem in lining. Turn and press double-fold hem in curtain. Tack weights inside fold of curtain hems at seams and stitch curtain hems.

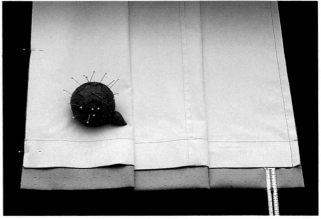

2) **Place** lining on curtain, right sides together, so lining is 1½" (3.8 cm) above curtain hem. Pin and stitch ½" (1.3 cm) seams on sides.

3) **Turn** curtain right side out. Center lining so side hems are equal width. Press side hem with seam allowance toward center. Continue to the top edge of the curtain.

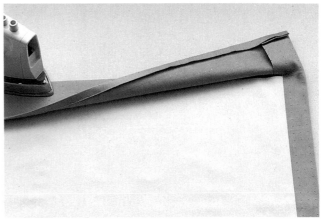

4) **Press** ½" (1.3 cm) seam allowance across upper edge of curtain. Fold upper edge of curtain down an amount equal to depth of casing and heading. Lining ends at foldline.

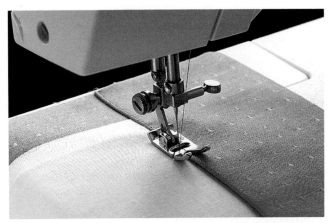

5) Stitch close to the folded edge to form casing. For curtains with headings, stitch the heading the desired depth.

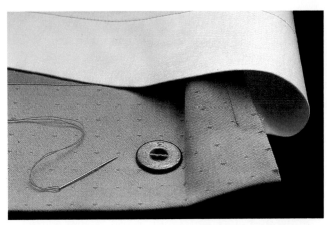

6) Hand-tack weights along lower edge of curtain inside side hems.

7) Turn side hems back diagonally below lining to form a miter. Slipstitch miter in place.

8) Make French tacks about 12" (30.5 cm) apart between hem and lining, using double thread. Take two stitches near top of hem and directly across in lining, leaving 1" (2.5 cm) slack in thread. Make blanket stitch over thread; secure with knot in lining.

How to Line Curtains to the Edge

1) Cut curtain and lining the same size. Turn, press and stitch equal lower hems in curtain and lining. Place right sides of curtain and lining together with lower hems even. Pin sides and upper edge.

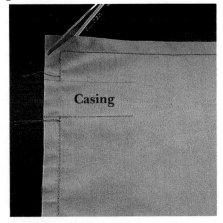

2) Mark casing and heading depth on lining. Join lining and curtain with ½" (1.3 cm) seam on sides and upper edge, leaving opening on both sides at casing line. Diagonally trim upper corners. Press the upper seam open.

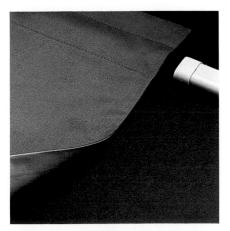

3) Turn curtain right side out. Press seams flat. Stitch casing and heading. Insert curtain rod in casing. Hang curtain and fold lining to right side so contrasting fabric shows; secure with tieback.

Pleated Draperies

Pleated draperies are easy to sew with pleater tape, which eliminates tedious, complicated measuring.

Pinch pleats are the traditional pleated heading for draperies. Each pinch pleat is actually three small pleats grouped together at regular intervals. Pleater tape for pinch pleats has evenly spaced pockets woven into it; special four-pronged pleater hooks inserted into the pockets draw up the pleats.

Select pleater tape that gives the desired drapery fullness. Some pleater tapes are designed to give an exact double fullness; others allow for more or less than double fullness, depending on how the pockets are used. Determine the drapery fullness according to the fabric weight, following guidelines for curtain fullness (page 59).

Panel draperies are stationary pleated panels that hang at the sides of the window.

Draw draperies can be closed to cover the entire width of the window. These draperies hang on traverse rods and pull open to one side only (one-way draw) or to both sides (two-way draw).

Before cutting fabric or tape, prepleat the *tape only* using pleater hooks to determine the finished width of the draperies and the pleat position. Pleat tape to the width of the drapery panel and hang it on the rod. Adjust pleats as necessary so the last pleat of the panel is at the corner of the rod return. Do not position pleats on the return or at the center of two-way draperies where panels overlap. Remove pleater hooks and measure tape to determine the finished width of drapery panels, as in steps 1 and 2, opposite.

✂ Cutting Directions

After pleating tape to correct size, cut pleater tape for each panel so that panels have pockets in the same position. Add ½" (1.3 cm) at each end of pleater tape for finishing.

Cut decorator fabric so width is the length of the pleater tape plus 4" (10 cm) to allow for 1" (2.5 cm) double-fold side hems. Seam fabric if necessary, allowing 1" (2.5 cm) for each seam. For length, cut fabric finished length, plus 6½" (16.3 cm) to allow for 3" (7.5 cm) double-fold hem and ½" (1.3 cm) for turning under on upper edge.

YOU WILL NEED

Decorator fabric for draperies.

Pleater tape to match style of heading.

Pleater hooks and end pins.

How to Sew Unlined Pinch-pleated Draperies

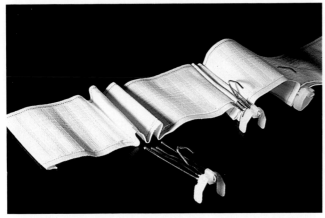

1) Prepleat pleater tape to finished width of drapery panel. Leave space unpleated at one end of tape for overlap and at other end for return.

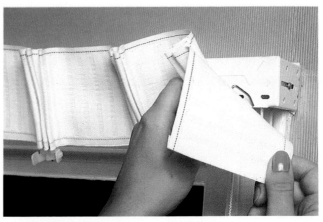

2) Position the pleater tape on installed traverse rod and adjust pleats if necessary. Fold ends under ½" (1.3 cm). Remove hooks. Cut drapery panels using pleater tape as guide.

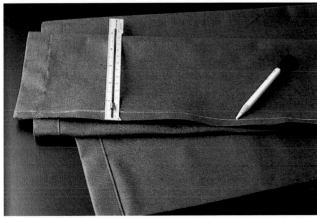

3) Turn under double-fold hem on lower edge and double-fold hems on sides; stitch. Mark ½" (1.3 cm) from upper edge on right side of drapery.

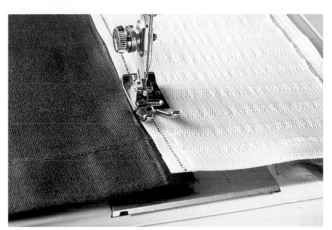

4) Pin upper edge of pleater tape, pocket side up, along marked line so that pleater tape overlaps drapery ½" (1.3 cm). Stitch ¼" (6 mm) from edge of pleater tape.

5) Fold pleater tape to inside of drapery so it is even with finished upper edge of drapery; press. Stitch lower edge and both sides of tape, following guideline on tape, if marked.

6) Insert hooks. Push prongs all the way up into pleats. Adjust folds between hooks.

Curtain Basics

Curtains are a traditional favorite for window fashions. They are flat, nonpleated panels, so they are easier to clean and press than many other window treatments.

Curtains are often made of lightweight or sheer fabrics. Heavier fabrics such as linen, chintz, or textured or polished cotton look best for formal, floor-length curtains. Lighter, crisper fabrics work well for casual, sill-length and cafe curtains. Sheer curtains are usually two and one-half to three times the fullness of the finished width; heavier fabrics require only double fullness.

Mount curtains at windows on stationary rods or poles. Rods may be plain, covered with shirred fabric between the curtain panels, or wide and flat such as Continental™ and cornice rods.

Casings, also known as rod pockets, are hems stitched in place along the upper edge of curtains. The hems are open at both ends so a curtain rod or pole can be inserted.

Headings are optional on curtains. The heading creates a decorative ruffle above the casing along the upper edge of the curtain.

Linings add weight and body to curtains. Although a lining may not be necessary, it can improve a curtain's appearance and give it a custom look.

Tab top curtains have fabric loops instead of a casing along the upper edge. These curtains are used with decorative brass or wooden poles.

Ruffled curtains have a graceful appearance. Ruffles add weight to curtains and make them hang and drape more attractively.

Tiebacks are separate fabric strips which hold curtains open and emphasize the drape of the curtain. Tiebacks can be straight, shaped or ruffled and are usually stationary on panel curtains.

Shower curtains are flat, one-piece, hemmed curtains with evenly-spaced holes along the upper edge for hanging with hooks or rings.

Casing Styles for Curtains

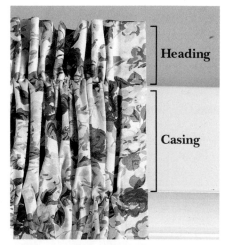

Simple casing is stitched along the upper edge of the curtain. It may be used for sheer curtains that hang behind draperies, a valance or cornice.

Heading creates a ruffled edge above casing. Headings are from 1" to 5" (2.5 to 12.5 cm) deep, depending on curtain length and weight of the fabric.

Wide casing and heading are used with a Continental or cornice rod. They are well suited for floor-length curtains, where casing and heading depth should balance with curtain length.

Hems

If you have measured, figured and cut accurately, your curtains should fit windows perfectly once they are hemmed. For the neatest and easiest hems, follow the procedure used in professional workrooms: sew the lower hems first, the side hems next, and casings and headings last.

Side and lower hems of unlined curtains are almost always double to provide strength, weight and stability. The easiest way to make a double-fold hem is to press it in place on an ironing board or padded work surface. Use a seam gauge to measure each fold. As you make the fold, pin the fabric to the padding, placing the pins so they do not interfere with pressing. If side edges are on the selvage, cut off selvage or clip it every 1" to 6" (2.5 to 15 cm).

Curtains hang better when hems are weighted or anchored. Sew small weights into the hems at the lower corners and bottoms of seams to keep the curtain from pulling or puckering. Use heavier weights for full-length curtains, lighter weights for lightweight fabrics and shorter curtains.

How to Sew Double-fold Hems

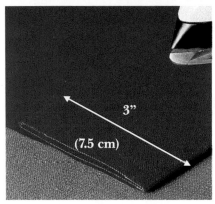

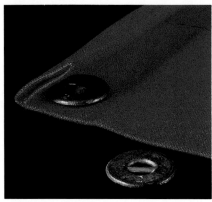

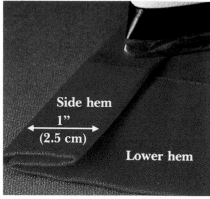

1) Turn a scant 3" to 4" (7.5 to 10 cm) to wrong side on lower edge of curtain. Pin along cut edge. Press fold. Fold under another 3" to 4" (7.5 to 10 cm); pin and press. Secure hem using one of the methods below.

2) Turn a scant 1" to 1½" (2.5 to 3.8 cm) to the wrong side for side hems. Pin and press. Fold under another 1" to 1½" (2.5 to 3.8 cm); pin and press. Tack weights inside the second fold at side corners.

3) Press the side hems in place. When the hems have been pressed, finish them with straight stitching, machine blindstitching or fusible web.

Three Ways to Finish Curtain Hems

Straight-stitch on folded hem edge, using 8 to 10 stitches per inch (2.5 cm). When stitching three layers of fabric, lessen pressure slightly and stitch slowly.

Machine blindstitch to make stitches almost invisible on right side. After pressing, fold hem back to right side, leaving a fold of fabric ⅛" (3 mm) from hem edge. Set machine to blindstitch. Adjust zigzag stitch to take tiny bite into curtain only.

Fuse hem in place. Tuck strip of fusible web between pressed hem and curtain. Follow manufacturer's instructions for fusing, using damp press cloth for additional steam. Most fusibles require 15 seconds for permanent bonding.

60

How to Sew a Simple Casing

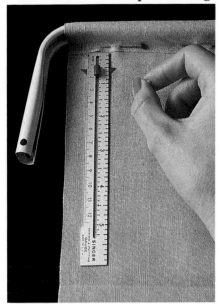 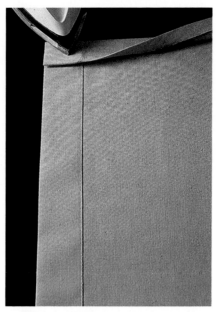 

1) Determine casing depth by loosely pinning a curtain fabric strip around the rod. Remove rod and measure the distance from the top of the strip to the pin. Add ½" (1.3 cm) to be turned under.

2) Press under ½" (1.3 cm) along upper cut edge of curtain panel. Fold over again and press to form a hem equal to amount measured in step 1.

3) Stitch close to folded hem edge to form casing, backstitching at both ends. If desired, stitch again close to the upper edge to create a sharp crease appropriate for flat or oval curtain rods.

How to Sew a Casing with a Heading

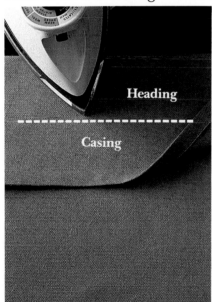  

1) Determine the depth of the casing as directed in step 1, above. Determine the depth of heading, opposite. Press under ½" (1.3 cm) along upper cut edge of the curtain panel. Fold and press again to form hem equal to casing plus heading depth.

2) Stitch close to folded edge, backstitching at both ends. Mark heading depth with a pin at each end of panel. Stitch again at marked depth. To aid straight stitching, apply a strip of masking tape to the bed of the machine at heading depth, or use seam guide.

3) Insert rod through casing and gather curtain evenly onto rod. Adjust heading by pulling up the folded edge so the seam is exactly on the lower edge of the rod. A wide heading may be made to look puffy and more rounded by pulling the fabric out on each side.

How to Sew a Continental® or Cornice Rod Casing with a Heading

1) Measure window after rod has been installed to determine total length. Add 15½" (39.3 cm): 5½" (14 cm) for the casing and seam allowance, 8" (20.5 cm) for the double-fold hem, and 2" (5 cm) for 1" (2.5 cm) heading. For a deeper heading, add twice the desired heading depth.

2) Turn under ½" (1.3 cm) on upper edge of curtain and press. Fold over again 6" (15 cm) for casing and heading. Stitch 1" (2.5 cm) from upper folded edge to form heading. Stitch close to folded edge to form casing.

3) Insert rod through casing and gather curtain evenly onto rod. Hang on installed brackets. For a wide heading, use two Continental or cornice rods, installed one above the other. Add 10" (25.5 cm) for second casing.

How to Make a Shirred Pole or Rod Cover

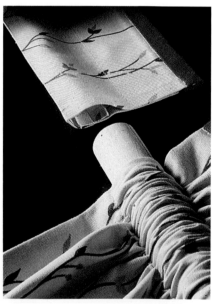

1) Cut fabric two and one-half times the length of pole area to be covered; cut width equal to circumference of pole plus 1½" (3.8 cm). For pole cover with a heading, add amount equal to twice the heading depth.

2) Stitch ½" (1.3 cm) hems on short ends. Fold strip in half lengthwise, right sides together, and pin long edges together. Stitch ½" (1.3 cm) seam. Press seam open. Turn cover right side out.

3) Press cover so that seam is at back of pole. To form heading, stitch again at appropriate distance from upper folded edge. If desired, add narrow binding to upper edge, opposite. Gather pole cover onto rod between two curtain panels.

Customizing Rod-pocket Curtains

Bindings, borders, ribbon or contrasting returns give curtains individuality and style. These decorative touches customize curtains and require little additional sewing time.

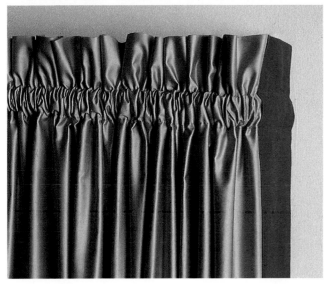

Contrasting returns. Cut fabric strips the width of return plus 1" (2.5 cm), and the cut length of curtain. Allow for ½" (1.3 cm) side seam on one edge of the curtain. Press under ½" (1.3 cm) on one long edge of strip. Pin right side of strip to wrong side of curtain, unpressed raw edges even; stitch. Press strip to right side; fuse or edgestitch edge to right side of curtain. Finish curtain.

Narrow binding. Construct basic curtain. Cut 2½" (6.5 cm) strip of fabric with length equal to finished width of panel plus 1" (2.5 cm). Press under ½" (1.3 cm) on one long side and each short end. Pin unpressed edge to upper edge of curtain, right sides together; stitch. Press folded edge of binding over upper edge. From right side, stitch in the ditch.

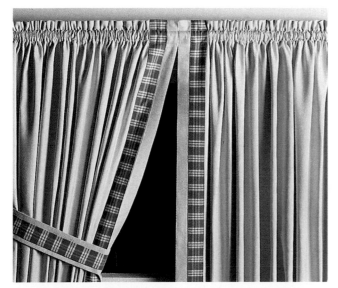

Edgestitched ribbon banding. Cut fabric trims two times the finished width of banding, length equal to cut length of curtain. Press and stitch 1" (2.5 cm) double-fold side hems on curtain. Press trim, wrong sides together and raw edges meeting at center. Pin trim with outer edge covering side hem stitching line. Edgestitch trim close to folded edges. Finish curtain.

Fused border. Construct basic curtain. Cut fabric trim two times the width of finished band, and the finished length of curtain plus 1" (2.5 cm). Press trim wrong sides together and raw edges meeting at center; press under ½" (1.3 cm) on short ends. Cut strips of fusible web slightly narrower than finished trim; insert between curtain and trim. Fuse in place.

Bishop Sleeve Curtains

These elegant pouffed curtains are simply rod-pocket curtains with extra length allowed for blousing. The bishop sleeve look is achieved with tiebacks pulling the curtain tight to the window frame. Any number of poufs may be used. Arrange and tie the poufs in a position that is in proportion to the window length and width.

The poufs are balanced on each side of the tieback because the curtain rod extends 6" to 8" (15 to 20.5 cm) on each side of the window. If side space is limited, they may also hang straight on the outer edge, with the pouf draping only to the center of the window.

Tiebacks are tight on this curtain, in contrast to loose-fitting tiebacks on most curtain panels. For a decorative effect, use tasseled tiebacks or floppy bows with long streamers. Or use cord to tie the poufs so tiebacks do not show. As a finishing touch, the soft, flowing look of the bishop sleeve curtains can be repeated with puff or balloon valances (page 116).

✂ Cutting Directions

Cut panels 2 to 2½ times wider than finished width. To finished length, add 12" (30.5 cm) extra for each pouf and 12" (30.5 cm) more to puddle on the floor; add allowance for double top heading and rod pocket. Add 2" (5 cm) for double bottom hem if puddling on floor, or 8" (20.5 cm) for double bottom hem if curtains come to the floor.

YOU WILL NEED

Decorator fabric for curtains.

Tiebacks and cup hooks for each pouf.

Flat curtain rod or Continental® rod.

How to Sew a Bishop Sleeve Curtain

1) Turn under and stitch double 1" (2.5 cm) side hems. Turn under and stitch rod pocket and heading. Stitch double bottom hems.

2) Insert rod; hang and gather panels evenly. Determine location of poufs by tightly bunching the panel with your hands and lifting it to different positions until you find a pleasing proportion.

3) Mark tieback position. Attach cup hook behind pouf to hold tieback. Tissue paper can be tucked into the pouf to improve blousing if fabric does not have as much body as you would like.

Rod-pocket Swags & Cascades

This swagged window treatment is not only easy to sew, but is also easier to install than most swags. Just insert the drapery rod into the rod pockets and adjust the gathers evenly. When a print fabric is used, choose one of the colors in the print as the accent color in the swags.

Swags may be used with or without cascades. Cascades add a more vertical appearance to the window treatment. When swags and cascades are used with underdraperies, make the cascades to match the draperies so they blend in, or make them from an accent color in the swags to contrast with the draperies.

Triple fullness is recommended for this window treatment. At this fullness, each cascade covers about 15" (38 cm) of the window width; each swag covers about 10" to 12" (25.5 to 30.5 cm) of the width. If you are not making cascades for the sides of the window, determine the number of swags you need by dividing the width of the window by 10" (25.5 cm); round up or down, if necessary, to the closest number. If you are making cascades, first subtract 30" (76 cm) from the width of the window; then divide the remaining width by 10" (25.5 cm) to determine the number of swags.

✄ Cutting Directions

To determine the depth of the rod pocket, add 1" (2.5 cm) ease to the width of the drapery rod. The cut length of each swag panel is equal to two times the desired finished length, two times the depth of the rod pocket, two times the depth of the heading, 3" (7.5 cm) for pouffing, and 1" (2.5 cm) for seam allowances.

One fabric width will make three swags. If two fabrics of different widths are being used, cut the wider fabric to the same width as the narrower one. Cut each fabric to the calculated length, and then cut lengthwise into thirds.

The short point of the cascades is equal to the finished length of the swags. The long point should be at least 12" (30.5 cm) longer than the short point, but may be two-thirds the length of the window, sill-length, or apron-length. If used with underdraperies, the long point is usually two-thirds the length of the draperies.

The cut length of the cascades is equal to the finished length at the long point, the depth of the rod pocket, the depth of the heading, and 2" (5 cm) for seam allowances. For each cascade, you will need one cut length of each of the two fabrics.

YOU WILL NEED

Decorator fabrics in two contrasting colors.

Flat drapery rod; projection of rod must be at least 2" (5 cm) more than projection of underdraperies or other undertreatment.

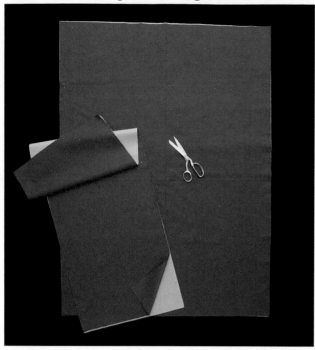

1) Place face fabric and lining right sides together. Mark width of fabric into three equal panels; cut.

2) Stitch panels of face fabric and lining together around all four sides in ½" (1.3 cm) seam, leaving 6" (15 cm) opening at upper edge for turning; trim corners. Turn right sides out; press.

3) Measure combined depth of rod pocket and heading from upper edge of panel; fold and press to lining side at this depth. Measure combined depth of rod pocket and heading from lower edge of panel; fold and press to face-fabric side at this depth.

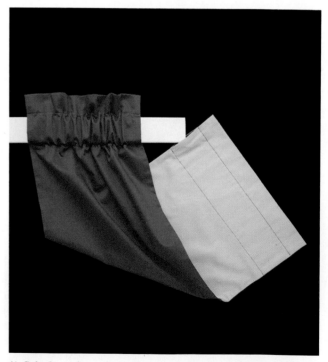

4) Stitch rod pockets. Insert drapery rod into rod pocket at upper edge. Then fold panel under, and insert drapery rod into rod pocket at lower edge. Repeat for remaining swag panels.

How to Sew Rod-pocket Cascades

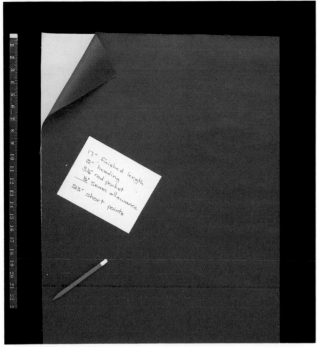

1) **Place** face fabric and lining right sides together. Determine length at short points by adding finished length of swag, depth of heading, depth of rod pocket, and ½" (1.3 cm) seam allowance. On inner sides of cascades, measure this distance from upper edge; mark short points.

2) **Draw** a line on each cascade from marking for short point to lower edge of outer side, or long point. Cut on marked line.

3) **Stitch** panels around all four sides in ½" (1.3 cm) seam, leaving 6" (15 cm) opening at upper edge for turning; trim corners. Turn right sides out; press.

4) **Measure** combined depth of rod pocket and heading from upper edges of cascades; fold and press to lining side at this depth. Stitch rod pockets. Insert drapery rod into rod pockets.

Curtains with Attached Valances

Curtains with attached valances have a clean, updated look. Self-styling tape sewn at the top of the curtain gathers the upper edge in an attractive pattern. These stationary curtains can be made as two separate panels with attached valances, hanging at the sides of the window. Or, for another look, two panels that meet in the center and share an attached valance can be held back at the sides of the window with decorative hardware or tiebacks.

For best results, curtains with attached valances are made from lightweight fabric. The curtain panels may be lined, if desired. The valances can be made from either matching or coordinating fabric. The bottom of the valance is bound with a contrasting fabric, accenting the lower edge and eliminating the need for a hem.

Select a self-styling tape that will gather the upper edge in the desired pattern. Mount either style of treatment on a decorator rod with rings. Or, if desired, use a standard curtain rod to mount a treatment with two panels under one valance.

Two curtain panels share one continuous attached valance (opposite). The curtain top is gathered into even pencil pleats, using self-styling shirring tape. Smocking tape, used in the separate curtain panels above, gathers the upper edge into a unique design.

Types of Self-styling Tapes

Self-styling cords and hook loops are woven into the styling tapes to create several different looks. Shirring tape **(a)** draws curtain panels into narrow, evenly spaced pencil pleats. Smocking tape **(b)** creates soft, alternating pleats for a look that resembles smocking. Two rows of smocking tape can be applied for a more dramatic effect. Pleating tape **(c)** is used to create a classic pinch-pleated look. If using this tape, plan spacing so that pleats form at the front corner of the return edge and at least 2" (5 cm) from the inner edge.

✂ Cutting Directions

Determine the desired finished length of the curtain. If using a decorative rod with rings, measure from the pin holes in the rings to the desired length. If using a standard curtain rod, measure from the top of the rod to where you want the lower edge of the curtain; then add ½" (1.3 cm) so the curtain will extend above the rod. Determine the desired finished width of the curtain, including returns. Divide this amount by two for a curtain with two panels under one valance.

Cut fabric for the curtain panel with the cut length equal to the desired finished length plus 8½" (21.8 cm). The cut width of the fabric is equal to the finished width, including returns, multiplied by the desired fullness plus 6" (15 cm) for double-fold 1½" (3.8 cm) side hems. Fullness is determined by the self-styling tape; most tapes require two-and-one-half times fullness.

If lining is desired, cut lining fabric with the cut length equal to the cut length of the curtain fabric minus 5" (12.5 cm) and cut width equal to the cut width of the curtain.

Cut fabric for the valance with the cut length equal to the desired finished length of the valance plus ½" (1.3 cm). For a single-panel curtain, the cut width of the valance is the same as the cut width of the curtain panel. For a two-panel curtain with one attached valance, the cut width of the valance is equal to the combined cut widths of the two panels minus 6" (15 cm).

Cut strips of fabric, 2" (5 cm) wide, to bind the lower edge of the valance. The length of the binding strip after seaming is equal to the cut width of the valance minus 5" (12.5 cm).

YOU WILL NEED

Decorator fabric, for curtain and valance.

Contrasting fabric, for binding the lower edge of the valance.

Drapery weights.

Self-styling tape.

Floss holder or small square of thin cardboard.

Decorator rod with rings; or standard curtain rod.

Drapery pins.

Pin-on rings and cup hooks or tenter hooks, for securing returns to wall.

Decorative holdbacks; or tieback holders and tiebacks (page 94), for curtain with two panels that meet in the center and share an attached valance.

How to Sew a Curtain with an Attached Valance

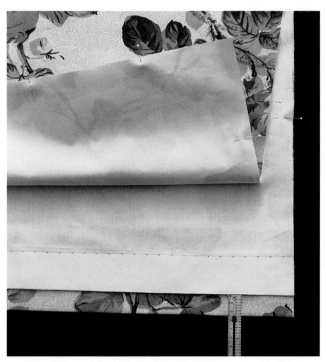

1) Seam fabric widths together as necessary for the curtain panel. At lower edge of curtain panel, press under 4" (10 cm) twice to wrong side; stitch to make double-fold hem, using blindstitch or straight stitch. Repeat for lining, if desired, pressing under 2" (5 cm) twice. For unlined curtain, omit step 2.

2) Pin lining and curtain panel wrong sides together, aligning the upper and side edges. Lower edge of the lining will be 1" (2.5 cm) above the lower edge of curtain. Baste along the upper edge within ½" (1.3 cm) seam allowance.

3) Press under 1½" (3.8 cm) twice on sides of the curtain; if lined, fold the lining and curtain as one fabric. Tack drapery weights inside the side hems, about 3" (7.5 cm) from lower edges. Stitch to make double-fold hems, using blindstitch or straight stitch.

4) Seam valance fabric widths together as necessary. Seam binding strips together with diagonal seams; trim to ¼" (6 mm). Press seams open. Press under ⅜" (1 cm) along one long edge.

(Continued on next page)

5) Stitch remaining edge of binding strip to lower edge of the valance, right sides together, stitching ½" (1.3 cm) from raw edges; begin and end binding strip 2½" (6.5 cm) from sides of valance. Press seam allowances toward binding.

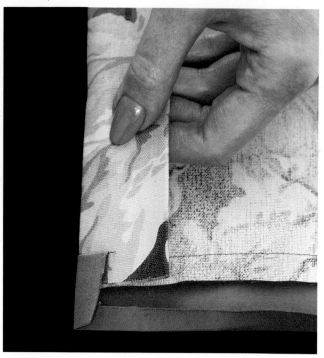

6) Press under 1½" (3.8 cm) twice on sides of the valance. Stitch to make double-fold hems, using blindstitch or straight stitch.

7) Turn binding strip over lower edge of valance, encasing raw edges. From right side of valance, pin binding in place along seamline, catching pressed edge of binding on wrong side.

8) Stitch in the ditch from the right side by stitching in the well of the seam.

9) Pin right side of valance to wrong side of curtain panel, matching upper raw edges. For curtain with two panels under one valance, butt inner edges of curtain panels. Stitch ½" (1.3 cm) seam; press open.

10) Fold the valance to front side of curtain along seamline; press.

11) Cut self-styling tape 3" (7.5 cm) longer than the width of curtain panel. Turn under 1½" (3.8 cm) on ends of tape, and use pin to pick out cords. Side of tape with hook loops is right side.

(Continued on next page)

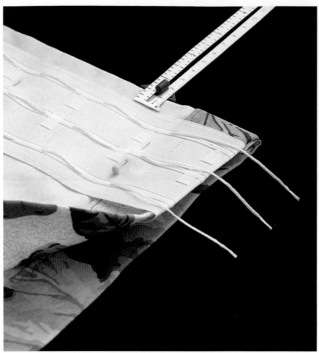

12) Lay curtain facedown on flat surface. Pin self-styling tape to curtain, with upper edge of tape ½" (1.3 cm) below upper edge of curtain; pin through curtain and valance. (Hook loops are at upper edge of tape.) Tuck turned-under ends of tape between curtain and valance.

13) Stitch along top and bottom edges of the tape; do not catch cords in stitching. For smocking tape, stitch again close to remaining cords.

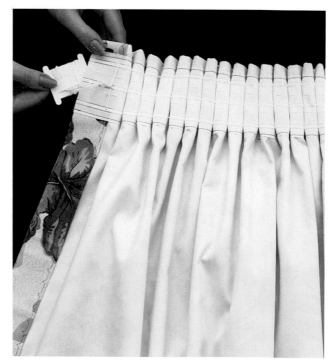

14) Secure the cords at both ends of tape, using one or two overhand knots to prevent cords from being pulled out. Pull cords at one end to gather curtain to finished width, as determined by the styling tape. Adjust fullness evenly.

15) Knot the cords securely at sides of curtain. Wind excess cord around floss holder or small square of thin cardboard; tuck into space between curtain and valance, or secure to back of curtain.

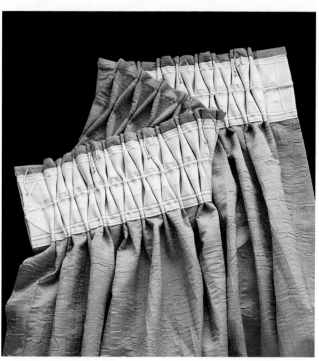

16) Standard curtain rod. Insert drapery pins at ends of the panel, with remaining pins evenly spaced, about 3" (7.5 cm) apart; tops of pins should be ½" (1.3 cm) from top of curtain.

16) Decorative rod. Insert drapery pins at inner ends of panels and at front corners of returns. Insert the remaining pins, evenly spaced, about 3" (7.5 cm) apart, with tops of pins ¼" (6 mm) from top of curtain.

17) Standard curtain rod. Hook drapery pins over the rod.

17) Decorative rod. Insert drapery pins into eyes of rings. Attach pin-on ring to inner edge of return, and secure to a cup hook or tenter hook in wall.

Hourglass Curtains

Hourglass curtains take their name from their shape. They are held taut between sash rods at the top and bottom of the window glass, and then pulled in at the center to create the hourglass shape. Use tension rods, instead of sash rods, for mounting inside a window frame.

Because these curtains are held tight to the glass, they are a practical treatment for doors. They also work well on windows where there is not room for a return. They allow sunlight to get in and, for extra airiness, are attractive in lace and sheer fabrics.

You will need to take two length measurements: the length at the center of the curtain and the *adjusted* length at the sides. The adjusted length accommodates the pinching in of the fabric at the center of the window. Estimate 2" (5 cm) extra at the sides for every 12" (30.5 cm).

✂ Cutting Directions

Cut the fabric 2 to 2½ times the width of rod. Cut the length as measured in step 1, right. Add allowance for rod pockets and headings at top and bottom of curtain plus 1" (2.5 cm) to turn under.

YOU WILL NEED

Lightweight decorator fabric for curtains.

Two sash rods or tension rods; mount rods before measuring.

How to Sew an Hourglass Curtain

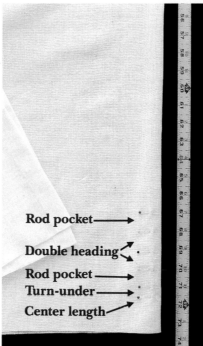

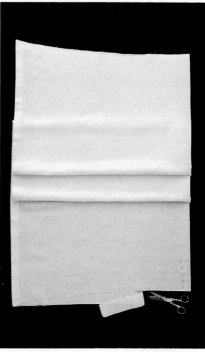

Rod pocket
Double heading
Rod pocket
Turn-under
Center length

1) Measure for side finished length. With a tape measure or string, plan the curve of the hourglass shape on the door or window. The narrowest part of hourglass should be no less than one-third the width of the glass.

2) Turn under and stitch double 1" (2.5 cm) side hems. Fold panel in half lengthwise; on the fold, mark the center finished length, plus rod pocket and heading allowance. Be sure markings are equal at both ends of fabric.

3) Mark a gentle curved line from side length at hemmed edge to center length about 3" (7.5 cm) from center fold. Line should not have any curve at the fold. Cut on marked line at top and bottom.

4) Stitch rod pockets and headings at top and bottom of curtain, easing in excess fullness. Insert sash rods.

5) Mount curtain. With string or tape measure, pull panel into hourglass shape at midpoint and measure for tieback. Add 2" (5 cm) for overlap. For tiebacks, see pages 94 to 99. To sew rosette, see page 299.

Sunburst Curtains

A sunburst curtain dresses a Palladian window while diffusing the light. Designed to perfectly outline the arch shape, this sheer rod-pocket curtain is custom-fitted for your window.

Flexible plastic tubing, which shapes easily to curve around the window opening, is inserted into the rod pocket at the upper edge. Drapery cord, inserted into the opposite casing, holds the gathers at the center. A large rosette (pages 160 and 161) is used to finish the treatment.

Trace the shape of the inside window frame onto paper to make a pattern. Fitting adjustments can be made on the curtain, using the pattern, before it is installed.

✂ Cutting Directions

The cut width of the fabric is equal to one and one-half to two times the measurement of the curved line on the pattern, depending on the fullness desired. Railroad the fabric whenever possible to prevent seams (page 27).

To determine the cut length of the fabric, divide the length of the lower straight line on the pattern by two; then add 4½" (11.5 cm). This allows for a double ½" (1.3 cm) heading and a double 1" (2.5 cm) rod pocket at the outer edge, a double ½" (1.3 cm) casing at the center, and ½" (1.3 cm) for ease.

YOU WILL NEED

Sheer drapery fabric for curtain and rosette.

3/8" (1 cm) flexible plastic tubing (page 47), cut to fit curve at inside edge of window frame.

Sockets for 3/8" (1 cm) round rodding.

1" (2.5 cm) cup hooks; one for every 8" to 10" (20.5 to 25.5 cm) around curve of window, plus one for center of sunburst.

Nylon drapery cord; binder clips or clamps.

How to Sew and Install a Sunburst Curtain

1) Seam fabric widths, if necessary. Press under ½" (1.3 cm) twice at sides; stitch to make double-fold hems. Press under 1½" (3.8 cm) twice at upper edge; stitch rod pocket close to first fold, then 1" (2.5 cm) away. Press under and stitch double ½" (1.3 cm) rod pocket on lower edge.

2) Tie safety pin to one end of drapery cord; thread through casing at lower edge. Pull up cord as tightly as possible, and tie ends together; trim excess cord. This becomes center of sunburst.

3) Insert plastic tubing into casing at upper edge, gathering fabric. Pin or tape paper pattern to heavy cardboard or foam core board. Aligning heading of curtain to marked arc on pattern, clamp ends of tubing to cardboard; distribute gathers evenly and pin heading in place. Clamp center at lower edge.

4) Pull curtain taut toward center to remove slack, using double strands of thread. Cover center with a small half-circle of matching fabric, if necessary for neater appearance on outside of window treatment. Make rosette (pages 160 and 161); hand-stitch to center.

5) Screw sockets at ends of bottom window frame. Screw cup hooks into window frame at 8" to 10" (20.5 to 25.5 cm) intervals around arch, with hook openings facing into the room; position all cup hooks the same distance from edge of window frame. Screw one cup hook at center of bottom window frame.

6) Insert ends of tubing into sockets. Snap tubing into cup hooks around inside curve of window. Hook center of sunburst into cup hook at center of bottom window frame. It may be necessary to trim tubing to fit around window.

Buttonhole Curtain Panels

Simple in style, these no-fuss, unlined curtains have fresh appeal. The flat fabric panels slide onto the curtain rod through buttonholes, creating a curtain with soft, rolling curves.

✂ Cutting Directions

Determine the desired finished length of the panels by measuring from ½" (1.3 cm) above the top of the rod to the desired finished length of the curtain. Determine the necessary length of the buttonholes; the buttonhole length is equal to one-half the measurement around the rod plus ¼" (6 mm).

The facing and turn-under at the top of the panel is equal to the length of the buttonholes plus 1½" (3.8 cm). The hem allowance at the bottom is equal to 6" (15 cm); this allows for a 3" (7.5 cm) double-fold hem. The cut length of each panel is equal to the desired finished length plus the facing and turn-under at the top plus the hem allowance at the bottom.

Determine the cut width of the fabric by multiplying the length of the rod times two; if you are sewing two curtain panels, divide this measurement by two to determine the cut width of each panel. For each panel, add 4" (10 cm) to allow for 1" (2.5 cm) double-fold side hems; if it is necessary to piece the fabric widths together, also add 1" (2.5 cm) for each seam.

YOU WILL NEED

Lightweight to mediumweight decorator fabric.
Pole set or decorative curtain rod.

How to Sew a Buttonhole Curtain Panel

1) Seam fabric widths, if necessary, for each curtain panel. Trim seam allowances to ¼" (6 mm); finish, using zigzag or overlock stitch, and press to one side. At lower edge, press under 3" (7.5 cm) twice to wrong side; stitch close to inner fold.

2) Press under ½" (1.3 cm) on the upper edge. Then press under an amount equal to buttonhole length plus 1" (2.5 cm). Stitch close to inner fold.

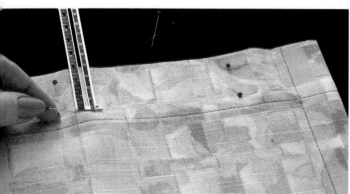

3) **Press** under 1" (2.5 cm) twice on the sides; stitch close to the inner fold. Pin-mark placement for even number of buttonholes on top of panel, centered on faced area; space end buttonholes 2" (5 cm) from sides, and remaining buttonholes 4" to 5" (10 to 12.5 cm) apart.

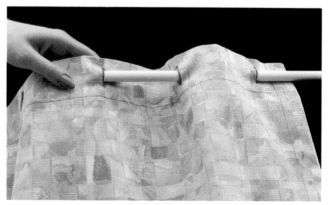

4) **Stitch** vertical buttonholes. Weave panels onto pole or rod. Hang curtains.

Scalloped Curtains

For an interesting effect, the upper edge of curtain panels can be scalloped. This design detail works for stationary curtain panels that are attached to a rod by tabs or by clip-on or sew-on rings. Curtains attached by rings can also be made to traverse the rod and cover the window when necessary. Scalloped curtains may be lined or unlined, in any desired length. The hem may fall to a casual length just ½" (1.3 cm) below the window frame, to a more formal length ½" (1.3 cm) above the floor, or break at the floor with 2" (5 cm) of extra length. The scalloped edge is finished with a facing, using the same fabric as the curtain or a coordinating fabric.

Select mediumweight fabric with enough body to hold the shape of the scallop. If a print is selected, check to see that light from the window will not cause the facing to shadow through to the right side of the curtain.

For best results, the curtain should be made with returns on the outer edges to block side light. A tab or ring is positioned at the outer front corner, and the return is attached to the wall. For curtains with two panels that meet in the center, both panels should end with a tab or ring at the center edge.

When more than one width of fabric is used in a curtain panel, the scallop widths vary slightly from one fabric width to the next. This is done to avoid placing tabs or rings directly over a seam, making the seam highly visible. A seam is least visible if it is positioned 3" (7.5 cm) to the outside of the nearest tab or ring. This may result in scallop widths in the center of the panel being slightly narrower than the remaining scallops. Scallop depths are all equal, however, and fullness can be distributed so that tabs or rings are spaced evenly along the rod, making the difference in scallop width unnoticeable in the finished treatment.

Before mounting the rod above the window, consider the distance any rings or clips hang below the rod, as this will determine the highest point of the upper edge of the curtain. If making tab curtains, wrap a cloth tape measure over the rod to determine the desired length of the tab. Also determine the depth of the scallops. Shallow scallops of 2½" to 3" (6.5 to 7.5 cm) are appropriate for cafe curtains on a small window, whereas deep 8" (20.5 cm) scallops create a dramatic effect on floor-length curtains. Depending on how high the rod is mounted and the depth of the scallops, part of the upper window frame and even the glass may be exposed by the scallops.

Deep scallops and a breaking hem exaggerate the length of elegant jacquard curtains (opposite). Scalloped cafe curtains in a fresh, flowery print (above) capture the carefree mood of a breakfast nook.

✂ Cutting Directions

Mount the rod in the desired location above the window. Determine the finished length of the curtain by measuring from the clip, ring, or desired distance below the rod for tabs to where you want the lower edge of the curtain. The cut length of the decorator fabric is equal to the finished length of the curtain plus 8" (20.5 cm) for the bottom hem plus ½" (1.3 cm) for the seam allowance at the upper edge.

Determine the desired finished width of the curtain. The finished width of traversing curtains with rings is determined by measuring the length of the rod plus returns. The finished width of stationary panels is determined only by the space they cover plus returns. Multiply this amount by two times fullness. Divide this amount by the fabric width and round up or down to the nearest whole or half width, to determine the number of fabric widths needed. If the curtain is to be split between two panels, use only full and half widths in each panel.

Cut fabric for the facing, with the length equal to the scallop depth plus 4" (10 cm) and the width equal to the cut width of the curtain fabric.

The cut length of the lining is equal to the cut length of the decorator fabric minus the scallop depth minus 8" (20.5 cm).

If making tab curtains, cut a 3" (7.5 cm) strip of fabric for each tab, 1" (2.5 cm) longer than the desired finished length. You will need five tabs for the first full width plus four tabs for each additional full width and two tabs for each additional half width in each curtain panel.

Cut paper for the pattern, 2" (5 cm) longer than the desired scallop depth and 6" (15 cm) narrower than the seamed width of the curtain panel. This will be the finished width after hemming.

YOU WILL NEED

Decorator rod; clip-on rings or sew-on rings, if desired.

Decorator fabric, 48" to 54" (122 to 137 cm) wide, for curtains.

Matching or contrasting fabric, for facing.

Matching or contrasting fabric, for tabs, if desired.

Lining fabric, optional.

Paper, pencil, string, for making scallop pattern.

Drapery weights.

Pin-on rings and cup hooks or tenter hooks, for securing returns to wall.

How to Sew Unlined Scalloped Curtains

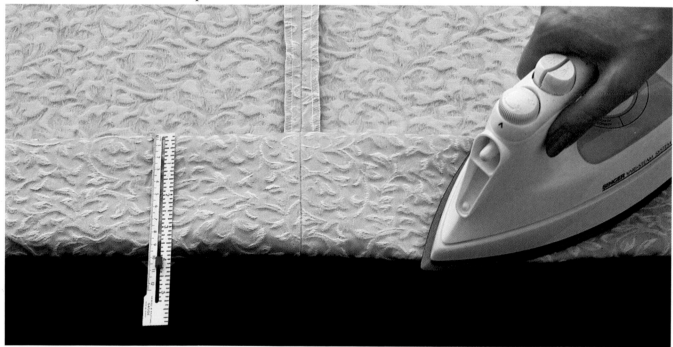

1) Seam fabric widths together as necessary for each curtain panel, adding any half widths at the return ends of the panels. Repeat for facings. At lower edge of curtain panel, press under 4" (10 cm) twice to wrong side; stitch to make double-fold hem, using blindstitch or straight stitch.

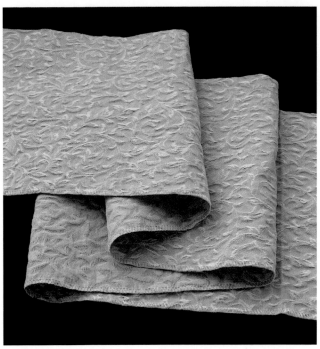

2) Finish the lower edge of the facing, using overlock, or turn under ¼" (6 mm) twice and stitch, using straight stitch.

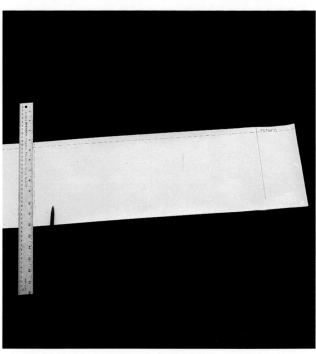

3) Mark ½" (1.3 cm) seam allowance across upper edge of pattern. Mark depth of return on one end of pattern; mark seam positions.

4) Mark point on upper seamline ½" (1.3 cm) away from return. Mark a point 3" (7.5 cm) beyond first seam from return.

5) Fold paper to divide space between marks into four equal parts if space represents whole width, or into two equal parts if space represents half width; crease to mark. Unfold.

(Continued on next page)

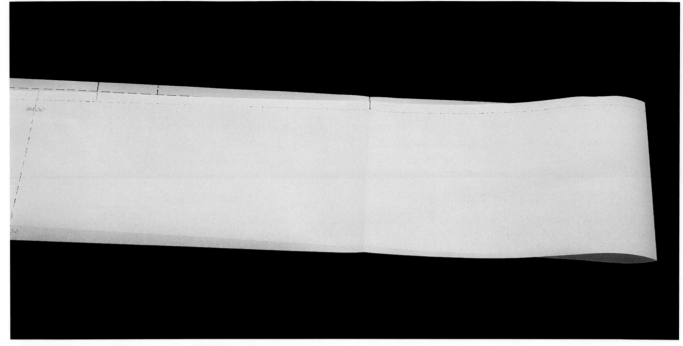

6) **Divide** any additional whole widths, falling between return end and opposite end of panel, into four equal parts, placing marks for tabs or rings nearest seams 3" (7.5 cm) beyond seams.

7) **Mark** point ½" (1.3 cm) from end; divide end width into four equal parts.

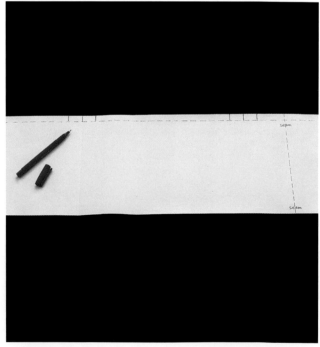

8) **Mark** scallop end points on the upper seamline, 1" (2.5 cm) on each side of the marks. This allows for ½" (1.3 cm) seam allowances in the scalloped edge and 1" (2.5 cm) space for tabs or rings.

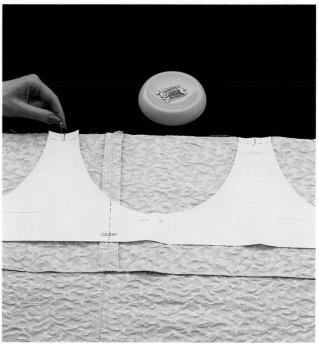

9) Mark depth of scallop in first space from return, measuring from upper edge of pattern; draw scallop from end points through depth mark. Refold, and cut first set of scallops.

10) Repeat step 9 for each set of scallops. Place the facing over the curtain panel, right sides together, matching upper and side edges. Pin pattern over facing, aligning upper edges and seam marks; cut scallops. Transfer mark for return. For curtains without tabs, omit steps 11 to 13.

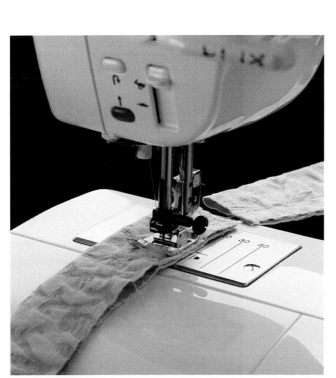

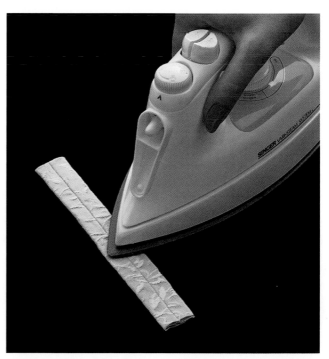

11) Fold each tab in half lengthwise, right sides together. Stitch ½" (1.3 cm) seam along cut edge; sew from one tab to the next, using continuous stitching.

12) Turn tabs right side out. Center seam in back of each tab; press.

(Continued on next page)

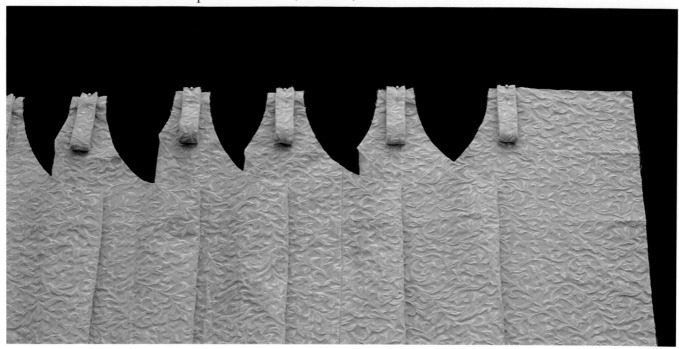

13) Fold each tab in half, aligning raw edges. Pin or baste tabs in place on right side of curtain, aligning raw edges of tabs to the upper edge of curtain and centering tabs between scallops. Pin tab at the return end with outer edges on return mark. Pin tab at the opposite end 3" (7.5 cm) from side of panel.

14) Pin facing to upper edge of curtain, right sides together, aligning raw edges. Stitch ½" (1.3 cm) seam. Zipper foot may be used to stitch close to tab. Trim seam; clip curves. Turn right side out, aligning outer raw edges; press.

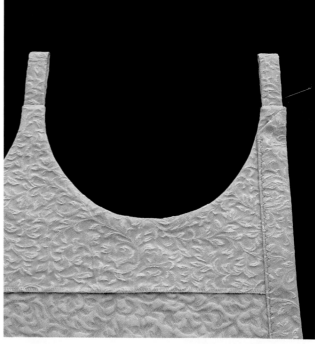

15) Press under 1½" (3.8 cm) twice on sides, folding facing and curtain panel as one fabric. Tack drapery weights inside the side hems, about 3" (7.5 cm) from lower edges. Stitch to make double-fold side hems, using blindstitch or straight stitch. Fold hem under diagonally at upper corner, if necessary; hand-stitch.

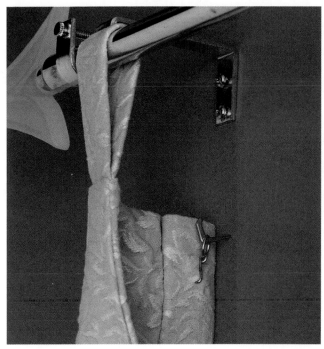

16) Hang curtain from the rod, using tabs or clip-on or sew-on rings. Attach pin-on ring to the inner edge of return, and secure to a tenter hook or cup hook in wall.

17) Space tabs or rings evenly on the rod as desired. Train the curtain so fabric in scallops rolls toward window; fabric at tabs or rings rolls outward, forming soft folds.

How to Sew Lined Scalloped Curtains

1) Follow step 1 on page 86. Seam lining widths together. Press under 2" (5 cm) twice at lower edge of lining; stitch to make double-fold hem. Pin facing to upper edge of lining, right sides together; stitch ½" (1.3 cm) seam. Press toward facing.

2) Follow steps 3 to 14 on pages 87 to 90. Align outer edges of facing and lining to outer edges of curtain. Lining will be 1" (2.5 cm) shorter than curtain panel. Complete curtain, following steps 15 to 17, folding lining and curtain panel as one fabric.

Tent-flap Curtains

Stylish tent-flap curtains require a minimum amount of fabric and provide a tailored, uncluttered look. Choose two fabrics that complement each other for the outer fabric and the lining. The lining is just as important as the outer fabric.

✄ Cutting Directions

Cut each panel half the width of the mounting board plus return, plus 2" (5 cm) for seam allowances and overlap; cut length as measured from the top of the mounting board to desired finished length, plus the depth of the mounting board and ½" (1.3 cm) for seam allowance. Cut face fabric and lining panels the same size.

YOU WILL NEED

Decorator fabric and lining for curtains.

Mounting board: For outside mount, board should extend at least 1" (2.5 cm) on each side of window frame and be deep enough to clear window by 2" (5 cm). For inside mount, cut 1" × 2" (2.5 × 5 cm) to fit inside window.

Two tieback holders or two wooden blocks.

Two angle irons for mounting.

Heavy-duty stapler, staples.

How to Sew a Tent-flap Curtain

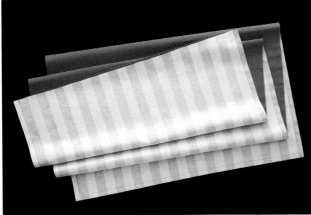

1) Pin face fabric to lining, right sides together, and stitch three sides in ½" (1.3 cm) seam, leaving upper edge open.

2) Press one seam allowance back to make it easier to turn a crisp, sharp edge. Trim seam allowance across corners. Turn panels right side out, and press.

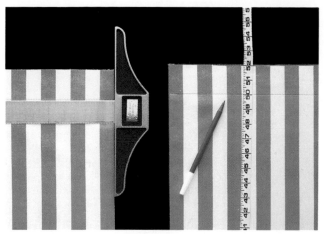

3) Mark finished length across the top of the panels, making sure that both panels are exactly even and that end is at perfect right angle to sides.

4) Align panel length marking with front edge of mounting board. Staple panel to board, starting at return. At corner, make diagonal fold to form a miter. Panels overlap about 1" (2.5 cm) at center.

5) Mount board with angle irons positioned at edge of window frame.

6) Fold the front edges of the panels back to side edges, and adjust opening. Measure to be sure they are even on both sides.

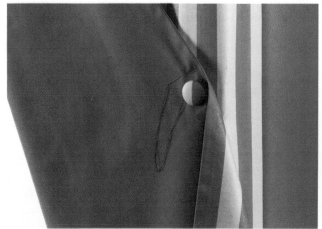

7) Hand-tack two layers together, and finish with decorative or covered button. Or hand-tack ties at front edge and sides. To maintain projection at sides, attach panel to tieback holder or wooden block attached to window frame behind ties.

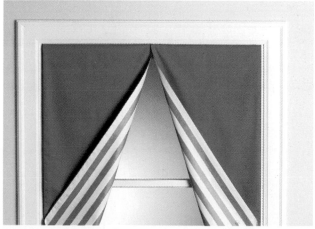

Inside mounting. Cut panels half the finished width of mounting board, plus 2" (5 cm). Sew as for steps 1 to 3. Mount panels on top of board. Fold flap; tack to side of curtain. At side, sew ring to curtain back; attach to cup hook inside frame.

Tiebacks

Tiebacks are a decorative way to hold curtains open. Make them straight or shaped, plain, bound, ruffled or shirred. Use matching or contrasting solids, coordinating prints or bordered fabrics. Interface all tiebacks to add stability.

An easy way to make tiebacks the proper length is to complete and hang the curtains before sewing the tiebacks. Cut a strip of fabric that is 2" to 4" (5 to 10 cm) wide; experiment by pinning it around the curtains to determine the best tieback length. Slide the strip up and down to find the best location for tiebacks. Mark the wall for positioning cup hooks, which will be used to fasten the tiebacks. Remove the strip and measure it to determine the finished size.

✂ Cutting Directions

For straight tiebacks, cut a piece of heavyweight fusible interfacing the finished length and two times the finished width. To cut fabric, add ½" (1.3 cm) on all sides for seams.

For shaped tiebacks, cut a strip of brown paper for pattern, 4" to 6" (10 to 15 cm) wide and slightly longer than the tieback. Pin the paper around the curtain and draw a curved shape around the edge of the paper. Experiment by pinning and trimming the paper to get the effect you want. Cut two pieces of fabric and heavyweight fusible interfacing for each tieback. Cut interfacing same size as pattern. To cut fabric, add ½" (1.3 cm) on all sides for seams.

YOU WILL NEED

Decorator fabric for tiebacks.

Heavyweight fusible interfacing.

Brown paper for pattern.

Fusible web strips, length of finished tieback width.

Two ⅝" (1.5 cm) brass or plastic rings for each tieback.

Two cup hooks.

How to Sew Straight Tiebacks

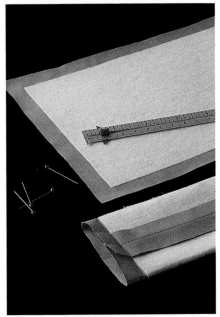

1) Center fusible interfacing on wrong side of tieback and fuse. Press the short ends under ½" (1.3 cm). Fold tieback in half lengthwise, right sides together. Stitch ½" (1.3 cm) seam, leaving short ends open. Press open.

2) Turn tieback right side out. Center seam down back and press. Turn pressed ends inside. Insert fusible web at each end and fuse. Or slipstitch closed.

3) Hand-tack ring on back seamline at each end of tieback, ¼" (6 mm) from edge **(a)**. Or press corners diagonally to inside to form a point; slipstitch or fuse corners in place. Attach ring **(b)**.

How to Sew Shaped Tiebacks

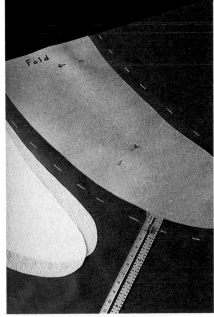

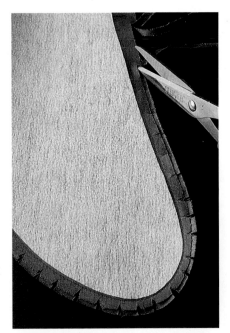

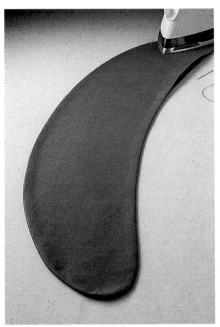

1) Position pattern on fold to cut fabric and interfacing. Center interfacing on wrong side of each tieback piece and fuse.

2) Pin tieback pieces, right sides together. Stitch ½" (1.3 cm) seam, leaving 4" (10 cm) opening on one long edge for turning. Grade seam allowances; notch or clip curves at regular intervals.

3) Turn tieback right side out; press. Insert fusible web at opening and fuse. Or slipstitch closed. Hand-tack rings at each end of tieback ¼" (6 mm) from the edge.

Bound Tiebacks

Binding emphasizes the graceful line of a curved tieback and allows you to pick up an accent color from the room decor or from the curtain fabric. Shaped tiebacks are easier to bind than straight tiebacks because the bias binding will ease around curves.

✄ Cutting Directions

Cut two pieces of fabric and two pieces of fusible interfacing from the pattern; do not add seam allowances to tieback. Cut 2" (5 cm) wide bias strips (page 40), 1" (2.5 cm) longer than the distance around the tieback.

How to Bind Shaped Tiebacks

1) Position pattern on fold to cut fabric and interfacing. Fuse interfacing to wrong side of tieback. Pin wrong sides of tieback together.

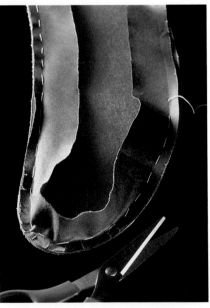

2) Press under ½" (1.3 cm) on one end of bias strip. Starting with pressed end, baste strip to tieback, right sides together, clipping to ease around curves. Stitch strip ½" (1.3 cm) from edge.

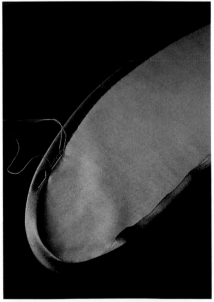

3) Press bias strip over edge of tieback. Turn under cut edge of bias strip to meet seamline; slipstitch. Hand-tack rings to ends of tieback.

Ruffled Tiebacks

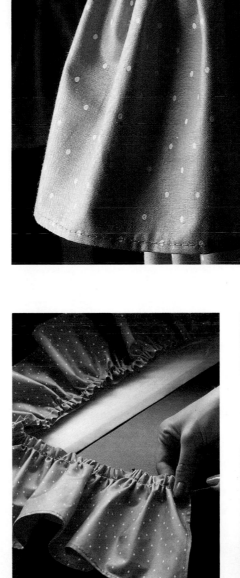

Adding ruffled tiebacks changes the appearance of the curtains and the look of a window. Make ruffles from a matching or coordinating fabric in a width that suits the length of the curtain. Purchased pregathered lace or eyelet ruffles may be used to reduce sewing time.

✂ Cutting Directions

Cut ruffle the desired width plus 1" (2.5 cm) for seams, and two and one-half times the finished length.

Cut a straight tieback and interfacing (page 94). The tieback should be in proportion to the ruffle width, usually less than half as wide.

How to Sew Ruffled Tiebacks

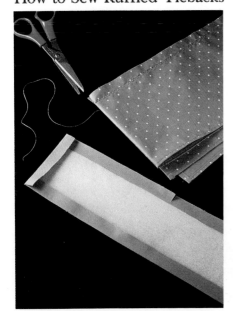

1) Fuse interfacing to wrong side of tieback. Press under ½" (1.3 cm) on one long side and both ends of tieback. Stitch a ¼" (6 mm) hem on one long side and both ends of ruffle. Fold ruffle and tieback into fourths; mark folds with snips.

2) Zigzag over a cord ⅜" (1 cm) from raw edge. Pin ruffle to tieback, right sides up; match snips and raw edges. Pull up cord until ruffle fits tieback. Distribute gathers evenly and pin. Stitch ruffle ½" (1.3 cm) from edge.

3) Fold tieback in half lengthwise, wrong sides together. Pin the folded edge over ruffle seam. Edgestitch across ends and along gathered seam. Hand-tack the rings to ends of tieback.

Jumbo Tiebacks

Knotted

Cut cording and fabric strips the finished length of the tieback plus 20" (51 cm) for the knot. Encase cording (page 158, steps 4 to 6). Tie big knot near center. Cut tieback to desired length. Trim cording out of ends. Turn ends to inside; slipstitch closed. Tack curtain ring on each end.

Twisted

Cut cording and fabric strips two-and-one-half times the finished length of tieback. Encase jumbo cording (page 158, steps 4 to 6). Trim cording out of ends. Turn ends to inside; slipstitch closed. Hand-stitch ends of tubes together, and twist. Tack curtain ring on each end.

Shirred

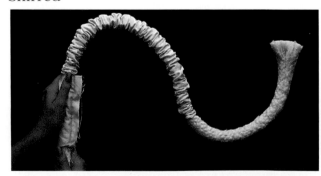

Cut cording three times the tieback length. Cut fabric strips two times the tieback length and 2" (5 cm) wider than circumference of cording. Encase cording (page 158, steps 4 to 6), gathering fabric evenly. Turn ends to inside; slipstitch closed, catching cording in stitching. Attach rings.

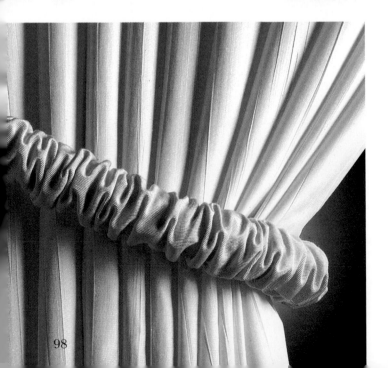

Shirred Insert Tiebacks

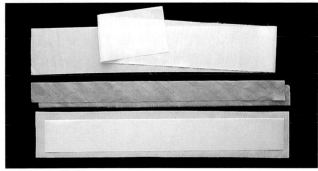

1) Cut insert two times finished length plus 2" (5 cm) and finished width plus 1" (2.5 cm). Cut lining 2" (5 cm) longer and 1" (2.5 cm) wider than finished tieback. Cut buckram ¼" (6 mm) narrower than finished size. Cut bias strips for welting (page 40) two times the finished length, plus 4" (10 cm) extra for finishing ends.

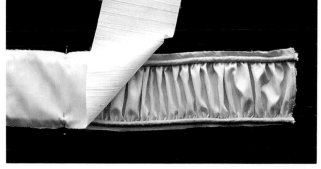

2) Gather both edges of the insert. Make welting as on page 40, step 1. Machine-baste welting on right side of shirred strip in ⅜" (1 cm) seam. Pin right side of lining to right side of strip. Stitch ½" (1.3 cm) seam. Turn right side out.

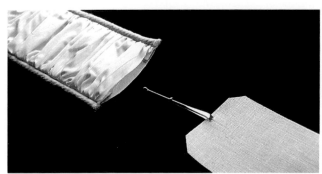

3) Trim buckram to slight point at one end. Attach bodkin to pointed end, and insert buckram between gathered insert and lining.

4) Trim 1" (2.5 cm) of cording out of welting at ends. Turn under a double ½" (1.3 cm) hem at ends, and slipstitch in place. Attach rings in center of tieback.

Roller Shades

Mount roller shades inside the window opening with ¼" (6 mm) or less clearance around the edges to increase the energy efficiency of a window. Roller shades can also be hung on brackets on the frame or wall outside the window. For inside mounting, measure from outside edges of brackets. If you do not want the roller to show, use reverse brackets, and cut the roller to fit.

Select a firmly woven fabric that bonds well. Water-resistant and stain-resistant fabrics that are treated with silicone do not bond.

✂ Cutting Directions

Cut fabric 1" to 2" (2.5 to 5 cm) wider than jamb or bracket measurement, and 12" (30.5 cm) longer than area to be covered top to bottom. Cut fusible backing with same dimensions.

YOU WILL NEED

Fabric and fusible shade backing for shade.

Wooden slat, ¼" (6 mm) shorter than finished width of shade.

Roller to fit window width.

Staple gun with ¼" (6 mm) staples, masking tape or other strong tape and white glue.

Shade pull (optional).

How to Make a Roller Shade

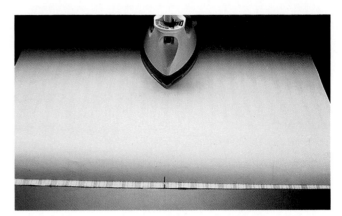

1) **Mark** center at upper and lower edges of fabric and fusible backing. Place the wrong side of the fabric to the resin side of the backing, matching edges and center markings.

2) **Fuse** according to manufacturer's directions for time and temperature, working from center to outside and from top to bottom. Allow shade to cool before moving so bond is permanently set.

3) **Use** a yardstick to mark cutting lines on sides of shade; distance between cutting lines should be equal to finished width of shade. Use a carpenter's square or cutting board for right angles.

4) **Cut** sides carefully with smooth, even strokes or use rotary cutter. Apply liquid fray preventer or small amount of white glue along each edge. Let dry completely.

5) **Fold** under 1½" (3.8 cm) along lower edge for a straight hem and slat pocket. Use carpenter's square to check right angles at corners.

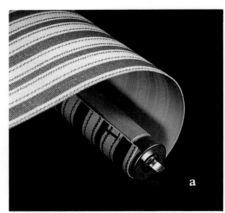

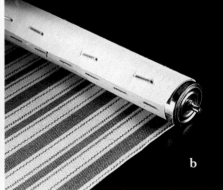

6) **Stitch** 1¼" (3.2 cm) from folded edge, using long stitches to form a pocket for the slat. Press pocket. Insert the slat. Attach shade pull if desired.

7) **Position** roller under or over top of shade, depending on how shade is to roll. To attach roller under shade, place flat pin to the right (**a**); to attach roller over shade, place round pin to the right (**b**). Make sure wrong side of hem is turned so it will not show when shade is hung. Staple or tape shade to roller.

Butterfly Roman Shades

This simple, yet stylish, window treatment has the sleek smoothness of a flat Roman shade, with draped softness at the lower edge. Excess length is folded up and secured, forming a swag at the lower hem when the shade is down. As the shade is drawn up, the folds stack in the center and flare at the sides, creating a butterfly effect. The shade is lined to give it extra body and protect the fabric from sunlight. A dowel, inserted into a pocket in the lining, adds stability to the shade.

This Roman shade style works best if the finished width does not exceed 49½" (126.3 cm). A shade of this width can be made from 54" (137 cm) fabric, with no seaming necessary. Plan to mount the shade above the window frame, so that the finished length from the top of the mounting board to the highest point of the hem is evenly divisible by six.

✂ Cutting Directions

Cut the decorator fabric with the length equal to the desired finished length of the shade plus 26¾" (68 cm); this allows for the bottom swag, hem allowance, and mounting. The cut width of the decorator fabric is equal to the desired finished width of the shade plus 4½" (11.5 cm); this allows for double ¾" (2 cm) side hems and twice the ¾" (2 cm) projection of the mounting board. Cut a strip of decorator fabric to cover the mounting board (page 53).

Cut the lining fabric with the length equal to the cut length of the decorator fabric plus 1¼" (3.2 cm) and the width equal to the desired finished width of the shade plus 1½" (3.8 cm).

YOU WILL NEED

Decorator fabric.

Lining fabric.

⅜" (1 cm) wooden dowel, with length equal to two-thirds the finished shade width minus ½" (1.3 cm).

½" (1.3 cm) plastic rings, number as determined in diagram on page 32.

1 × 2 mounting board, cut to desired finished width of shade.

Staple gun and staples.

Three screw eyes.

Shade cord; fabric glue; drapery pull.

Drill and drill bits.

8 × 2½" (6.5 cm) flat-head screws, for installing shade into wall studs; or molly bolts or toggle anchors, for installing shade into drywall or plaster.

Awning cleat; screws.

How to Make a Diagram of the Shade

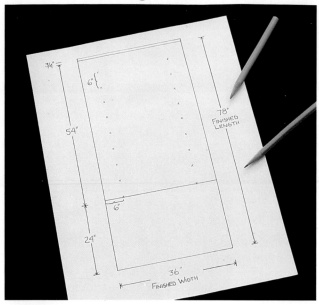

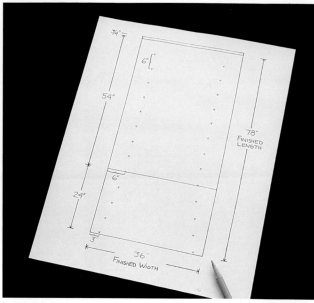

1) Diagram back side of the shade, indicating ring placement marks. Draw a line 24" (61 cm) from the bottom of the shade, indicating the dowel pocket. Plan two vertical rows of rings from the dowel pocket to 6¾" (17 cm) from top of shade, each positioned one-sixth of the shade width from the hemmed sides; space rings 6" (15 cm) apart vertically.

2) Mark positions for two rings in center of the lower hem, each a distance from outer edge equal to one-sixth of the shade width minus 3" (7.5 cm). Remaining three rings in each row are spaced evenly along a line between dowel pocket ring and lower ring.

How to Sew a Butterfly Roman Shade

1) Mark line across lining 26⅝" (67.5 cm) from the lower cut edge. Fold the lining, right sides together, along the marked line; pin. Stitch ⅝" (1.5 cm) from the fold, forming dowel pocket. Press pocket toward lower edge.

2) Insert dowel into dowel pocket and slide it to center of lining; tack through dowel pocket to hold the dowel in place.

3) Press under ¾" (2 cm) twice on sides of shade fabric. Place lining over shade fabric, wrong sides together, matching upper and lower edges; at sides, place lining under hems, up to second foldline.

4) Pin side hems to lining; blindstitch in place. Press under 1" (2.5 cm) of lining and shade fabric twice at lower edge; pin. Blindstitch in place.

5) Finish upper edge of shade and lining together, using overlock or zigzag stitch. Place shade facedown on flat surface. Mark a line ¾" (2 cm) from finished upper edge, indicating top of shade. Mark locations for rings, as determined in diagram; place marks for rings at ends of dowel, on dowel pocket stitching line.

6) Pin through both layers of fabric at center of ring markings, with pins parallel to bottom of shade. Fold shade in accordion pleats at pins, to position shade for attaching rings.

7) Attaching rings by machine. Attach rings by placing fold under the presser foot with ring next to fold at mark. Set zigzag stitch at widest setting; set stitch length at 0. Stitch over ring, securing it with about eight stitches. Secure the stitches by stitching in place for two or three stitches, with stitch width and length set at 0.

(Continued on next page)

7) Attaching rings by hand. Tack rings by hand, using double strand of thread, stitching in place through both fabric layers for four or five stitches.

8) Cover mounting board (page 53). Align upper edge of shade to the back of narrow top edge of mounting board, centering shade on board so hemmed sides extend beyond board. Staple shade to mounting board; wrap sides over ends of board, and staple in place on top of board, forming squared corners.

9) Decide whether draw cord will hang on left or right side of shade. Install screw eyes on the narrow underside of mounting board, aligning two of them to rows of rings; install third screw eye 1" (2.5 cm) from end of board on draw side.

10) Place shade facedown on flat surface. String first row of rings, opposite the draw side. Run the cord through rings from bottom to top and across the shade through three screw eyes; extend cord about halfway down draw side of shade.

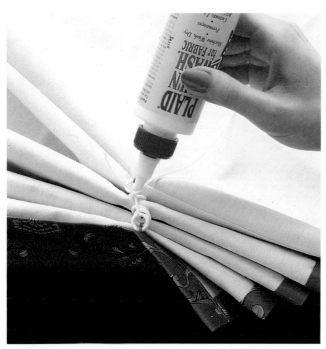

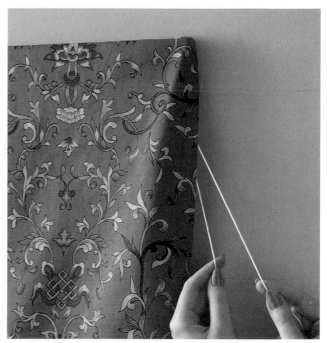

11) String remaining row of rings, running the cord through two screw eyes and extending cord about halfway down draw side. Tie lower five rings of each row together securely. Apply fabric glue to knot and end of cord to prevent knot from slipping.

12) Mount the shade above the window, following instructions for the Roman shade with ¾" (2 cm) projection on page 103. Adjust length of cords, with shade lowered, so the tension on both cords is equal. Tie cords together just below screw eye.

13) Insert ends of the cord into top of the drapery pull; knot ends.

14) Screw awning cleat into window frame or wall. When shade is raised, wrap cord around the awning cleat to hold at desired height.

Scarf Swags

Scarf swags are an adaptation of the traditional swag window treatment, which consists of a swag draped across the top of the window, and cascades draped at the sides. A scarf swag can look like an elegant, traditional window treatment or can have a more contemporary, unstructured look. Scarf swags are suitable for nearly any size or shape of window, including arch windows.

The scarf swag is created from a long, lined rectangle of fabric, and is folded and draped at the window. The swag can be shaped to form rosettes at the corners of the treatment, using special U-shaped swag holders, or can be draped over tieback holders.

The swag holders or tieback holders may be installed at the outer corners of the window frame or on the wall, positioned up and out from the corners. For arch windows, shown opposite, the brackets can be installed symmetrically or asymmetrically around the arch of the window.

After deciding on the placement of the brackets, determine the length of the cascades at the sides of the window. For good proportion, cascades are often two-thirds the length of the window or end at the window sill. On large windows, they may be floor-length, or even longer, to "puddle" onto the floor. An asymmetrical look can be achieved by making one cascade noticeably longer than the other.

Mediumweight decorator fabric, such as chintz and sateen, is recommended. Avoid heavyweight fabrics, because they do not drape well and may not fit into a swag holder. Select a contrasting lining to accent the folds of the cascades. If a patterned fabric with a one-way design is used, the fabric for one cascade must be turned in the opposite direction and stitched to the swag portion of the treatment.

If the swag holders can be seen from the side view, cover the extensions of the brackets with rod panels for a more finished appearance. The cascade-length panels are placed over the extensions before the brackets are installed.

✂ Cutting Directions

Cut outer and lining fabrics the length calculated, below. The entire width of both fabrics is used; if outer fabric and lining are of two different widths, cut the wider fabric to match the narrower width.

If rod panels are desired for the brackets at the top of the cascades, cut two pieces of fabric for each rod panel, 7" (18 cm) wide by the length of cascade plus 1¾" (4.5 cm) for the rod pocket and the seam allowance. One piece may be cut from the outer fabric and one from the lining, or both pieces may be cut from the outer fabric.

YOU WILL NEED

Decorator fabric and contrasting lining.

Swag holders or tieback holders (page 47).

Drapery hooks, one per rosette; or wire.

How to Calculate Yardage for a Scarf Swag

Drape cord or tape measure across window, between swag holders or tieback holders, to simulate the planned shape of each swag. Add desired length of cascades to this measurement. For swag with rosettes, add 24" (61 cm) for each rosette.

How to Sew a Scarf Swag

1) Place outer fabric and lining right sides together. At one selvage, measure in 18" (46 cm) from each end of fabric; draw a line from these points diagonally to the corners of the opposite selvage. Trim away triangular pieces of fabric at each end.

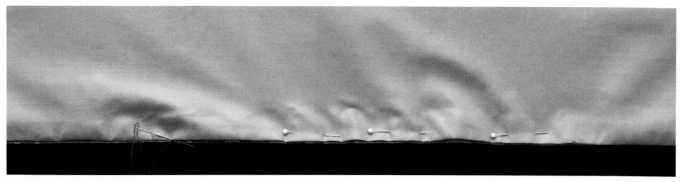

2) Stitch around all four sides in ½" (1.3 cm) seam, leaving 12" (30.5 cm) opening at center for turning. Press seams open. Turn right side out; stitch opening closed. Press edges.

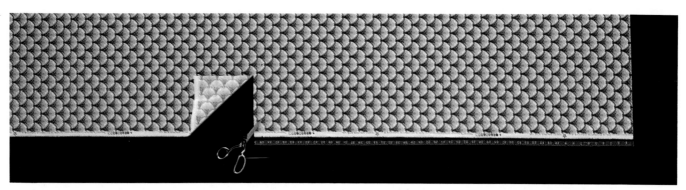

Fabric with one-way design. 1) Determine length of one cascade from lower edge up to tieback holder or swag holder; add 1" (2.5 cm) to this measurement. Measure this distance from one end of fabric; cut across width.

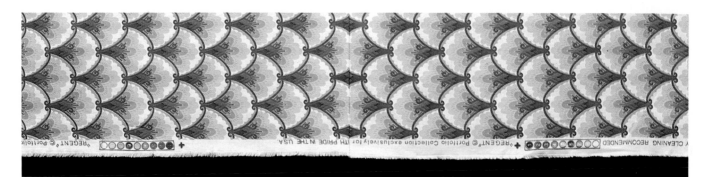

2) Turn fabric so design goes in opposite direction; stitch ½" (1.3 cm) seam. Seam will be concealed in rosette.

How to Sew a Rod Panel

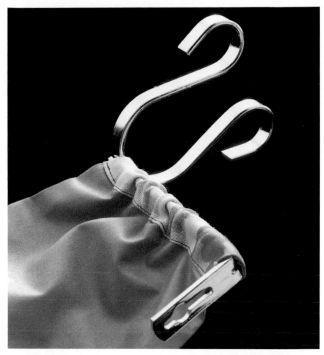

1) Place two rod panel pieces right sides together. Stitch around long sides and lower edge in ½" (1.3 cm) seam. Clip corners; turn right side out, and press. Fold under ¼" (6 mm) at upper edge to wrong side; then fold under 1" (2.5 cm). Stitch near second fold, forming rod pocket.

2) Slide rod pocket over extension of swag holder. Mount bracket onto wall or window frame.

How to Fold and Install a Scarf Swag

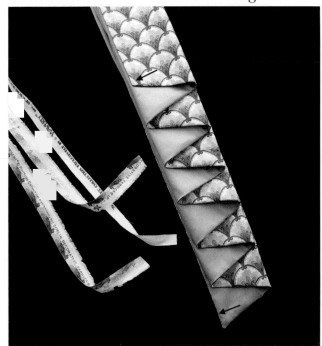

1) Lay scarf swag on long surface, such as floor, with lining side up. Accordion-fold entire width of swag in about 4" (10 cm) folds, beginning at longer side; both edges must face in same direction (arrows).

2) Tie folded swag with remnants of fabric every 18" to 24" (46 to 61 cm). This keeps folds in place, making swag easier to handle during installation.

(Continued on next page)

3) Place swag over bracket extensions, with shorter side facing down and in toward window. Drape folded swag portion the amount planned. If window treatment is to be symmetrical, check to see that cascade lengths are even. Remove ties.

4) Pull gently on lower folds for a deeper swag; pull gently on upper folds, toward brackets, to decrease amount of draping at top of swag. Adjust folds as desired; secure at brackets, using safety pins.

5) Measure down from bracket 24" (61 cm). Fold this 24" (61 cm) portion of fabric in half, forming 12" (30.5 cm) loop, with shorter side facing forward; do not twist swag. Bring fabric through U-portion of bracket, as shown; widen U-portion, if necessary for thickness of fabric. Keep fabric in accordion folds, with shorter side and contrasting folds facing window.

6) Adjust rosette portion so cascades are even in length if window treatment is to be symmetrical. Gently squeeze U-portion of bracket closed at the top as much as possible, to prevent rosette from sliding out of bracket during shaping. Secure top of bracket with a piece of wire or a drapery hook.

7) **Pull** the inside fold in middle of fabric loop, spreading fabric apart.

8) **Form** the rosette by continuing to pull out the fabric folds.

9) **Tuck** top and bottom of rosette back into bracket to round out the rosette, preventing peaks. Secure rosette as necessary with pins.

10) **Adjust** folds of cascades as necessary to achieve desired drape.

Swags with Side Drapes

This swag is a valance draped across the top of a window, with a fabric drape at the sides. Swags can be draped from post-type drapery holdbacks mounted at or above the corners of a window frame, or they can be draped around decorative finials at the ends of curtain rods.

To simplify the construction of the elegant and graceful lined swag (right), shape a fabric panel to size with two easy window measurements. Measure the width between holdbacks or finials. Measure finished length from top of hardware to point on side of window where you want the drape to end. The cut length of panel equals the width, plus twice the length, plus 1" (2.5 cm) for seam allowances. Line the panel to the edge to eliminate hems and headings; then use shirring tape to gather the fabric for draping. To save cutting time, cut the decorator fabric and lining together.

Save even more time by making a swagged valance or curtain from a fabric with no apparent right or wrong side, such as gauze, handkerchief linen, silk broadcloth, or lace. Drape artfully over a decorative rod. There is no need to line or shirr the panel. To finish edges and ends, fuse or glue hems for a custom look without taking a stitch. Swag can also be tied to finials with separate bows or tasseled cords.

How to Make a No-sew Swag

1) Drape tape measure across window between finials of decorative rod to estimate finished width of swag. Measure finished length. The cut length of panel equals the finished width, plus twice the finished length, plus two hem allowances; allow extra fabric for draping adjustments.

2) Drape fabric over rod to test effect. If fabric panel is too wide, trim side edges for desired effect. Mark hems, and fuse or glue them. Drape finished panel over rod, and adjust fabric into soft folds. Tie cord around folds at corners to hold in place. Knot soft or slippery fabrics around finials to anchor swag.

How to Sew Lined Swag with Side Drape

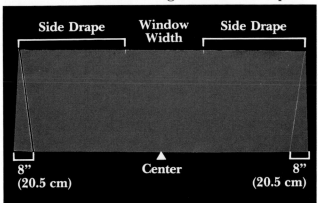

1) Measure and mark center and window width. On opposite side, mark 8" (20.5 cm) in from each corner. Layer decorator fabric and lining, and cut diagonally to opposite corner on each side.

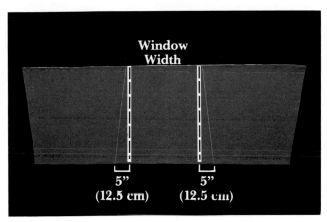

2) Sew lining to panel, with right sides together. At center of shorter edge, leave an opening for turning. Trim corners. Turn right side out; press. Fuse or glue opening closed. On lining, mark shorter edge of panel 5" (12.5 cm) out from the width markings.

3) Position 2-cord shirring tape on diagonal lines from window width mark on long side to 5" (12.5 cm) mark on short side.

4) Stitch shirring tape between each set of marks. Knot cords of tape at shorter edge. Pull up cords to gather swag. Mount on drapery holdbacks and adjust folds.

Basic Valances

Balloon valance. A balloon valance, above, gives simple sheers or draperies a soft, casual look. This valance, with bottom hem draped into swags, looks complicated but is actually easy to sew. It is a basic rod-pocket curtain, shortened to valance length. Each swag is created with shade tape or by tying cord through plastic rings. The balloon valance can be used on a curtain rod, a cafe pole, or a Continental® rod.

For graceful draping, make balloon valances about 28" (71 cm) long. To determine cut length, add to the finished length allowances for the heading, rod pocket, and double lower hem. To determine cut width, allow triple fullness if using sheer or lightweight fabric, or 2 to 2½ times fullness for medium-weight decorator fabrics; allow for double side hems.

Flat valance. A flat valance, right, takes little fabric and even less sewing time. It is a plain fabric panel with rod pockets for a pair of curtain rods. The simple, tailored style of this valance can complement contemporary or traditional decor. Choose a medium to heavyweight fabric with a crisp, firm hand; or back lightweight fabric with a layer of fusible interfacing. Textured fabrics such as cotton jacquard, raw silk, cotton velvet, and synthetic suede are appropriate as are quilted fabrics and needlework such as trapunto.

To determine cut length, install the rods so the distance between them equals the desired finished length. Most valances are made 12" to 14" (30.5 to 35.5 cm) long, depending on the proportion to window size. To measure, pin a tape measure around the top rod, down, and around the bottom rod. Add 1" (2.5 cm) for turning under the raw edges. To determine the cut width of a flat valance, measure the length of the curtain rod, including returns. Add 3" (7.5 cm) for side hems.

Puff valance. A puff valance, right, has a light, airy look. It is a natural for sheers and other lightweight fabrics. Combine a puff valance with shades, curtains, or blinds for a layered window treatment, or use it alone as a decorative accent.

This valance is made from a strip of fabric cut large enough to form a self-lining. To determine cut length, double the finished length of the valance; add heading and rod-pocket allowances. To determine cut width, use triple fabric fullness for sheer and lightweight fabric or 2½ times the finished width for mediumweight fabric; add 4" (10 cm) for double side hems.

How to Sew a Balloon Valance

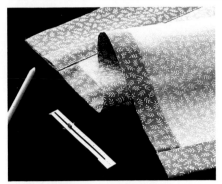

1) Make double side and bottom hems. Turn upper raw edge under ½" (1.3 cm), and press. Fold edge over to form heading and rod pocket; mark stitching lines. Stitch as marked.

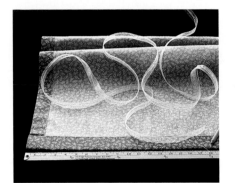

2) Mark location for shade tape at lower edge of shade. Swags should hang at even intervals across valance, about 8" to 12" (20.5 to 30.5 cm) apart; if width is double fabric fullness, tapes should be 16" to 24" (40.5 to 61 cm) apart.

3) Cut strips of shade tape 24" (61 cm) long, making sure that the first tack over the cord is at the top of the hem. Stitch tape in place. Pull up cord from both ends, and tie. Tuck cords into swag.

How to Sew a Flat Valance

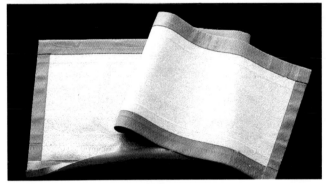

1) Turn under raw edges at sides ½" (1.3 cm). Press. Turn under 1" (2.5 cm), and stitch side hems. Fold fabric to wrong side to form rod pockets on upper and lower edges, turning under raw edges ½" (1.3 cm). Stitch rod pockets.

2) Insert rods through rod pocket at top and bottom to install valance at window. Valance takes shape of rods and has custom upholstered look. For quick trim, fuse grosgrain ribbon over stitching lines.

How to Sew a Puff Valance

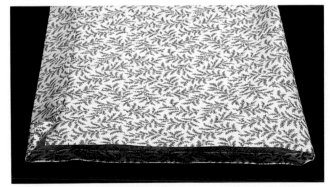

1) Make double side hems. Turn upper raw edge under ½" (1.3 cm), and press. Fold edge over to depth of heading. Bring lower raw edge up, and lap ½" (1.3 cm) under heading. Stitch along folded edge to form heading. Stitch parallel row below folded edge to form rod pocket.

2) Slip rod through rod pocket to install valance. Pull fabric layers apart along length of valance to create puffs. If valance seems limp, stuff with tissue paper or plastic drycleaning bags for fuller look.

117

Valances from Lace Tablecloths

Create shirred valances using oval lace tablecloths with decorative, shaped edges. One oval tablecloth is cut to make the swag and two cascade panels for this valance, as shown on page 120. The only sewing required is stitching the rod pocket and the side hems on the cascades.

This valance is best suited for wide windows. The length and width of the swag and cascades varies with the

size of the tablecloth and the depth of the rod pocket and heading.

To determine the tablecloth size to use, allow for one and three-fourths to two and one-half times fullness. Add the width and length of the tablecloth; then subtract 4" (10 cm) for the side hems of the cascades. Divide this measurement by 1.75 to 2.5, to determine the range of window widths for this tablecloth size. The chart on the opposite page lists common oval tablecloth sizes and the window widths they will cover.

The cut length of the swag panel is equal to one-half the width, or shortest dimension, of the tablecloth, because the tablecloth is cut in half lengthwise. The cut length of the cascade panels is equal to one-half the length, or longest dimension, of the tablecloth. The finished length of the valance panels, from the top of the heading to the lower edge, is equal to the

cut length of the panels minus a 1" to 2" (2.5 to 5 cm) heading depth minus the rod pocket depth minus ½" (1.3 cm) turn-under. The rod pocket depth is one-half the measurement around the rod plus ¼" (6 mm) for ease. If desired, the swag panel can be cut shorter; usually this also decreases the width of the panel.

✂ Cutting Directions

Determine the necessary tablecloth size; then cut the panels as on page 120, steps 1 and 2.

YOU WILL NEED

Oval lace tablecloth.
Decorative curtain rod or pole set.

Tablecloth and Window Measurements

Common oval tablecloth sizes	Window widths
52" × 70" (132 × 178 cm)	47" to 67" (120 to 170.5 cm)
60" × 84" (152.5 × 213.5 cm)	56" to 80" (142 to 203.5 cm)
60" × 92" (152.5 × 234 cm)	59" to 85" (149.8 to 216 cm)
60" × 104" (152.5 × 264.5 cm)	64" to 91" (163 to 231.5 cm)
70" × 108" (178 × 274.5 cm)	70" to 99" (178 to 251.5 cm)
70" × 126" (178 × 320 cm)	78" to 110" (198 to 280 cm)

Cutting Plan for a Valance from an Oval Lace Tablecloth

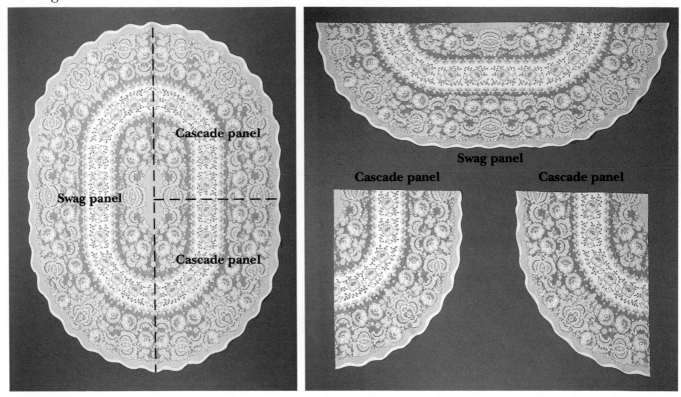

Oval tablecloth is cut to make the swag and two cascade panels for this valance, as shown. The tablecloth is cut in steps 1 and 2, below.

How to Sew a Valance from an Oval Lace Tablecloth

1) Fold the lace tablecloth in half lengthwise; cut along the fold.

2) Set aside one tablecloth section for the swag panel. Fold remaining section in half crosswise; cut along fold to make two cascade panels.

3) Adjust the length of swag, if desired, by trimming desired amount from upper cut edges. Turn up 1" (2.5 cm) twice to wrong side on side edge of cascade; stitch close to the inner fold. Repeat on remaining cascade, making sure panel is reverse of first panel.

4) Press up ½" (1.3 cm) to wrong side on upper edge. Then press up an amount equal to rod-pocket depth plus heading depth; take up fullness with small tucks on each side or ease in any excess fullness.

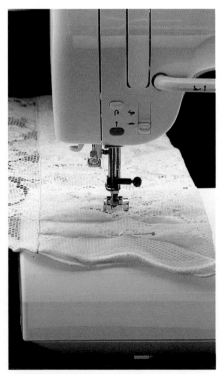

5) Stitch close to inner fold. Stitch again at depth of heading, using seam guide or tape on bed of sewing machine as guide for stitching.

6) Repeat steps 4 and 5 on the cut edge of the swag panel.

7) Insert pole or curtain rod into rod pockets, gathering the fabric evenly. Hang valance.

Mock Cornices

Top treatments that resemble cornices can be made without carpentry or upholstery techniques. Mock cornices are mounted on flat curtain rods that measure 4½" (11.5 cm) wide. Fusible fleece applied inside the rod pocket gives the treatment a padded look. The top and bottom of the rod pocket are accented with fabric-covered welting or twisted welting. For added flair, a pleated or gathered skirt is sewn below the rod pocket.

These versatile top treatments can be used to dress up windows that have existing treatments, such as vertical or horizontal blinds, pleated shades, or curtains. In some cases, they may provide a totally new look, using existing wide flat rods.

For best results, select a lightweight fabric that can be successfully railroaded (page 27) to eliminate the need for seams in the rod pocket. The skirt can be seamed in the center, with the seam hidden in a pleat or gathers. Two skirt lengths and both rod-pocket pieces can be cut from one width of 54" (137 cm) decorator fabric, if the skirt length does not exceed 16" (40.5 cm).

✂ Cutting Directions

Determine the desired finished width of the valance, the depth of the returns, and the desired finished length of the skirt. Preshrink decorator fabric and lining by steaming.

Cut a strip of decorator fabric for the front of the rod pocket, 6" (15 cm) wide, with the length equal to the desired finished width of the valance, including returns, plus 1" (2.5 cm) for end seams plus ½" (1.3 cm) for ease. Cut a strip of decorator fabric for the back of the rod pocket, 6" (15 cm) wide, with the length equal to the cut length of the front rod-pocket strip plus 1" (2.5 cm). Cut a strip of lining fabric for the front rod-pocket facing, with the same length and width as the front rod-pocket strip.

Cut decorator fabric for the skirt, with the length equal to the desired finished length plus 4½" (11.5 cm). For a gathered skirt, the cut width is twice the desired finished width, including returns. For a pleated skirt, determine the cut width by making a pattern. Plan the number of pleats, pleat depth, and direction; avoid overlapping pleats to minimize bulk. Mark ½" (1.3 cm) seam allowances and returns at the ends. Cut the skirt lining to the finished length plus ½" (1.3 cm) and the same width as the decorator fabric.

Cut bias fabric strips, if making fabric-covered welting, as on page 40, step 1.

Cut a strip of fusible fleece, 5" (12.5 cm) wide, with the length equal to the finished width of the valance, including returns, plus ½" (1.3 cm) for ease.

YOU WILL NEED

Decorator fabric.

Lining fabric.

Fusible fleece.

Fabric-covered welting, twisted welting, or ⁵⁄₃₂" **(3.8 mm) cord and fabric,** for making fabric-covered welting.

Flat curtain rod, 4½" (11.5 cm) wide, with adjustable mounting brackets to obtain necessary projection.

Self-adhesive hook and loop tape.

Mock cornice with a gathered skirt (opposite) has a soft, relaxed look. Knife-pleated skirt and twisted welting create a crisp, tailored mock cornice (above).

How to Sew a Mock Cornice with a Gathered Skirt

1) Center fusible fleece strip on the wrong side of the front rod-pocket strip; fuse in place, following manufacturer's instructions.

2) Make fabric-covered welting (page 40) and attach it to upper and lower edges of front rod-pocket strip, if desired; begin and end welting ½" (1.3 cm) from ends of strip. Or attach purchased welting.

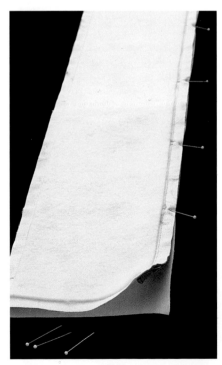

3) Place front rod pocket over the front rod-pocket facing strip, right sides together, aligning edges; pin along lower edge and ends.

4) Stitch ½" (1.3 cm) seam along lower edge and ends, using zipper foot and stitching with facing side down. Crowd cording by stitching just inside previous stitches.

5) Clip lower corners diagonally; turn front rod pocket right side out, and press. Baste upper edges together within ½" (1.3 cm) seam allowance.

6) Seam fabric for skirt, if necessary; repeat for skirt lining. Pin skirt and lining, right sides together, along lower edge. Stitch 2" (5 cm) from raw edges.

7) Press 2" (5 cm) hem allowance away from lining. Pin skirt to lining, right sides together, along sides, aligning upper edges; skirt will form fold even with lower edge of hem allowance. Stitch ½" (1.3 cm) side seams.

8) Clip lower corners diagonally. Press the lining side seam allowances toward lining. Turn skirt right side out, realigning upper edges; press. Baste the upper edges together.

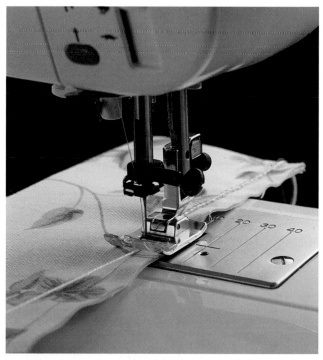

9) Zigzag over a cord on right side of skirt within ½" (1.3 cm) seam allowance of upper edge.

(Continued on next page)

10) Divide skirt into eighths; pin-mark. Divide lower edge of back rod pocket into eighths, beginning and ending 1" (2.5 cm) from ends. Pin wrong side of skirt to right side of back rod pocket along lower edge, matching pin marks and raw edges.

11) Pull gathering cord on skirt to fit lower edge of back rod pocket; pin in place. Stitch ½" (1.3 cm) from raw edges. Press seam allowances toward back rod pocket.

12) Pin back rod pocket to front rod pocket along upper edge, right sides together; ends of back rod pocket extend 1" (2.5 cm) beyond ends of front rod pocket. With the front rod pocket on top, stitch ½" (1.3 cm) seam, using zipper foot; crowd cording.

13) Press seam allowances toward back rod pocket. Turn under ends of back rod-pocket strip ½" (1.3 cm) twice, encasing ends of seam allowances; stitch.

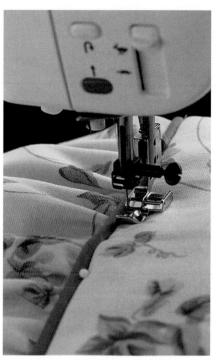

14) Turn skirt and back rod pocket down behind rod pocket. From the right side, pin skirt in place along the seamline at lower edge of rod pocket, just above welting.

15) Stitch in the ditch from the right side by stitching in the well of the seam above the welting, using a zipper foot.

16) Insert the curtain rod into rod pocket. Mount rod on bracket. Pull taut toward returns; secure returns to the sides of brackets, using self-adhesive hook and loop tape.

How to Sew a Mock Cornice with a Pleated Skirt

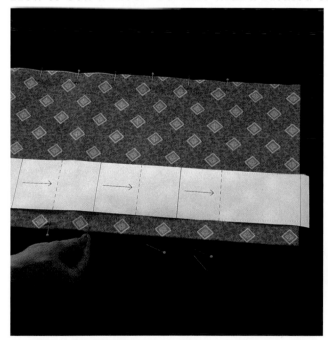

1) Make pattern for pleated skirt; pleat pattern to test for accurate width. In pattern shown, knife pleats are folded on solid lines and aligned to dashed lines in direction of arrows. Follow steps 1 to 8 on pages 124 and 125. Transfer pattern markings to right side of skirt on upper and lower edges.

2) Pin pleats in place along upper and lower edges of skirt; press. Baste along upper edge. Pin wrong side of skirt to right side of back rod pocket along lower edge; stitch. Press seam allowances toward the rod pocket. Complete mock cornice, following steps 12 to 16, opposite and above.

Valances with Clustered Gathers

Valances with clustered gathers are simple top treatments that may be used with shades or blinds. Soft, clustered gathers are spaced evenly across the width of the valance, and decorative cording, knotted at each cluster, is used for embellishment.

The valance is mounted outside the window frame on a mounting board that can be positioned at the top of the window frame or on the wall above the window. The finished width of the valance should be at least 2" (5 cm) wider than the outside measurement of the window frame. If there is no undertreatment, a 1 × 3 board can be used. With an undertreatment, use a mounting board that will project out from the window frame enough so the valance will clear the undertreatment by 2" to 3" (5 to 7.5 cm).

For attractive gathers, make the valance from a soft decorator fabric. For nondirectional prints, the valance may be constructed on the crosswise grain. For directional prints, piece the fabric as necessary, matching the pattern. Plan the placement of seams to fall within a cluster of gathers, if possible. The valance is constructed with a self-lining; therefore, a pattern printed on lightweight or light-colored fabric may show through to the right side. Test the fabric by folding a piece in half and holding it up to a light or a window to see if the pattern shows through.

✂ Cutting Directions

The cut width of the fabric is equal to the length of the mounting board plus two times the width, or projection, of the mounting board plus 1" (2.5 cm) for ½" (1.3 cm) seam allowances plus 6" (15 cm) for each clustered gather. Space clustered gathers from 7" to 10" (18 to 25.5 cm) apart along the front of the mounting board.

The cut length of the fabric is equal to two times the desired length of the valance plus 1" (2.5 cm) for ½" (1.3 cm) seam allowances; the finished length of the valance may range from 12" to 16" (30.5 to 40.5 cm), depending on the size of the window.

YOU WILL NEED

Decorator fabric.
Cording.
Mounting board.
Heavy-duty stapler.

Angle irons, one for each end of mounting board and one for every 45" (115 cm) interval across the width of the board.

Pan-head screws or molly bolts.

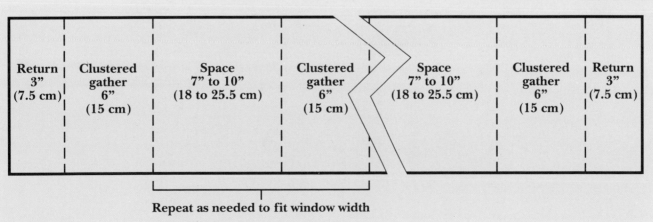

| Return 3" (7.5 cm) | Clustered gather 6" (15 cm) | Space 7" to 10" (18 to 25.5 cm) | Clustered gather 6" (15 cm) | Space 7" to 10" (18 to 25.5 cm) | Clustered gather 6" (15 cm) | Return 3" (7.5 cm) |

Repeat as needed to fit window width

Determine the number and spacing of clustered gathers and the amount of fabric needed for the *returns* that wrap around the sides of the mounting board, using the guide above. Plan for a clustered gather at each end of the board; space additional clustered gathers about 7" to 10" (18 to 25.5 cm) apart. Allow 6" (15 cm) of fabric for each clustered gather.

How to Sew a Valance with Clustered Gathers

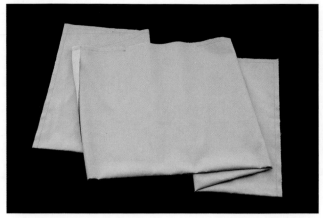

1) Seam fabric widths, if necessary. Fold the fabric in half lengthwise, with right sides together and raw edges even; pin. Stitch ½" (1.3 cm) from raw edges; leave 8" (20.5 cm) opening on upper edge for turning.

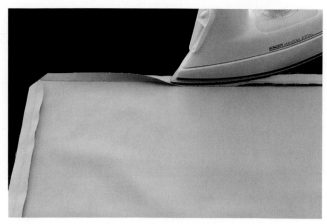

2) Trim corners diagonally. Press the seam allowances open at edges. Turn the valance right side out. Press edges, folding in the seam allowances at the opening. Slipstitch opening closed.

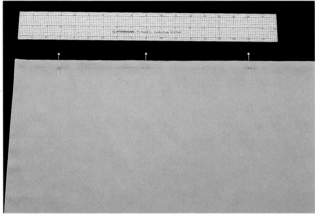

3) Pin-mark a distance equal to width of mounting board on each end of valance at seamed upper edge. Pin-mark placement of clustered gathers at the upper edge of the valance.

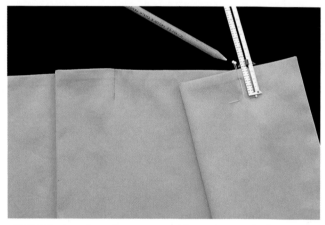

4) Fold pleat in valance, matching pin marks for each clustered gather. Mark a line parallel to fold, 1½" (3.8 cm) deep at pin mark. Stitch in place on the marked line. Repeat for remaining clustered gathers.

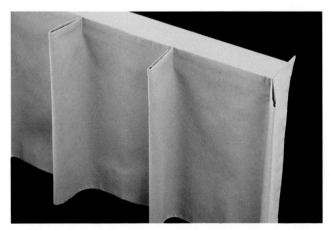

5) Check fit of valance around the mounting board. Adjust pleats, if necessary for accurate fit.

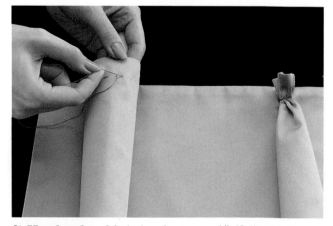

6) Hand-gather fabric in pleat area 1" (2.5 cm) from upper edge; secure with hand stitching. Repeat for remaining clustered gathers.

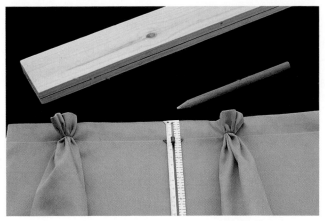

7) Mark center of mounting board around edges on sides and face of board, using pencil. Mark valance 1" (2.5 cm) from upper edge, using chalk pencil.

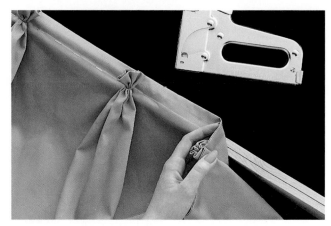

8) Staple valance to board, aligning marked line on board with marked line on valance; place staples between clustered gathers.

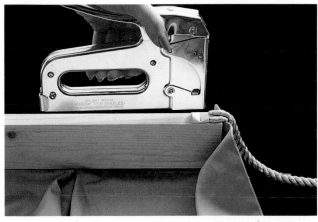

9) Unravel the ends of cording so individual cords lie parallel and flat; secure the ends with masking tape. Staple taped ends to back side of mounting board.

10) Tie a knot in cording to align with first cluster; secure cording to valance over the staples, using hot glue. Hold cording in place on both sides of cluster until glue sets.

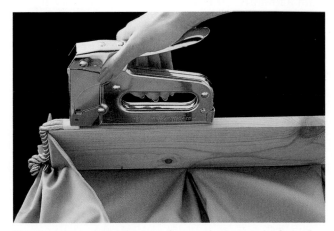

11) Continue knotting and securing remainder of cording to the valance. Secure ends of cording and staple to back of board as in step 9.

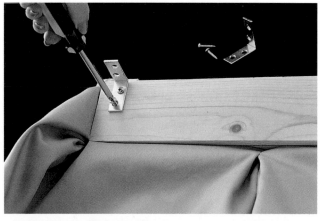

12) Secure angle irons to the bottom of mounting board, near ends and at 45" (115 cm) intervals, using pan-head screws. Secure angle irons to top of window frame or into the wall studs, using pan-head screws; if securing to drywall or plaster, use molly bolts.

Handkerchief Valances

This easy, tailored valance features a 3" (7.5 cm) band at the lower edge, which is simply an extension of the contrasting lining. The valance can be used alone or over another window treatment, such as blinds or underdraperies. It works well for small windows, without being overpowering, but this banded styling is also attractive on larger windows.

A handkerchief valance should be mounted as an outside mount (pages 52 and 53). The board can either be mounted at the top of the window frame or on the wall above the window. The finished width of the valance should be at least 2" (5 cm) wider than the outside measurement of the window frame or undertreatment; the finished width does not include the fabric drop at the sides of the valance.

✂ Cutting Directions
The cut width of the outer fabric is equal to the length of the mounting board plus two times the return of the valance plus 1" (2.5 cm) for seam allowances. The fabric may be railroaded if the design is not directional (page 27). Fabric that cannot be railroaded will require piecing if the cut width of the valance is wider than the fabric width; when the fabric is pieced, add the necessary extra width for seam allowances. To determine the cut length of the outer fabric, add the projection of the mounting board to the desired finished length of the valance; then

subtract 2" (5 cm) from this measurement to allow for seam allowances and for a 3" (7.5 cm) contrasting band at the lower edge.

Cut the contrasting lining the same width as the outer fabric. To determine the cut length of the lining, add the projection of the mounting board to the desired finished length of the valance; then add 4" (10 cm) to this measurement to allow for seam allowances and for a 3" (7.5 cm) contrasting band at the lower edge.

Cut fabric to cover the mounting board (page 53).

YOU WILL NEED

Decorator fabric in two contrasting colors for outer fabric and lining.

Mounting board, cut to the desired finished width of valance. Mounting board must be at least 2" (5 cm) wider than projection of window frame or undertreatment.

Angle irons, one for each end and one for every 45" (115 cm) interval across the width of the mounting board.

Heavy-duty stapler; staples.

Pan-head screws or molly bolts (page 52).

How to Sew a Handkerchief Valance

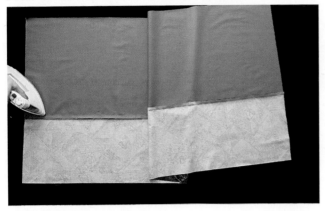

1) Seam fabric widths, if necessary. Place outer fabric and lining right sides together, matching the lower edges; stitch ½" (1.3 cm) seam. Press seam toward outer fabric.

2) Place outer fabric and lining right sides together, matching upper edges. Stitch ½" (1.3 cm) seams at sides and upper edge; leave an 8" (20.5 cm) opening at center of upper edge for turning. Trim corners diagonally. Press seam allowances open at edges.

3) Turn valance right side out. Press edges, folding in seam allowances at center opening.

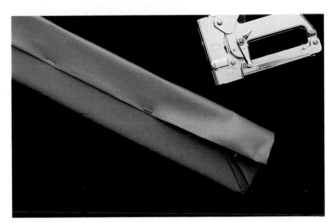

4) Cover mounting board with fabric (page 53); staple fabric in place at 4" (10 cm) intervals, folding under raw edges.

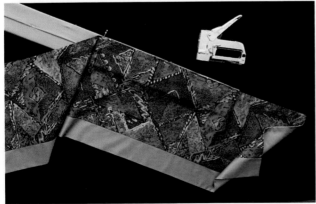

5) Mark center of mounting board; mark center of valance at upper edge. Place valance, right side up, on mounting board, aligning upper edge of valance to back edge of board; match center markings. Near back edge, staple valance to board at center. Working from center to sides, staple valance to board at 4" (10 cm) intervals, with one staple close to each end.

6) Screw angle irons to bottom of mounting board, positioning one at each end and spacing them at 45" (115 cm) intervals. Install valance on window frame or wall (pages 52 and 53). Adjust the drape at ends of valance.

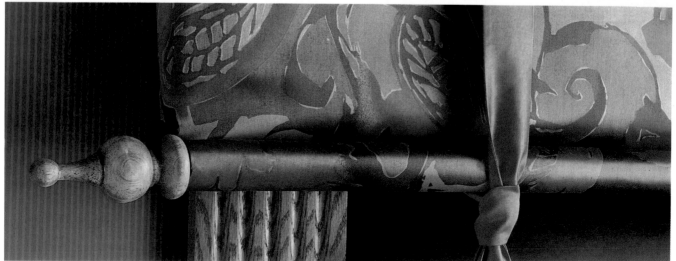

Outside mounted stagecoach valance has side returns; finials may be added at ends of wood pole, if desired.

Stagecoach Valances

This stationary, tailored top treatment features decorative ties and resembles the curtains used in the stagecoaches of the past. The valance may be lined with matching or contrasting fabric. The lining shows when the stagecoach valance is rolled at the lower edge.

A stagecoach valance is attached to a mounting board and is frequently mounted inside the window frame. When an inside mount is used, the finished width of the valance is ¼" (6 mm) less than the measurement inside the window frame, and the window treatment is attached to a 1" × 1" (2.5 × 2.5 cm) mounting board.

For an outside mount, side returns are added to the valance. The return is the distance from the wall to the front edge of the mounting board. The mounting board can either be mounted at the top of the window frame or on the wall above the window. The finished width of the valance should be at least 2" (5 cm) wider than the outside measurement of the window frame or 2" (5 cm) wider than the width of an undertreatment.

The ties are usually spaced 24" to 36" (61 to 91.5 cm) apart. If they are spaced farther apart, the valance fabric may buckle between the ties. If possible, plan the placement of the ties so they will be aligned with any existing vertical lines in the window.

✂ Cutting Directions

If this treatment is used on a window that is wider than the fabric width, railroad the fabric whenever possible (page 27). If the fabric cannot be railroaded, plan the placement of the seams so they will be concealed under the ties.

For an inside mount, the cut width of the face fabric is equal to the finished width of the valance plus 1" (2.5 cm) for seam allowances. For an outside mount, the cut width of the face fabric is equal to the finished width of the valance plus two times the return plus 1" (2.5 cm) for seam allowances.

The cut length of the face fabric is equal to the finished length plus the width of the mounting board plus 12" (30.5 cm) for a rolled effect at the lower edge plus 1" (2.5 cm) for seam allowances.

Cut the matching or contrasting lining the same size as the face fabric.

Cut two fabric strips for each tie location, with the cut width of each strip two times the finished width of the tie plus ½" (1.3 cm) for seam allowances. The finished width of the ties in the photo is 2" (5 cm). The fabric strips may be cut on the crosswise grain, with the cut length of the strips equal to the width of the fabric. Cut fabric to cover the mounting board (page 53).

YOU WILL NEED

Decorator fabric for valance and mounting board.

Matching or contrasting fabric for lining.

Contrasting fabric for ties.

1⅜" (3.5 cm) wood pole, cut to finished width of valance after it is stitched.

Mounting board, cut ¼" (6 mm) shorter than the finished width of valance after it is stitched. For inside mount, use 1" × 1" (2.5 × 2.5 cm) board. For outside mount, use a board at least 2" (5 cm) wider than projection of window frame or undertreatment.

Heavy-duty stapler; staples.

Angle irons, one for each end and one for every 45" (115 cm) interval across the width of the mounting board; pan-head screws or molly bolts (page 52) for outside mount.

Pan-head screws (page 52) for inside mount.

How to Sew an Inside-mounted Stagecoach Valance

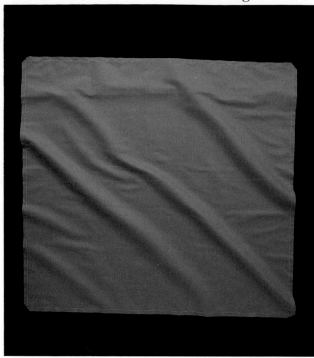

1) Seam fabric widths as necessary. Place face fabric and lining right sides together, matching raw edges. Stitch ½" (1.3 cm) seams around all sides; leave an 8" (20.5 cm) opening at center of upper edge for turning. Trim corners diagonally.

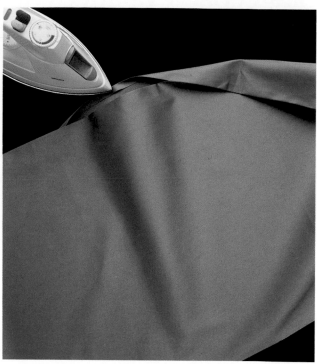

2) Turn valance right side out. Press edges, folding in seam allowances at center opening.

3) Cut two 3" (7.5 cm) circles. Attach to ends of wood pole, using fabric glue or spray adhesive.

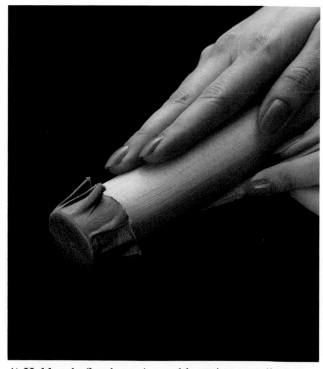

4) Hold pole firmly against table; using pencil, draw line on pole where it touches table.

5) Center pole on right side of valance at lower edge; staple in place, aligning lower edge of valance to marked line on pole.

6) Roll up valance to desired finished length. Anchor pole in place with pins.

7) Fold fabric strips for ties in half lengthwise, right sides together. Stitch long edge and one short end, using ¼" (6 mm) seam allowance. Trim diagonally across corners, turn tie right side out, and press. Two ties are used at each placement.

8) Mark desired placement of ties at upper edge of valance. Staple valance to covered mounting board (page 53), aligning upper edge of valance to back edge of board. Do not place staples at markings for ties.

(Continued on next page)

How to Sew an Inside-mounted Stagecoach Valance (continued)

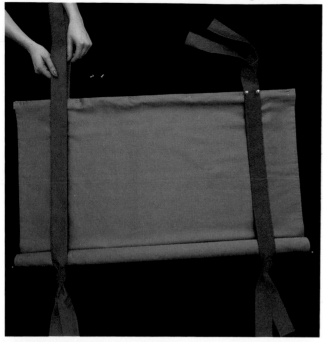

9) Sandwich valance between two ties at placement marks; tack in place, using map tacks. Tie finished ends; adjust length of ties from upper edge, for desired effect, making sure all ties are the same length. Staple ties to board. Trim excess ties at top.

10) Mount valance by screwing board inside window frame, using #8 gauge 1½" (3.8 cm) pan-head screws. Predrill the holes, using ⅛" (3 mm) drill bit.

How to Sew an Outside-mounted Stagecoach Valance

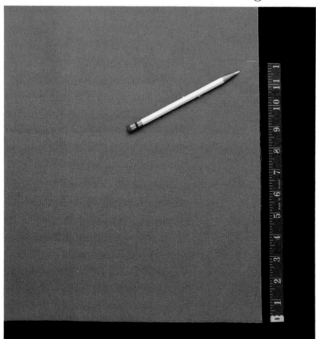

1) Seam fabric widths as necessary. Fold face fabric in half lengthwise, right sides together. At sides, mark a line 12½" (31.8 cm) from lower edge; this is the amount needed for rolled effect plus seam allowance.

2) Draw line in from side at marked line, the amount of one return. Draw line, parallel to side, down to lower edge; cut out section through both layers. The cut width at lower edge should now be the finished width of valance plus 1" (2.5 cm). Repeat for lining.

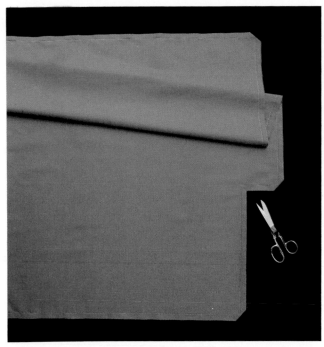

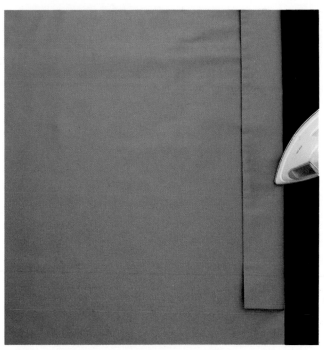

3) Place face fabric and lining right sides together, matching raw edges. Stitch ½" (1.3 cm) seams around all sides; leave an 8" (20.5 cm) opening at center of upper edge for turning. Clip and trim corners.

4) Turn valance right side out. Press edges, folding in seam allowances at center opening. Press returns lightly. Complete steps 3 to 7 on pages 136 and 137.

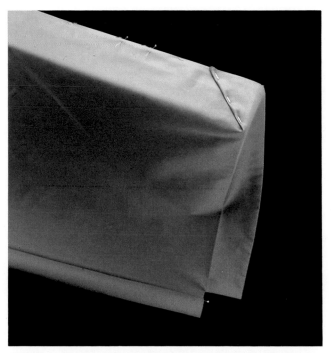

5) Mark desired placement of ties at upper edge of valance. Staple valance to covered mounting board (page 53), aligning upper edge of valance to back edge of board and centering upper edge on board, with returns extending at ends of board. Do not place staples at markings for ties.

6) Miter corners of returns; staple in place. Finish valance with ties, as in step 9, opposite. Mount as on pages 52 and 53.

Pillows

Pillows

Pillows can add softness and texture to a room for a decorative finishing touch. Basic techniques and instructions for several pillow designs are included on the following pages.

For most pillows, cut the pillow top and back 1" (2.5 cm) wider and longer than the finished size of the pillow. If using a pillow form, cut the fabric 1" (2.5 cm) wider and longer than the form. To prevent dog-eared corners on square or rectangular pillows, taper the corners of the fabric (page 144).

A zipper closure can be added to make it easier to clean the pillow cover. An invisible zipper can be inserted along one side for an inconspicuous closure; use the special zipper foot designed for applying invisible zippers.

If the pillow has welting, it may be easier to add a seam and insert the zipper on the pillow back. To make a zippered pillow cover that has a back seam, cut the pillow front 1" (2.5 cm) wider and longer than the finished size of the pillow, or 1" (2.5 cm) wider and longer than the pillow form. Cut one pillow back piece the width of the pillow front and 3¾" (9.5 cm) long; cut another piece, the width of the pillow front and 2¼" (6 cm) shorter than the length of the pillow front.

When the pillow cover is completed, insert a pillow form, or fill the cover with polyester fiberfill or quilt batting. Push fiberfill or batting into the corners and along the sides as necessary to fill out the pillow. Even when a pillow form is used, you may want to add fiberfill or batting to the corners and sides.

Pillow Fabrics, Forms & Fillings

To choose the right fabric for your pillow, consider how the pillow will be used and where it will be placed in your home. For a pillow that will receive hard wear, select a sturdy, firmly woven fabric that will retain its shape.

Pillows get their shape from forms or loose fillings. Depending on their washability, loose fillings may be stuffed directly into the pillow covering or encased in a separate liner for easy removal. For ease in laundering or dry cleaning, make a separate inner covering or liner for the stuffing, using lightweight muslin or liner fabric, or use purchased pillow forms. Make the liner as you would a plain pillow (page 142), fill it with stuffing, and machine-stitch it closed. Choose from several kinds of forms and fillings.

Standard polyester forms are square, round and rectangular for knife-edge pillows in sizes from 10" to 30" (25.5 to 76 cm). These forms are nonallergenic, washable, do not bunch, and may have muslin or polyester outer coverings. Choose muslin-covered forms for pillows with hook and loop tape closings. The loose muslin fibers do not catch on the rough side of the tape.

Polyurethane foam is available in sheets ½" to 5" (1.3 to 12.5 cm) thick for firm pillows and cushions. Some stores carry a high-density foam, 4" (10 cm) thick, for extra firm cushions. Since cutting the foam is difficult, ask the salesperson to cut a piece to the size of your pillow. If you must cut your own foam, use an electric or serrated knife with silicone lubricant sprayed on the blade. Polyurethane foam is also available shredded.

Polyester fiberfill is washable, nonallergenic filling for pillows or pillow liners. Fiberfill comes in loose-pack bags or pressed into batting sheets of varying densities. For a smooth pillow, sew an inner liner of batting, then stuff with loose fill. Soften the hard edges of polyurethane foam by wrapping the form with batting.

Kapok is vegetable fiber filling, favored by some decorators because of its softness. However, kapok is messy to work with and becomes matted with use.

Down is washed, quill-less feathers from the breasts of geese and ducks. Down makes the most luxurious pillows, but it is expensive and not readily available.

How to Prevent Dog-eared Corners

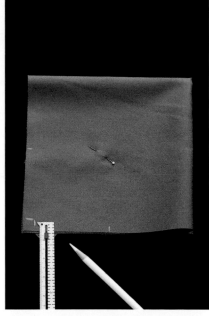 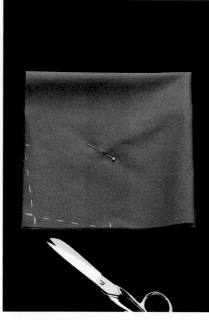 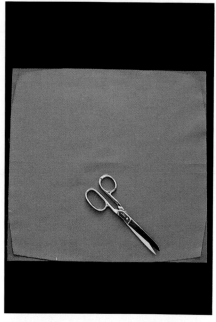

1) Fold pillow top into fourths. Mark a point halfway between corner and fold on each open side. At corner, mark a point ½" (1.3 cm) from each raw edge.

2) Mark lines, tapering from raw edges at center marks to mark at corner. Cut on marked lines.

3) Use pillow top as pattern for cutting pillow back so all corners are tapered. For zippered pillow cover, below, corners may be tapered on pillow back after the zipper is inserted.

How to Sew a Pillow with a Back Zipper

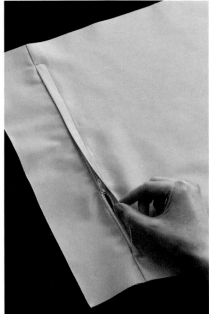 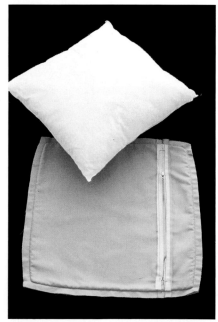 

1) Cut pillow pieces, opposite. Stitch pillow back pieces together in ¾" (2 cm) seam, basting in zipper area. Apply zipper that is about 2" (5 cm) shorter than the finished width of the pillow. To prevent dog-eared corners, taper corners of pillow front and back, above.

2) Apply welting (pages 39 and 145) to pillow front, if desired. Pin pillow front to pillow back, right sides together; stitch ½" (1.3 cm) seam. Turn right side out.

3) Stuff pillow cover by inserting pillow form. Push polyester fiberfill or quilt batting into corners of the pillow and along sides as necessary to fill out pillow.

How to Make and Attach Welting

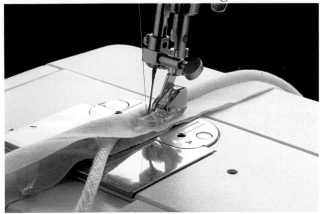

1) Cut fabric strips (page 40); seam strips together as necessary for desired length. Fold fabric strip around cording, wrong sides together, matching raw edges. Using a zipper foot, machine-baste close to cording; smooth cording as you sew, removing twists.

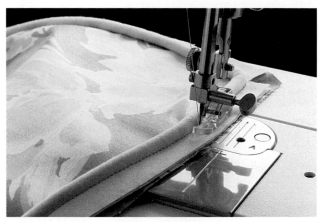

2) Stitch welting to right side of fabric over previous stitches, matching raw edges and starting 2" (5 cm) from end of welting; clip and ease welting at corners, or ease welting at curves.

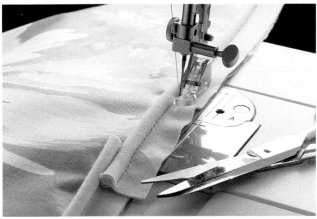

3) Stop stitching 2" (5 cm) from point where ends of welting will meet. Cut off one end of welting so it overlaps the other end by 1" (2.5 cm).

4) Remove stitching from one end of welting, and trim ends of cording so they just meet.

5) Fold under ½" (1.3 cm) of fabric on overlapping end of welting. Lap it around the other end; finish stitching welting to pillow front.

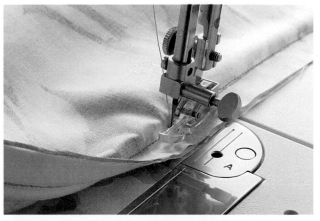

6) Stitch pillow back to pillow front, right sides together, using zipper foot; stitch inside previous stitching line, crowding stitches against welting. Leave opening on one side for turning, if pillow cover is not zippered.

Shirred Pillows

Shirred welting or boxing strips give pillows a formal look.

✂ Cutting Directions

For shirred box pillow, cut pillow front and back 1" (2.5 cm) larger than finished pillow. Cut boxing strip 1" (2.5 cm) wider than depth of form and two to three times longer than distance around form.

For shirred-welting pillow, cut pillow front and back 1" (2.5 cm) larger than finished pillow. For welting, cut fabric strips on the crosswise grain, wide enough to cover cord plus 1" (2.5 cm) for seam. The combined length of the strips should be two to three times the distance around the pillow.

YOU WILL NEED

Decorator fabric for pillow front and back and for welting or boxing strips.

Cord (twisted white cotton or polyester cable), if making shirred welting. Cut 3" (7.5 cm) longer than distance around pillow.

Gathering cord (string, crochet cotton or dental floss), if making shirred boxing strip.

Pillow form wrapped in polyester batting, or liner.

How to Make a Shirred Box Pillow

1) Join short ends of boxing strip with ½" (1.3 cm) seam. Zigzag over gathering cord ⅜" (1 cm) from long raw edges; avoid piercing cord with needle. Fold strip into fourths and mark both edges of folds with ⅜" (1 cm) clips.

2) Pin boxing strip to pillow front, right sides together, raw edges even, matching clips on boxing strip to pillow corners. Pull up the gathering cord to fit each side of the pillow.

How to Make and Attach Shirred Welting

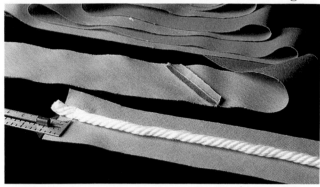

1) Cut and join welting strips (page 40). Press the seams open. Stitch one end of the cord to the wrong side of the welting strip, ⅜" (1 cm) from the end of the strip.

2) Fold welting strip around cord, wrong sides together, matching raw edges. Using zipper foot, machine-baste for 6" (15 cm), close to but not crowding cord. Stop stitching with needle in fabric.

3) Raise presser foot. While gently pulling cord, push welting strip back to end of cord until fabric behind needle is tightly shirred. Continue stitching in 6" (15 cm) intervals until all welting is shirred.

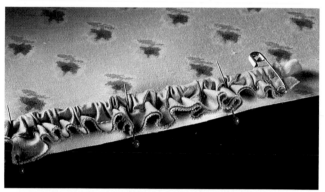

4) Insert pin through strip and cord at each end to secure cord. Distribute gathers evenly. Attach shirred welting to pillow front and join ends of cord as on page 145, steps 4 and 5.

3) Distribute gathers evenly. Stitch all four sides inside gathering row, shortening stitches for 1" (2.5 cm) on each side of corner. Take one or two stitches diagonally across each corner.

4) Pin the remaining long edge of the boxing strip to pillow back. Repeat steps 2 and 3, leaving 6" to 9" (15 to 23 cm) opening on one side to insert pillow.

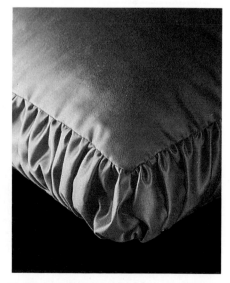

5) Turn pillow right side out. Press under seam allowances at the opening. Insert pillow form. Slipstitch opening closed.

Twisted Welting

Twisted welting, a decorative alternative to fabric-covered welting, has an attached tape, or lip, that can be stitched into the seams. Rayon welting, which has a shiny appearance, is more difficult to handle than cotton welting.

From the right side of the welting, the inner edge of the tape is not visible. For easier stitching and a more finished appearance on the front of the pillow, the welting is applied to the pillow back, right sides up. The ends of the welting can be twisted together to join them inconspicuously.

How to Attach Twisted Welting to a Pillow

1) Stitch twisted welting to pillow back, using zipper foot, with right sides up and edge of welting tape aligned to raw edge of fabric. Leave 1½" (3.8 cm) unstitched between ends; leave 3" (7.5 cm) tails.

2) Remove stitching from welting tape on tails. Separate cords; wrap transparent tape around ends to prevent raveling. Trim welting tape to 1" (2.5 cm) from stitching; overlap ends and secure with transparent tape. Arrange cords so those at right turn up and those at left turn down.

3) Insert cords at right end under welting tape, twisting and pulling them down until welting is returned to its original shape. Secure in place, using transparent tape or pins.

4) Twist and pull cords at left end over cords at right end until the twisted ends look like continuous twisted welting; check both sides of welting.

5) Position zipper foot on left side of needle; this will allow you to stitch in the direction of the twists. Machine-baste through all layers to secure welting at seamline, or cords may be hand-basted in place, if desired.

6) Place pillow back on pillow front, right sides together. Stitch as close to welting as possible, using zipper foot. If pillow cover is not zippered, leave an opening on one side for turning. With pillow front facing up, stitch again, crowding stitches closer to welting.

Sunburst Pillows

Framed with a ruffle and welting, this half-circle pillow can be made in any size and is an interesting accent on sofas and beds. The pillow shown is made from a pattern 18" (46 cm) across and 11½" (29.3 cm) high and has a 3" (7.5 cm) finished ruffle. When twisted welting is used, it is applied to the pillow back over the ruffle, for easier stitching and a more finished appearance on the front of the pillow. When fabric-covered welting is used, it is applied to the pillow front.

✂ Cutting Directions

Cut the pillow front and pillow back, using the pattern, opposite. For the ruffle, cut fabric strips two times the finished width of the ruffle plus 1" (2.5 cm) for seam allowances. For triple fullness, the combined length of the fabric strips is equal to three times the measurement along the curved edge of the pattern.

YOU WILL NEED

¾ yd. (0.7 m) decorator fabric, for pillow shown.

1½ yd. (1.4 m) twisted welting with welting tape or lip; or fabric-covered welting (pages 39 and 40).

Polyester fiberfill.

How to Make the Pattern for a Sunburst Pillow

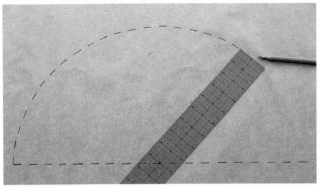

1) Draw a dotted line on paper equal to the desired diameter of circle. Using straightedge and pencil, mark half circle, measuring a distance equal to the radius from midpoint of dotted line.

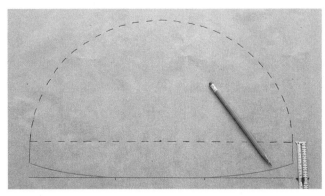

2) Extend lines straight down at sides for 1½" (3.8 cm). Draw line 2½"(6.5 cm) away from dotted line; divide into thirds, and mark. Draw slightly curved line between side and one-third markings. Cut on marked lines to complete pattern piece.

How to Sew a Sunburst Pillow

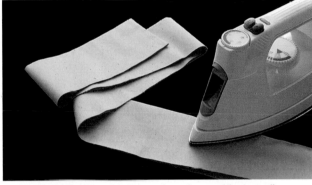

1) Stitch fabric strips together for ruffle in ¼" (6 mm) seams, right sides together. Fold pieced strip in half lengthwise, right sides together; stitch across ends in ¼" (6 mm) seam. Turn right side out; press. Stitch two rows of gathering threads on strip, ½" (1.3 cm) and ¼" (6 mm) from raw edge; or zigzag over cord as on page 146, step 1.

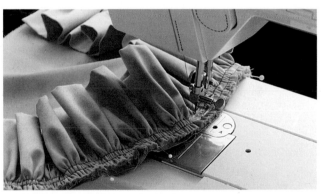

2) Divide strip and curved edges of pillow front and back into fourths; pin-mark. Place strip on curved edge of pillow back, right sides together, matching raw edges and pin marks; pull gathering threads to fit. Machine-baste ruffle, leaving pin marks in place.

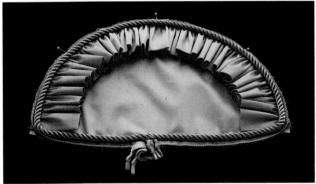

3) Machine-baste twisted welting around pillow back, over ruffle, and join ends as on pages 148 and 149. Or machine-baste fabric-covered welting around pillow front and join ends as on page 145.

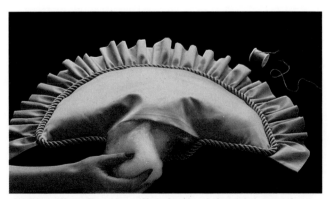

4) Pin pillow front to pillow back, right sides together, matching the pin marks. Stitch, using a zipper foot, crowding stitches against welting; leave 8" (20.5 cm) opening at bottom for turning. Stuff pillow with fiberfill, pushing it firmly into corners of pillow and along sides. Slipstitch opening closed.

Reversible Rosette Pillows

Perfect for the bedroom, a rosette pillow is simply a circular pillow cover tied around a pillow form. The pillow cover is lined to finish off the edges and to make it reversible. Select lightweight fabrics so the pillow cover can be gathered up tightly at the center; avoid fabrics that are stiff.

Twisted welting or fabric-covered welting is applied to the outer edge of the pillow cover. The welting defines the edge and helps the rosette stand out.

✂ Cutting Directions

For a 12" (30.5 cm) pillow, cut one 30" (76 cm) circle from the outer fabric and one from the lining. For a 14" (35.5 cm) pillow, cut 35" (89 cm) circles, or for a 16" (40.5 cm) pillow, cut 40" (102 cm) circles. To make it easier to mark and cut the circles, cut a square of each fabric, 1" (2.5 cm) larger than the diameter of the circle; then follow step 1, opposite.

Also cut a fabric strip, 2" × 18" (5 × 46 cm), to tie around the center of the pillow.

If fabric-covered welting is desired for the outer edge, cut bias fabric strips, with the combined length of the strips equal to the circumference of the circle. To estimate the length needed, multiply the diameter by three and one-half. The width of the bias strips depends on the size of the cording (page 39). For a 12" (30.5 cm) pillow, $\frac{5}{32}$" cording works well; for a larger pillow, use $\frac{8}{32}$" cording.

YOU WILL NEED

Decorator fabrics for outer fabric and lining.

Twisted welting with welting tape or lip; or cording and fabric for fabric-covered welting.

Circular pillow form.

How to Sew a Reversible Rosette Pillow

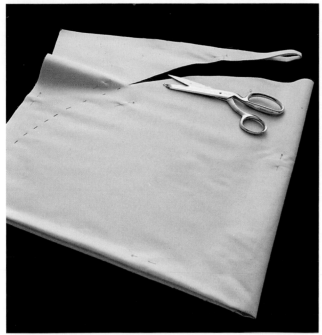

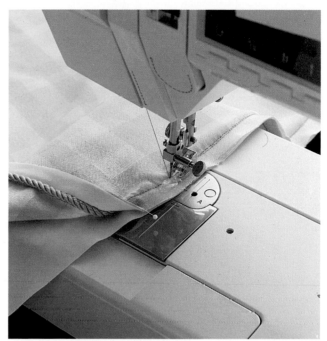

1) Fold fabric square into fourths, right sides together. Using straightedge and pencil, mark one-quarter of the circle on fabric, measuring a distance equal to the radius from the folded center of fabric. Cut on marked line through all layers; notch raw edge at foldlines. Use as pattern for cutting and notching remaining fabric circle.

2) Apply twisted welting to outer edge of one fabric circle, as on pages 148 and 149. Or make fabric-covered welting and apply to outer edge, as on page 145. Pin fabric circles, right sides together, matching notches; stitch close to welting, using zipper foot and leaving 6" (15 cm) opening for turning.

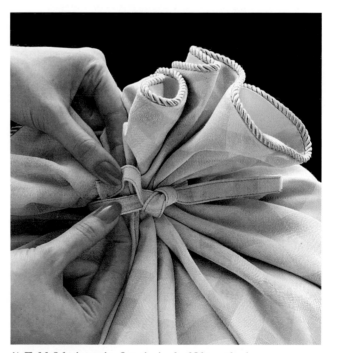

3) Turn pillow cover right side out; press. Slipstitch opening closed. Center pillow form on pillow cover; draw up fabric around pillow form, securing with rubber band. Adjust folds, arranging welting for desired effect.

4) Fold fabric strip for tie in half lengthwise, wrong sides together; press. Fold raw edges to center and press. Refold, and edgestitch on both long edges. Tie around bunched fabric, concealing rubber band and cinching in pillow cover tightly. Cut ends to desired length; tuck ends under tie to conceal them.

Pillow Shams with Buttoned Flaps

Offering a sleek, contemporary look, this easy-to-sew pillow sham features a contrasting flap, embellished with buttons. This style of pillow sham is designed to fit a 26" (66 cm) square pillow, often called a European square pillow. The sham has a generous overlapping closure at the center back to conceal the pillow. The buttoned flap on the front is a mock opening, for decorative detailing.

✂ Cutting Directions

Cut one 27" (68.5 cm) square from fabric, for the pillow front. Cut two 20" × 27" (51 × 68.5 cm) rectangles from fabric, for the pillow back. Cut one 14" × 27" (35.5 × 68.5 cm) rectangle from contrasting fabric, for the pillow flap.

YOU WILL NEED

Two coordinating decorator fabrics.

Five ¾" (2 cm) buttons.

26" (66 cm) square pillow form.

How to Sew a Pillow Sham with a Buttoned Flap

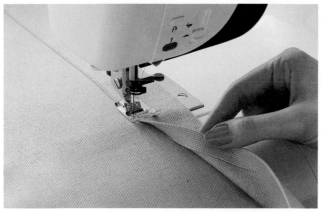

1) Press ½" (1.3 cm), then 1½" (3.8 cm), to wrong side, along one long edge of rectangle for flap. Stitch close to inner fold.

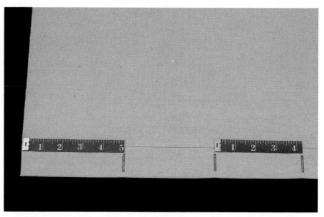

2) Mark buttonhole placement on hemmed edge of flap, 5" (12.5 cm) from each raw edge. Mark the placement of remaining buttonholes, spacing them 4¼" (10.8 cm) apart. Stitch vertical buttonholes at markings, centered on hemmed edge.

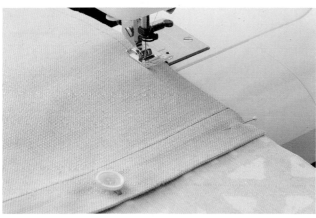

3) Place flap over pillow front, right sides up, matching raw edges at upper edge and sides. Mark placement for buttons; stitch buttons to pillow front. Reposition flap, and button over pillow front. Baste flap in place, ⅜" (1 cm) from raw edges.

4) Press ½" (1.3 cm), then 2" (5 cm), to wrong side, along one long edge of one pillow back piece. Stitch close to inner fold. Repeat for remaining back piece.

5) Position pillow back pieces over pillow front, right sides together, matching raw edges; hemmed edges overlap 8" (20.5 cm) at center. Pin in place.

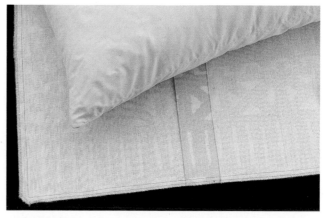

6) Stitch ½" (1.3 cm) seam around the pillow sham. Trim the corners diagonally; finish seam allowances, using zigzag or overlock stitch. Turn right side out; insert pillow.

Knotted-corner Pillows

On the knotted-corner pillow, jumbo welting forms pretzel-like knots and creates a border. Smaller versions of these pillows can accent sofas and chairs; larger ones can serve as comfortable floor cushions.

For creative detailing and easier sewing, the covered welting is pulled through self-fabric sleeves on all sides of the pillow. It is helpful to wrap the ends of the cording with masking tape to prevent the ends from fraying while you are handling the cording.

✄ Cutting Directions

Cut the pillow front and pillow back 1" (2.5 cm) longer and wider than the pillow form. Measure the height of the pillow form. Measure in from the corners of the pillow front and pillow back a distance equal to one-half the height of the pillow; mark with notches.

Measure the circumference of the jumbo cording loosely. Cut four fabric sleeves for the sides of the pillow, with the width of each sleeve equal to the circumference plus 1" (2.5 cm), and the length of each sleeve equal to the distance between the notches plus 2" (5 cm). If textured fabric is used, the fabric sleeves may need to be cut about ⅜" (1 cm) wider, so the fabric-covered cording can be pulled through the sleeve more easily.

Cut fabric strips to cover the jumbo cording, with the width of the strips equal to the width of the fabric sleeves and with the combined length of the strips equal to the length of the jumbo cording.

YOU WILL NEED

1¼ yd. (1.15 m) decorator fabric, for 20" (51 cm) pillow.

Jumbo cording, the length equal to the distance around the pillow plus about 60" (152.5 cm); each knot takes up 12" to 15" (30.5 to 38 cm), depending on the size of the cording.

Fusible web.

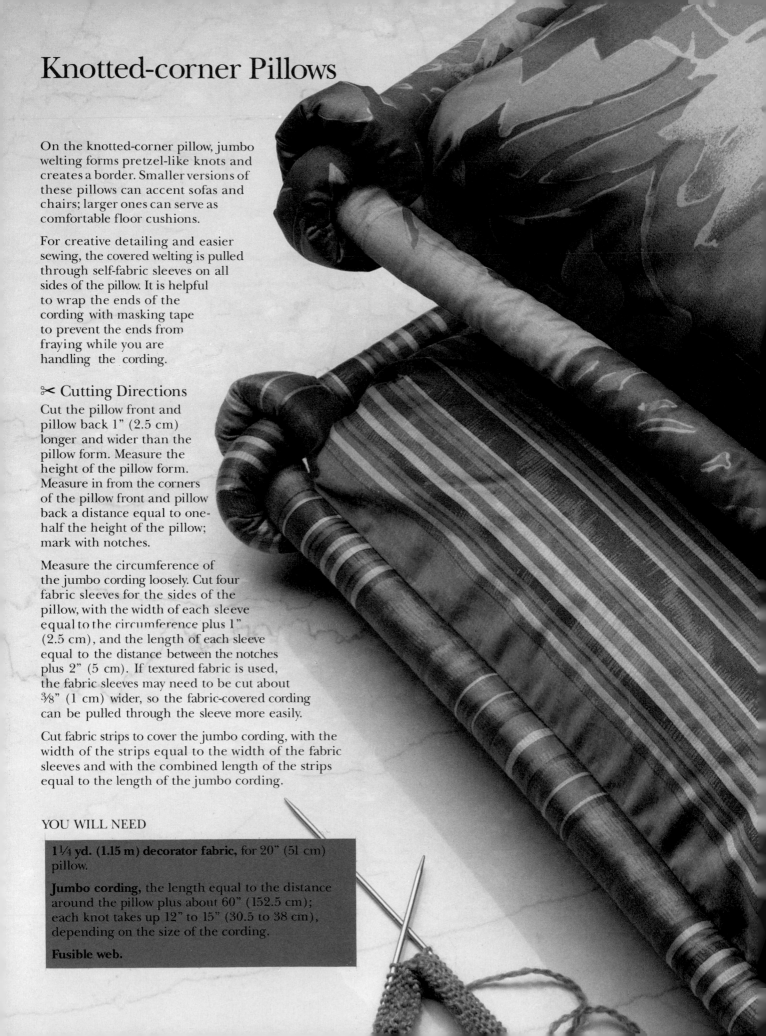

How to Sew a Knotted-corner Pillow

1) Mark notches on pillow front and pillow back, as on page 156. Press under 1" (2.5 cm) on short ends of fabric sleeves; fuse in place, using fusible web.

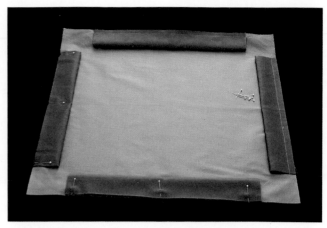

2) Fold fabric sleeves in half lengthwise, wrong sides together; pin to pillow front between the notches, matching raw edges. Baste strips in place on seamline.

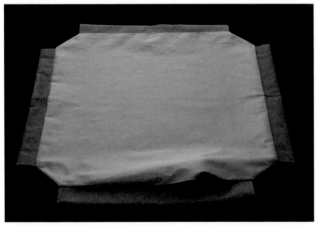

3) Pin pillow front to pillow back, right sides together. Stitch ½" (1.3 cm) seam on sides of pillow, stitching diagonally across corners between notches; leave an opening on one side for turning. Trim excess fabric at corners. Turn pillow cover right side out.

4) Fold fabric strip in half lengthwise, right sides together; stitch ½" (1.3 cm) seam. Turn right side out, using large safety pin or bodkin.

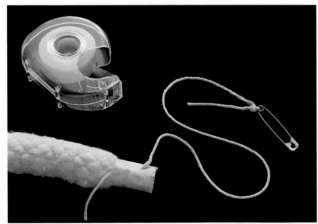

5) Cut piece of string the length of one side of pillow. Tie string around end of cording. Secure string to cording by wrapping it with tape. Attach safety pin or bodkin to end of string.

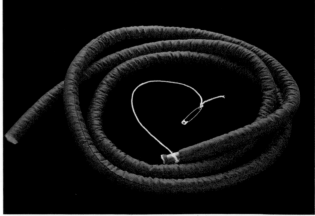

6) Pull cording through fabric strip to make welting. Tie string around end of welting; secure string to welting by wrapping it with tape.

7) Pull welting through fabric sleeve on pillow, leaving 1" (2.5 cm) tail at beginning. Tie overhand knot at end of sleeve.

8) Pull welting through next sleeve; tie another overhand knot. Repeat with remaining sleeves.

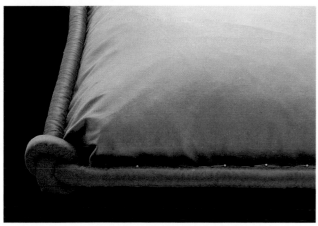

9) Insert pillow form, as on page 142; pin opening closed. Adjust all knots to same size. Turn seam on welting inward at knots.

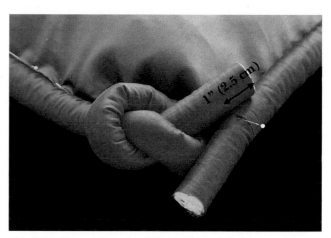

10) Cut off excess welting at end, so welting overlaps first sleeve 1" (2.5 cm), arrow. Mark welting at beginning of first sleeve.

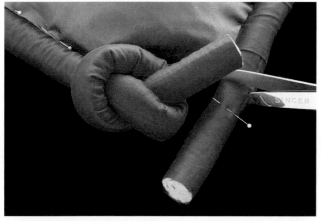

11) Pull end of welting out of first sleeve. Cut welting 1" (2.5 cm) beyond mark.

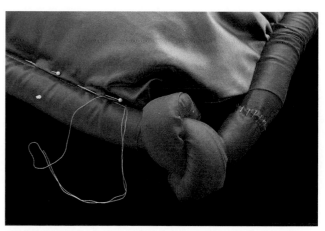

12) Whipstitch ends of welting together. Slide ends back into sleeve. Slipstitch opening on pillow closed.

Sash Pillows

Sash pillows coordinate well with scarf swag window treatments (page 109) and may have either a rosette or a tie at the center of the sash. The rosette can also be used at the center of the sunburst window treatment (page 80) for an arch, or Palladian, window.

✂ Cutting Directions

Cut two 17" (43 cm) squares of fabric for the pillow body and one 23" (58.5 cm) square for the sash. Cut bias strips for cording from contrasting fabric, with the total length of the strips equal to 2 yd. (1.85 m); piece the strips together as necessary. The width of the bias strips depends on the size of the cording (page 39).

For a pillow with a rosette, also cut one 25" (63.5 cm) circle for the rosette from constrasting fabric. To make

it easier to mark and cut the circle, cut a 26" (66 cm) square of fabric; then follow step 1 on page 153.

For a pillow with a tie, also cut one 5" × 6" (12.5 × 15 cm) rectangle for the tie from contrasting fabric.

YOU WILL NEED

½ yd. (0.5 m) decorator fabric for pillow body.

1½ yd. (1.4 m) contrasting decorator fabric for pillow with rosette, to make rosette, sash, and bias cording.

¾ yd. (0.7 m) contrasting decorator fabric for pillow with tie, to make tie, sash, and bias cording.

2 yd. (1.85 m) cording.

Pillow form, 16" (40.5 cm).

How to Make a Rosette

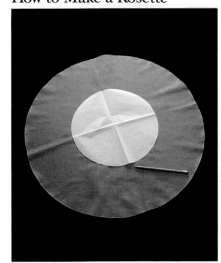

1) Mark center of rosette circle on right side of fabric, using a pencil. Make paper pattern of circle with 12" (30.5 cm) diameter; mark center. Match centers of fabric and paper circles; trace outline of paper circle onto right side of fabric.

2) Finish outer edge of circle, using zigzag or overlock stitch. Hand-baste on marked lines of small circle, using 1/2" (1.3 cm) running stitches. Pull basting stitches tight; secure threads. Hand-baste around outer edge and pull basting stitches tight; secure stitches, but do not cut thread tails.

3) Position eraser end of pencil on marked center of rosette. Push the center of smaller pouf through the opening at center of larger pouf; secure fabric on wrong side. Do not cut thread tails.

How to Sew a Sash Pillow with a Rosette

1) Fold 23" (58.5 cm) fabric square in half, right sides together. Stitch long edges together; press seam open. Turn tube right side out; center seam on underside of tube. Fold tube in half, matching raw edges. Press fold; do not press lengthwise edges.

2) Open out sash; hand-baste on pressed foldline. Pull basting stitches tight to cinch the sash at center.

3) Lay sash diagonally across pillow top, right sides up, pinning seams of sash at corners of pillow top. Trim excess sash fabric.

4) Make welting and apply to pillow top, as on page 145.

5) Place the pillow back on pillow front, right sides together. Stitch around all sides of pillow close to cording, using zipper foot; leave an opening on one side for turning.

6) Turn pillow right side out. Insert pillow form. Hand-stitch rosette to sash over basting stitches. Slipstitch opening of pillow closed

How to Sew a Sash Pillow with a Tie

1) Complete steps 1 to 5, opposite. Fold 5" × 6" (12.5 × 15 cm) rectangle of fabric in half lengthwise, right sides together. Stitch ½" (1.3 cm) seam along 6" (15 cm) side; turn right side out. Press flat, with seam centered on underside of tie.

2) Turn pillow right side out. Insert pillow form. Fold in one end of tie. Wrap tie around center of the sash, tucking raw edge into folded end; slipstitch in place. Turn tie so seam is under sash. Slipstitch opening of pillow closed.

Reversible Rolled Bolsters

The reversible rolled bolster is edged with welting for dimension and appeal. This soft pillow is actually a fabric cover and batting rolled together for easy construction. The bolster is lined to finish off the edges and to make it reversible. The ends of the bolster are tied with bows.

The striped fabric in the pillow above has been railroaded (page 27) so the stripes encircle the bolster. Extra yardage is needed for railroading.

✄ Cutting Directions

For pillow body, cut one 18" × 45" (46 × 115 cm) rectangle of decorative fabric and one of lining. For welting, cut bias fabric strips with combined length of strips equal to 3¼ yd. (3 m). The width of the bias strips depends on the size of the cording (page 39). For ties, cut two 1½" × 28" (3.8 × 71 cm) fabric strips.

Cut as many 12" × 30" (30.5 × 76 cm) rectangles of batting as necessary for 2" to 3" (5 to 7.5 cm) thickness.

YOU WILL NEED

½ **yd. (0.5 m) decorator fabric** for pillow body, or 1¼ yd. (1.15 m) if fabric is to be railroaded.

½ **yd. (0.5 m) contrasting fabric** for lining.

¾ **yd. (0.7 m) matching or contrasting fabric** for ties and welting.

3¼ **yd. (3 m) cording.**

Quilt batting.

How to Sew a Rolled Bolster

1) Round corners at one short end of rectangle. Make welting as on page 40. Machine-baste welting on right side of one fabric piece along sides and rounded end, matching raw edges and stitching over previous stitches; ease cording at corners and leave at least 3" (7.5 cm) of welting at ends.

2) Remove stitching from ends of welting. Trim cords ½" (1.3 cm) from raw edges of pillow fabric. Fold excess fabric strip back over welting, then diagonally, as shown. Pin, and stitch in place.

3) Pin fabric pieces, right sides together. Stitch on all sides, stitching as close as possible to welting; leave 6" (15 cm) opening at the end without welting. Notch out rounded corners to remove excess fullness. Turn right side out; press. Stitch opening closed.

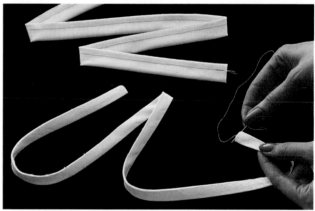

4) Fold each tie in half lengthwise, right sides together; stitch ¼" (6 mm) seam on long edge. Turn ties right side out, using loop turner; tuck in and slipstitch ends.

5) Center batting on finished rectangle. Roll fabric up to batting, starting from the end without welting.

6) Continue rolling fabric and batting together loosely. Tie ends tightly. Shape welting at ends for spiral effect.

Fringed Pillows

This no-sew pillow is created by simply raveling the edges of two fabric squares and tying the fringe together over the pillow form. The fringe can be knotted in a single row around the pillow, or in multiple rows for a heavier effect. The finished length of the fringe may range from 3" to 7" (7.5 to 18 cm), depending on the look desired.

For best results, select fabrics that ravel easily. Loosely woven casement fabrics work especially well. When working with white or off-white fabric, a white pillow form may be used. For colored fabrics, where the white pillow form would show through, you may want to substitute a simple knife-edge pillow in a color that blends with the fabric.

✂ Cutting Directions

Cut two fabric squares 12" to 20" (30.5 to 51 cm) larger than the pillow form, cutting the fabric exactly on the grainline. It may be helpful to pull the lengthwise and crosswise threads at the desired measurements and cut along the pulled threads.

YOU WILL NEED

Fabric that ravels easily.

Pillow form or purchased knife-edge pillow in a color that blends with fabric.

How to Make a Fringed Pillow

1) **Remove** threads, two or three at a time, along each edge of fabric piece until center woven area is ⅛" (3 mm) larger than pillow form. Repeat for remaining fabric piece.

2) **Center** the pillow form on wrong side of one fabric piece. Position remaining fabric piece, wrong side down, over pillow form; align lengthwise threads of top piece with crosswise threads of bottom piece.

3) **Tie** the threads from each fabric piece in a knot, starting at one corner, and working in clusters of about ½" (1.3 cm). Check periodically to make sure edges of fabric remain aligned at corners.

4) **Tie** second row of knots about ½" (1.3 cm) below first row, if desired, by using thread clusters from the adjacent knots, as shown. Repeat for third or fourth row of knots, if desired. Trim fringe to desired length.

Quick Pillows

Four Timesaving Pillows

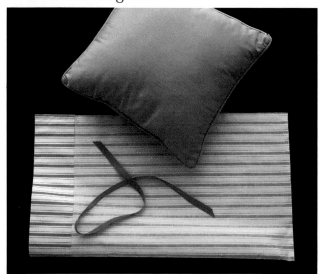

Sack pillow. Cut a 30" (76 cm) square. Turn under a deep hem on one side and fuse or stitch in place. Fold in half with right sides together and stitch raw edges together. Turn right side out. Insert pillow and tie a ribbon around open end.

Tie-on cover. Overlock the edge of large lace or decorator fabric square, or hem with narrow hem. Or make reversible slipcover by using two fabrics back to back. Tack ribbon tie or decorative cord at each corner. Lay pillow diagonally on slipcover, and fold corners over pillow. Tie closed.

Wrapped neckroll. Cut large fabric rectangle. Overlock raw edges, or hem with narrow hem. Wrap around foam bolster form or rolled quilt batt. Roll up excess fabric at each end, and tack. Tie ribbon or cord around rolled fabric.

Slip-on cover. Overlock one edge of both pillow cover sections, or hem with narrow hem. With right sides together, stitch remaining three sides in ½" (1.3 cm) seam. Clip corners. Turn right side out. Tack ribbon ties to open side. Insert fabric-covered pillow, and tie ribbons into bows.

Sewing for the Bedroom

How to Sew a Reverse Sham Bedcover

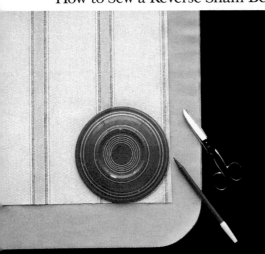

1) Fold face fabric and lining in half lengthwise. To round the corners at the foot of the cover and the top of the sham, line up corners evenly and use a saucer to mark curve. Cut on marked line.

2) Fold the bias strip in half lengthwise, wrong sides together; press. Stitch strip to curved sides on right side of cover and sham sections, stitching a scant ½" (1.3 cm) from edge. Ease strip around curves so it lies smooth when turned.

3) Pin lining to face fabric on both sections, right sides together in ½" (1.3 cm) seam; stitch around cover, leaving upper edge open. Trim corners, and turn both sections right side out.

Reverse Sham Bedcover

The reverse sham bedcover is an all-in-one cover for bed and pillows. It has an extra-deep flap at the top to fold back over the bed pillows, making the bed especially quick and easy to make.

The reverse sham technique can be adapted for comforters or full-size bedspreads. It also works as a sheet-weight bedcover for summer sleeping.

For a tailored feeling, without the look of separate pillow shams, add the sham extension to a comforter cover. Follow the instructions for a comforter cover (pages 176 to 179), leaving the upper edge open. Make the sham, and attach it as shown, below.

For versatility, use coordinating fabrics or sheets for the face and the lining and make the cover reversible. The edges are finished with a flat bias trim. If using a striped fabric, as shown here, the stripes may be mitered on the sham section for a decorative effect.

✂ Cutting Directions

Seam panels together as necessary for width. For the cover, cut the face fabric and lining the width of the bed, plus two times the drop plus 1" (2.5 cm) seam allowance; cut the length the length of the bed plus one drop, plus 1" (2.5 cm) for seam allowance.

For the sham, cut the face fabric and lining 28" (71 cm) deep and the same width as the cut width of the cover. This size is suitable for an average 20" (51 cm) pillow. For larger or smaller pillows, loosely measure over the curve of the pillow and add 1" (2.5 cm) for seam allowance. Cut sham in same direction as cover, matching stripes or motifs, unless stripes are mitered for decorative effect.

For contrasting trim, cut 2" (5 cm) bias strips (page 40) two times the finished length plus two times the finished width, plus extra for seam allowances.

YOU WILL NEED

Decorator fabric and lining for bedcover.
Contrasting fabric for bias trim.

4) Bastestitch raw edges together across open ends of cover and sham. To stitch concealed French seam, match *wrong* side of sham to *right* side of cover. Stitch ¼" (6 mm) seam; press. Trim, turn, press, and stitch ⅜" (1 cm) from fold.

4a) Alternative seam. Match *right* side of sham to *wrong* side of cover, and stitch ½" (1.3 cm) seam; trim. Finish seam with zigzag or overlock stitch, or apply tricot bias binding.

5) Place cover on bed with pillows on top of cover. Fold reverse sham back over pillows. Seam is inside when sham is turned back.

Basic Comforter Cover

Change the look of a bed with a covered comforter. It can replace a top sheet and blanket, and the removable cover of the comforter makes laundering easy. Sew your own comforter, or use a purchased one of down or of polyester batting.

Choose a washable, lightweight, firmly woven fabric for the cover. Sheets are good fabric choices because they do not require piecing. Seam decorator fabrics together by using a full fabric width in the center of the cover, with partial widths along the sides.

Leave a 36" (91.5 cm) opening in the back of the cover for inserting the comforter. Place the opening about 16" (40.5 cm) from the lower edge on the inside of the cover so it will not show at the ends. Use snap tape, hook and loop tape, a zipper or buttons for closure.

✄ Cutting Directions

Cut the front of the cover 1" (2.5 cm) larger than the comforter. Cut the back of the cover according to the closure method you choose. For button closures, add 5½" (14 cm) to back length. For a snap tape, hook and loop or zipper closure, add 1½" (3.8 cm) to back length.

Cut four small fabric strips for tabs, each about 2" (5 cm) square.

YOU WILL NEED

Decorator fabric or sheets for cover, and small amount of extra fabric for tabs.

Snap tape, hook and loop tape, zipper or buttons.

Gripper snaps to hold comforter in place.

How to Sew a Comforter Cover

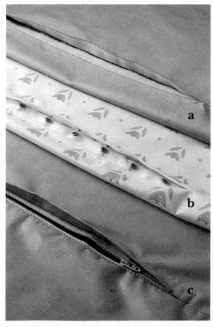

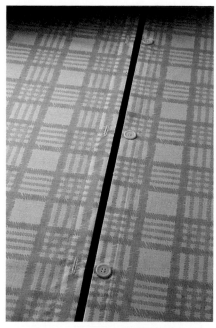

1) Press under 16" (40.5 cm) across the lower edge of the back, right sides together. If using tapes or zipper, snip the fold to mark ends of closure. Stitch ¾" (2 cm) from the fold; backstitch at snips and bastestitch across the closure area. Cut on fold; press seam open.

2a) Insert hook and loop tape (**a**), snap tape (**b**), or zipper (**c**) according to instructions for zipper closure (page 177).

2b) Cut back apart on 16" (40.5 cm) fold line for button closure. Press under ¼" (6 mm) then 1" (2.5 cm) hem on each edge; stitch. On hem of shorter piece, make buttonholes 10" to 12" (25.5 to 30.5 cm) apart; attach buttons opposite buttonholes.

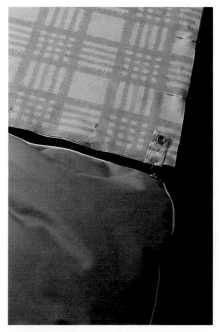

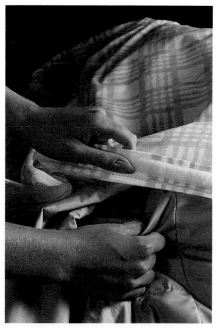

3) Pin cover front to cover back, right sides together. For button closure, pin the shorter piece first, lapping the longer piece over it.

4) Make tabs as on page 245, step 1. Attach socket side of snaps to tabs, and ball sides to corners of the comforter. Pin a tab at each corner of the cover, edges even.

5) Stitch front and back of cover together with ½" (1.3 cm) seam. Diagonally trim bulk from corners. Turn cover right side out. Insert comforter; snap cover to comforter at corners.

Welted Comforter Cover

Comforter covers can protect a new comforter or change the look of an existing one. Less bulky to handle than a full-size bedspread, a comforter cover is as easy to sew as a pillow sham. For a complete bed set, make the comforter cover, bed skirt, and pillow shams to coordinate.

The drop length of the comforter cover must be long enough to extend beyond the upper edge of the bed skirt and cover any blankets. The drop length is usually about 3" (7.5 cm) longer than the depth of the mattress. Purchased comforters may vary in drop length from 9" to 14" (23 to 35.5 cm). If the drop length is too short, jumbo welting or a ruffle can be added to the comforter cover.

To determine how many widths of fabric are needed, divide the total width of the comforter cover by the fabric width; round off to the next highest number. Most comforter covers require two fabric widths. Multiply the number of widths by the length of the comforter cover for the amount of fabric needed. Divide by 36" (100 cm) to determine the number of yards (meters).

✄ Cutting Directions

Determine the finished size of the comforter cover by measuring the size of the comforter. The finished comforter cover may be the same size as the comforter, or, for a snug fit on a down comforter, the comforter cover may be up to 2" (5 cm) shorter and narrower than the comforter.

The cut size of the comforter front is 1" (2.5 cm) wider and longer than the finished size. When more than one fabric width is required, cut one full width for the center panel of the comforter cover and two equal, partial-width panels for each side; add an extra ½" (1.3 cm) seam allowance to each panel for seaming them together. Cut the comforter back the same width as the comforter front, and 1½" (3.8 cm) shorter than the front. Cut a zipper strip 3½" (9 cm) wide and the same length as the cut width of the comforter back.

Cut fabric strips for plain or shirred jumbo welting (pages 39, 40, and 147).

YOU WILL NEED

Decorator fabric.

Two zippers, each 22" (56 cm) long.

Welting or ruffle, optional.

How to Sew a Welted Comforter Cover

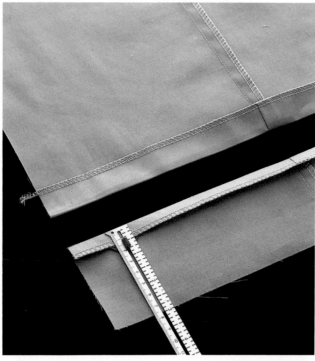

1) Overlock or zigzag upper edge of zipper strip and lower edge of comforter back. Press the finished edge of zipper strip under ½" (1.3 cm) and the finished edge of back under 1" (2.5 cm).

2) Place closed zippers face down on seam allowance of comforter back, with zipper tabs meeting in center and with edges of zipper tapes on fold. Using zipper foot, stitch along one side of zippers.

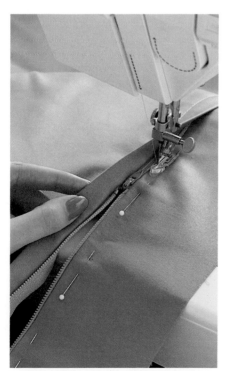

3) Turn right side up. Pin pressed edge of zipper strip along edge of zipper teeth; stitch close to pressed edge. Backstitch at ends of zippers.

4) Stitch across end of one zipper; then topstitch through all layers to stitch seam from zipper to side of comforter cover. Repeat at other end of zipper. Open zippers. (Contrasting thread was used to show detail.)

5) Apply welting and stitch comforter front to comforter back as for pillows (page 145). Turn comforter cover right side out; insert comforter.

Ideas for Comforter Covers

Make a comforter cover to coordinate with pillow shams and other room accessories. Because the construction of comforter covers is similar to that of pillow covers, most pillow designs can be adapted to make coordinating comforter covers.

Twisted welting and a coordinating ruffle have been added to this comforter cover, using the same basic construction as the sunburst pillow (page 150). The ruffle and the twisted welting are applied to the sides and the lower edge of the comforter back after the zipper is inserted; the upper edge is not ruffled.

Bows or rosettes can be tied at the corners of a comforter cover for an added detail that coordinates with bow picture hangers (page 302) or sash pillows (page 160).

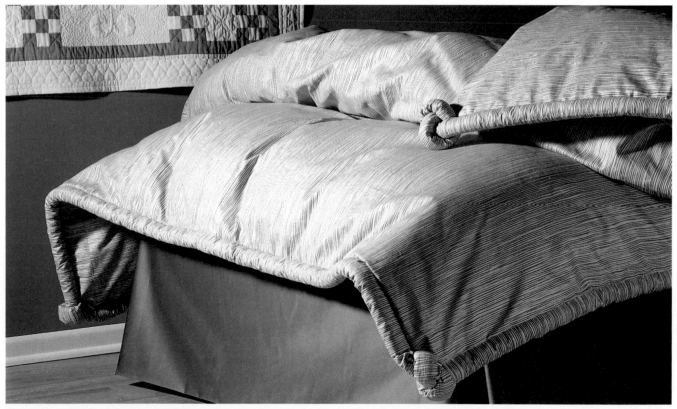

Knotted jumbo welting is added to this comforter cover to coordinate with the knotted-corner pillows (page 156). The jumbo welting is inserted into the fabric sleeves on three sides of the comforter cover; the upper edge of the comforter cover does not have welting.

Closure at the bottom of the duvet cover is created by overlapping the upper hemmed edges of the sheets and buttoning them in place.

Flanged Duvet Cover from Sheets

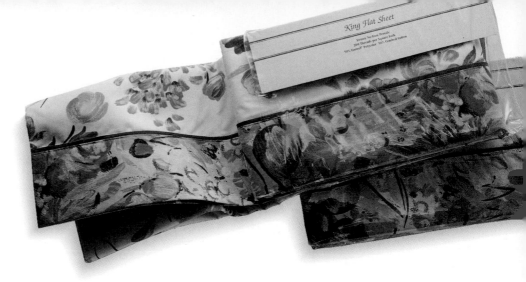

Make an easy-to-sew flanged duvet cover from two flat sheets. The upper hemmed edge of the sheet used for the top of the cover wraps to the underside at the foot of the bed and buttons in place. Flanged duvet covers are constructed larger than the duvet; the duvet fills out the center portion and the flanged edges increase the size of the cover. Use this style with traditional down comforters, which are often too small to provide the drop length necessary to conceal the mattress at the sides and foot of the bed. The flange size may range from 2" to 5" (5 to 12.5 cm).

Refer to the cutting directions below and the diagram at right to determine the cut size of the sheets for the desired finished size of the duvet cover. Then refer to the sheet measurement chart (right) to determine the sheet sizes required. When making a cover for a twin-size or full-size bed, it may be necessary to purchase a queen-size sheet for the top of the cover in order to have enough length for the underlap and closure. The top of the cover must equal the desired finished length of the duvet cover plus 8" to 10" (20.5 to 25.5 cm) for the underlap and closure. Prewash the sheets before cutting.

✂ Cutting Directions

Measure the down duvet. For a flanged duvet cover, place the duvet on the bed and determine the desired finished size of the cover, including the drop length; the drop length at the sides of the bed is usually 9" to 12" (23 to 30.5 cm), depending on the mattress depth. Compare these measurements to the actual size of the duvet to determine the width of the flange on the sides and lower edge; the inside dimensions of the cover can be slightly smaller than the measurements of the duvet.

The cut width of the top and bottom sheets is equal to the desired finished width of the duvet cover plus 1" (2.5 cm) for two ½" (1.3 cm) seam allowances. The cut length of the top sheet is equal to the desired finished length of the duvet cover plus 8" to 10" (20.5 to 25.5 cm) for the underlap and closure and ½" (1.3 cm) for the seam allowance. The bottom sheet is cut to length on page 182, steps 2 and 3.

Cutting Diagram for Flanged Duvet Cover Top

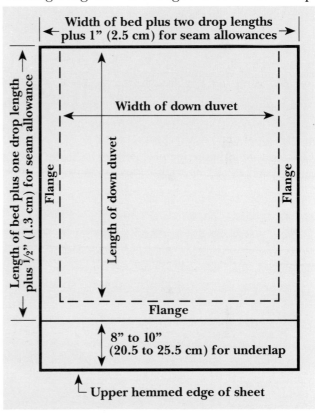

YOU WILL NEED

Two flat sheets.	**Twill tape;** four small
Buttons.	plastic rings.

Standard Flat Sheets

Sheet Size	Measurements
Twin	66" × 96" (168 × 244 cm)
Full	81" × 96" (206 × 244 cm)
Queen	90" × 102" (229 × 259.5 cm)
King	108" × 102" (274.5 × 259.5 cm)

How to Sew a Flanged Duvet Cover from Sheets

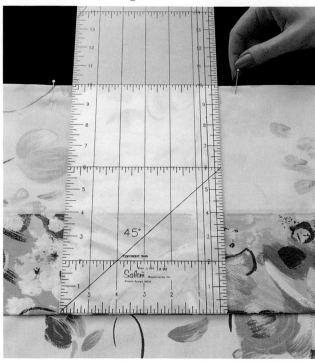

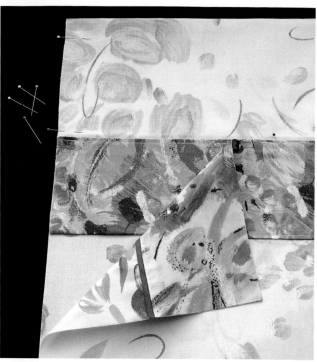

1) **Place** top sheet, right side up, on large, flat surface. On upper hemmed edge of sheet, fold 8" to 10" (20.5 to 25.5 cm) underlap, right sides together.

2) **Place** bottom sheet over the top sheet, right sides together, overlapping upper hemmed edges. Smooth sheets from the center out; pin layers together along sides and upper hemmed edge.

3) **Turn** sheets over; pin along lower edge. Trim lower edge of bottom sheet even with edge of top sheet. This edge will be at the upper edge of completed duvet cover.

4) **Stitch** ½" (1.3 cm) seam along the sides and the upper edge of duvet cover. Trim corners diagonally. Press seam allowances open.

5) Measure from edges of the duvet cover, and mark flange depth at each corner. Fold 20" (51 cm) strip of twill tape in half; baste to one layer of duvet cover at each marked corner as shown, so tape will be caught in stitching for flange.

6) Turn duvet cover right side out; press. Pin layers together. Measure from the edges of duvet cover, and mark depth of flange on sides and lower edge. Stitch on marked lines, pivoting at lower corners, to form flange; reinforce stitching at twill tape.

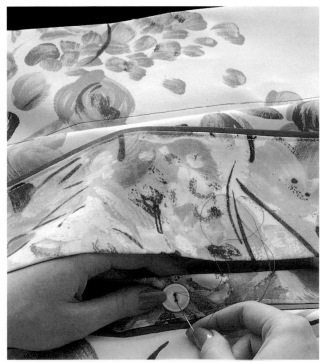

7) Mark the placement for the buttonholes on overlap, with end buttonholes about 6" (15 cm) from each side, and space remaining buttonholes about 12" (30.5 cm) apart. Stitch vertical buttonholes about ⅝" (1.5 cm) from folded edge. Stitch buttons to underlap.

8) Hand-stitch a plastic ring at each corner of duvet. Insert duvet in cover; secure twill tape to each ring with a bow.

Pillow Shams with Bordered Insets

The simple design of these pillow shams makes them suitable for many decorating styles. The pillow sham is easily constructed from three fabric panels that are pieced to create a bordered inset. Welting, stitched between the panels, provides additional detail. The side panels of the pillow sham fold to the back of the sham, creating an overlapping back closure. The pillow shams can be made to fit standard-size, queen-size, or king-size pillows.

✂ Cutting Directions

For each pillow sham, cut one center panel, one right side panel, and one left side panel, according to the chart, opposite.

YOU WILL NEED

Two coordinating decorator fabrics.
Purchased welting.

Cutting Chart for a Pillow Sham with a Bordered Inset

Pillow Size	Finished Size of Pillow Sham	Cut Size of Left Side Panel	Cut Size of Center Panel	Cut Size of Right Side Panel
Standard	20" × 26" (51 × 66 cm)	21" × 29" (53.5 × 73.5 cm)	21" × 15" (53.5 × 38 cm)	21" × 22" (53.5 × 56 cm)
Queen	20" × 30" (51 × 76 cm)	21" × 34" (53.5 × 86.5 cm)	21" × 17" (53.5 × 43 cm)	21" × 23" (53.5 × 58.5 cm)
King	20" × 36" (51 × 91.5 cm)	21" × 41" (53.5 × 104 cm)	21" × 21 (53.5 × 53.5 cm)	21" × 24" (53.5 × 61 cm)

How to Sew a Pillow Sham with a Bordered Inset

1) Pin welting to right side of center panel on side edges; position stitching line of welting ½" (1.3 cm) from raw edge of fabric. Trim the ends of welting even with edges of fabric.

2) Baste welting to center panel, using a zipper foot and ½" (1.3 cm) seam allowance.

3) Pin side panels to center panel, with right sides together and raw edges even. With the center panel facing up, stitch just inside previous stitching. Finish seams, using zigzag or overlock stitch. Press the seam allowances toward center panel.

4) Press ½" (1.3 cm), then 2" (5 cm), to the wrong side on short end of each side panel. Stitch close to inner fold.

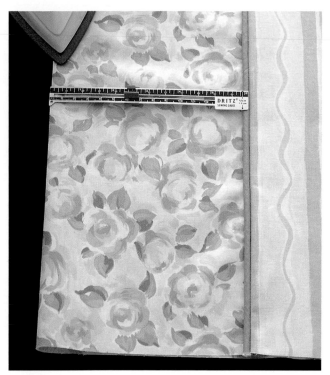

5) Fold under fabric at sides to make side panels that measure 6" (15 cm) for standard-size, 7" (18 cm) for queen-size, and 8" (20.5 cm) for king-size sham. Press fold in place.

6) Refold fabric at pressed folds, right sides together, lapping short back piece over long back piece; pin.

7) Stitch ½" (1.3 cm) seam on the two long sides of the sham. Finish seams, using zigzag or overlock stitch.

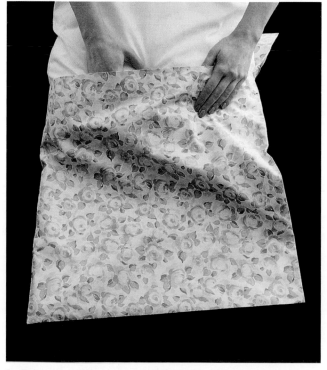

8) Turn the pillow sham right side out; press. Insert the pillow.

How to Sew a Tuck-pleated Pillow Sham

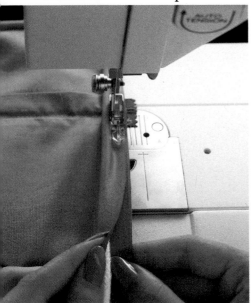

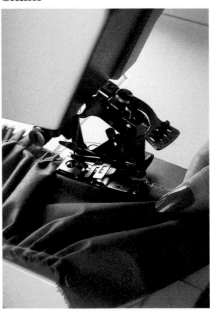

1) Insert zipper in back of sham, following instructions for zipper insertion in comforter (page 177). Cover cording and machine-baste to right side of back in ⅜" (1 cm) seam; join ends of welting (page 145).

2) Tuck-pleat the border strip, ⅜" (1 cm) from both edges, using ruffler attachment at 2 to 1 ratio. Keep fabric same side up when pleating. Steam press finished strip lightly to flatten tucks.

3) Cut two strips 1" (2.5 cm) longer than finished sham length, and two strips 1" (2.5 cm) longer than finished sham width. On wrong side of short strips, fold corner back; mark width of strip with pin. Unfold; mark stitching angle from pin to corner.

Tuck-pleated Pillow Shams

The mitered, tuck-pleated border on this sham is created using a ruffler attachment (page 35); the border may also be gathered (page 31). The finished sham should be the same size as the pillow.

The technique for mitering a border around a pillow is also used for attaching a mitered trim (page 36).

✂ Cutting Directions

Cut the back 1" (2.5 cm) wider and 1½" (3.8 cm) shorter than the finished size. Cut a back zipper strip the same width as the back and 3½" (9 cm) wide. Cut the center of the front 4" (10 cm) narrower and shorter than finished sham; cut border strips 3½" (9 cm) wide and 4 times the length and width of the sham, plus extra for seaming strips.

For welting, cut strips 1½" (3.8 cm) wide by two times the length plus two times the width of sham, plus extra for seaming.

YOU WILL NEED

Decorator fabric or sheets for sham.

Contrasting border fabric.

5/32" cording for welting.

Zipper, 22" (56 cm) long.

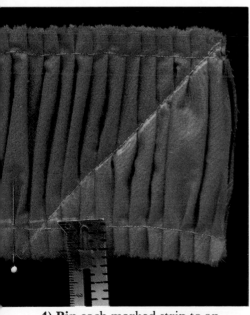

4) Pin each marked strip to an unmarked strip, and stitch from corner to ½" (1.3 cm) from raw edge; backstitch. Trim seams to ¼" (6 mm), and press open.

5) Pin inner edges of border to sham front; stitch one side at a time, backstitching (arrow) at both ends of seam.

6) Pin front to back, right sides together; stitch ½" (1.3 cm) from edge on all four sides. To finish, overlock or zigzag raw edges. Turn to right side; insert pillow.

Envelope Pillow Shams

These pillow shams open like an envelope, making it easy to insert pillows; the flap closes with hook and loop tape. Edged in plain or gathered jumbo welting, these pillows can be either traditional or contemporary. Make envelope pillow shams for any size bed pillow.

✂ Cutting Directions

Cut one rectangle of fabric for the pillow back/flap. The cut width is equal to the pillow width plus 1" (2.5 cm) for seam allowances; cut length is equal to one and two-thirds of the pillow length plus 1" (2.5 cm) for seam allowances.

Cut one rectangle of fabric for the pillow front. The cut width is equal to the pillow width plus 1" (2.5 cm) for seam allowances; cut length is equal to the pillow length plus 2" (5 cm) for seam and hem allowances.

Cut one rectangle of fabric for the flap facing. The cut width is equal to the pillow width plus 1" (2.5 cm)

for seam allowances; cut length is equal to two-thirds of the pillow length plus 5" (12.5 cm) for overlap.

Cut fabric strips for plain jumbo welting (pages 39 and 40) or gathered jumbo welting (page 147).

YOU WILL NEED

Decorator fabric for pillow.

Decorator fabric for welting. Allow up to ½ yd. (0.5 m) for plain jumbo welting, 1 yd. (0.95 m) for double-fullness gathered jumbo welting, or 1½ yd. (1.4 m) for triple-fullness gathered jumbo welting. Exact yardage depends on width of fabric, sizes of cording and pillow, and fullness of welting.

Jumbo cording, equal to the distance around the pillow back/flap.

1" (2.5 cm) hook and loop tape for closure.

How to Sew an Envelope Sham

1) Fold the pillow back/flap and flap facing in half lengthwise; mark end of flap 4" (10 cm) from fold for bed pillow or 3" (7.5 cm) from fold for accent pillow. Mark two-thirds the length of pillow on the edge opposite fold. Draw diagonal line between marks; cut on marked line. Round corners of flap and lower edges of pillow front and pillow back/flap.

2) Press under ½" (1.3 cm) twice on one crosswise edge of pillow front and on long crosswise edge of flap facing; stitch to make double-fold hems. Stitch loop side of hook and loop tape to flap facing, centered about 1" (2.5 cm) from short edge. Staystitch bias edges of flap and flap facing.

3) Place pillow front over pillow back/flap, right sides together, matching raw edges. Place flap facing over flap portion of pillow back/flap, right sides together, matching raw edges. Pin pillow front and flap facing together in lapped area; stitch a rectangle 2" × ½" (5 × 1.3 cm) at ends of overlap.

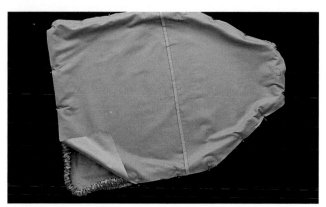

4) Make jumbo welting; apply to right side of pillow back/flap. Follow steps 1 to 4 on page 147 for gathered welting, or steps 1 to 5 on page 145 for plain welting. Place pillow front/flap facing on pillow back/flap, right sides together; pin.

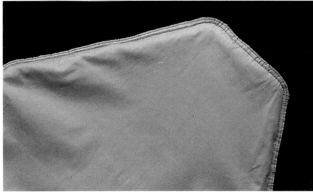

5) Stitch around pillow sham through all layers, using zipper foot; stitch inside previous stitching line. Finish seam allowances, using overlock stitch on serger or zigzag stitch on conventional machine.

6) Turn sham right side out; insert pillow. Pin hook side of hook and loop tape in position, under flap, on pillow front. Remove pillow and stitch tape in place.

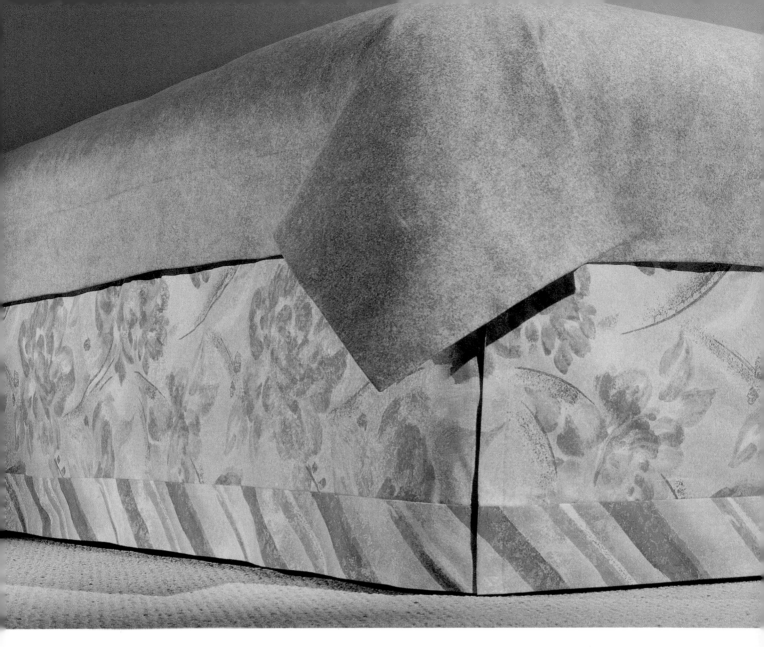

Banded Bed Skirt

A contrasting band provides interest along the lower edges of a tailored bed skirt. For a romantic touch, add a lace overlay to the band. The side panels are designed to overlap the end panel at the corners to conceal the bed frame. The split at the corners allows the bed skirt to be used with beds that have footboards. For best results, construct the bed skirt from decorator fabrics that have body.

✂ Cutting Directions

For the upper bed skirt panels, cut one piece of fabric for each long side of the bed skirt, on the lengthwise grain, with the cut width of each piece equal to the length of the box spring plus 4" (10 cm), to allow for two 1" (2.5 cm) double-fold side hems. Cut one piece for the foot of the bed on the lengthwise grain, with the cut width equal to the width of the box spring plus

6" (15 cm), to allow for two 1" (2.5 cm) double-fold side hems and two 1" (2.5 cm) underlaps. The cut length of the upper bed skirt pieces is equal to the distance from the top of the box spring to the floor minus 2½" (6.5 cm).

For the contrasting band, cut three pieces, with the cut width equal to the cut width of the three upper bed skirt pieces. The cut length of the band pieces is 7" (18 cm); this allows for ½" (1.3 cm) clearance at the floor.

YOU WILL NEED

Decorator fabric, for upper bed skirt panels.
Contrasting decorator fabric, for band.
Fitted sheet.
Flat lace edging, for optional overlay.

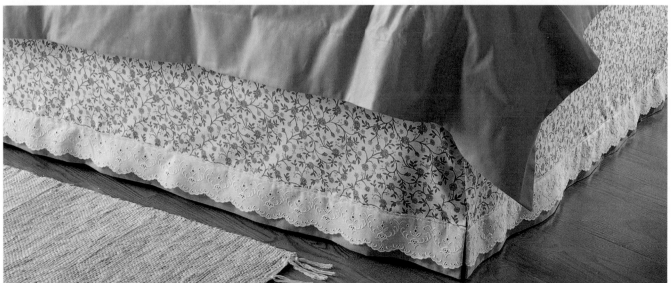

Banded bed skirts are made from two coordinating fabrics. Flat lace edging adds a feminine touch to the banded bed skirt above. Abstract prints are used for a contemporary look (top).

How to Sew a Banded Bed Skirt

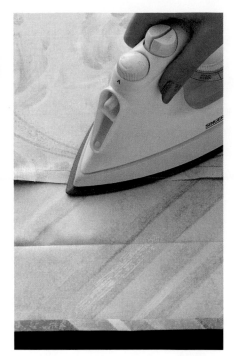

1) Place fitted sheet over the box spring. Using water-soluble marking pen or chalk, mark sheet along upper edge of box spring on each side and on foot of bed. Mark the corners at center of curve.

2) Press the band pieces in half lengthwise, wrong sides together. Press ⅜" (1 cm) to the wrong side on one long edge of each band.

3) Pin band piece to lower edge of corresponding skirt piece, with right sides together and raw edges even. Stitch ½" (1.3 cm) seam. Press the seam allowance toward band.

4) Fold the band along center fold; the pressed edge extends about ⅛" (3 mm) beyond the stitching, concealing the seam allowance. Stitch in the ditch in the well of the seam on the right side, catching the band on the back side.

5) Press up 1" (2.5 cm) twice to wrong side on ends of panels; stitch close to inner folds. Finish upper edge, using zigzag or overlock stitch. Staystitch a scant ½" (1.3 cm) from upper edge of skirt pieces for 2" (5 cm) on each side.

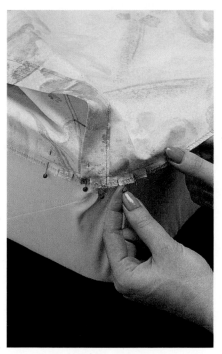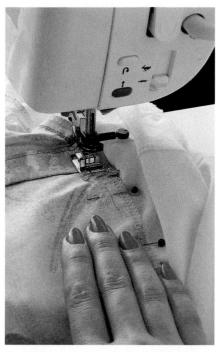

6) Lay the side pieces on top of the box spring, right side down; align ends with corner markings at foot of the bed. Pin upper edge of the bed skirt to the sheet, extending ½" (1.3 cm) seam allowance beyond marked line.

7) Lay panel for foot of bed on top of the box spring, right sides down, extending the ends 1" (2.5 cm) beyond the corner markings and overlapping side panels. Pin upper edge of bed skirt to sheet; clip the corners as necessary.

8) Remove the bed skirt and fitted sheet from bed. Stitch bed skirt to sheet, stitching ½" (1.3 cm) from raw edges.

How to Sew a Banded Bed Skirt with a Lace Overlay

1) Follow steps 1 to 5, opposite. Cut flat lace edging 2" (5 cm) longer than width of each skirt piece; finish ends, using zigzag or overlock stitch. Pin the lace to the skirt over band as desired, folding 1" (2.5 cm) at each end to back side. Topstitch in place.

2) Hand-stitch ends of lace in place. Stitch the lace to remaining skirt pieces. Complete the bed skirt as in steps 6 to 8.

Circular Ruffle Bed Skirt

The circular ruffle bed skirt has soft draping. Its simple style complements a tailored decor, but also works well for a room that is elaborately decorated, without detracting from other furnishings.

The circular ruffle bed skirt is easy to sew and requires less time than most bed skirts, because there are no gathers or pleats. To prevent the bed skirt from shifting out of position, the upper edge of the skirt is attached to a fitted sheet. If the bed does not have a footboard, the bed skirt is attached as one continuous strip. For a bed with a footboard, a split-corner bed skirt can be attached to the sheet in three sections.

✂ Cutting Directions

Determine the number of circular pieces required, as indicated in the chart, opposite. To make it easier

to cut the circles, cut fabric squares the size of the circle diameter; then cut the circular pieces, opposite.

The calculations given in the chart are based on a 15½" (39.3 cm) cut length. This gives an adequate amount of ruffling for any cut length up to at least 15½" (39.3 cm); you may have excess ruffling, which can easily be cut off during construction. The actual length of ruffling per circle is equal to the circumference of the inner circle minus 1" (2.5 cm) for seams and side hems.

YOU WILL NEED

Decorator fabric, in the yardage amount indicated in the chart, opposite.

Fitted sheet.

How to Cut Circles

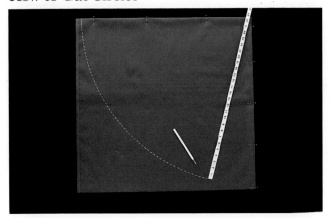

1) Fold the fabric square in half lengthwise, then crosswise, right sides together. Using straightedge and pencil, mark an arc on fabric, measuring from the folded center of fabric, a distance equal to the radius. Cut on marked line through all layers.

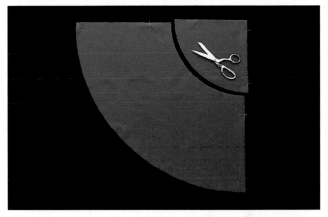

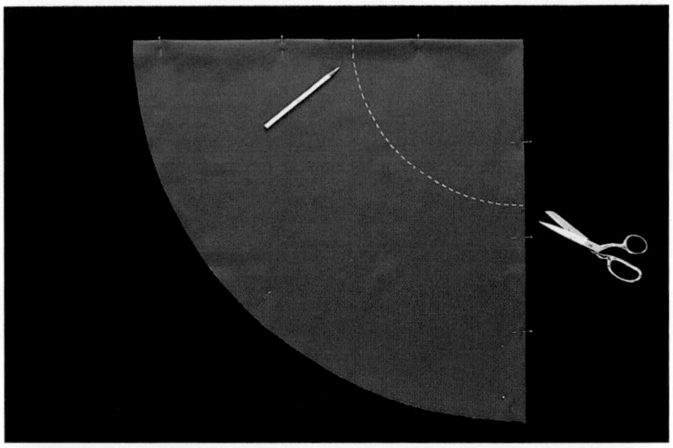

2) Add 1" (2.5 cm) to the drop length of bed skirt; measure and mark this distance away from arc. Draw second arc at this distance. Cut on marked line through all layers. Circumference of inner circle minus 1" (2.5 cm) determines length of ruffling per circle.

How to Cut Half-circles

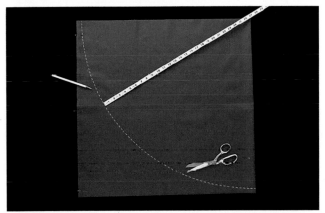

1) Cut rectangle across the width of fabric, with short sides equal to one-half the width of the fabric. Fold fabric in half, matching short sides. Using straightedge and pencil, mark an arc on fabric, measuring from the lengthwise fold, a distance equal to the radius. Cut on marked line through both layers.

2) Add 1" (2.5 cm) to the drop length of bed skirt; measure and mark this distance away from arc. Draw second arc at this distance. Cut on marked line through both layers.

Determining the Circular Pieces Needed

Diameter of Circles	Ruffling Length per Circle	Twin		Full		Queen		King	
		Circles Needed	Yardage Needed	Circles Needed	Yardage Needed	Circles Needed	Yardage Needed	Circles Needed	Yardage Needed
45" (115 cm)	47" (120 cm)	4	5 yd. (4.6 m)	4½	5⅝ yd. (5.15 m)	5	6¼ yd. (5.75 m)	5½	6⅞ yd. (6.3 m)
48" (122 cm)	58" (147 cm)	3½	4⅔ yd. (4.33 m)	3½	4⅔ yd. (4.33 m)	4	5⅓ yd. (4.92 m)	4½	6 yd. (5.5 m)
54" (137 cm)	76" (193 cm)	2½	3¾ yd. (3.45 m)	3	4½ yd. (4.15 m)	3	4½ yd. (4.15 m)	3½	5¼ yd. (4.8 m)
60" (153 cm)	95" (242 cm)	2	3⅓ yd. (3.07 m)	2½	4¼ yd. (3.9 m)	2½	4¼ yd. (3.9 m)	3	5 yd. (4.6 m)

How to Sew a Circular Ruffle Bed Skirt

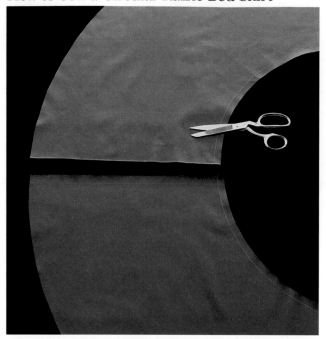

1) Cut circles for bed skirt (pages 196 and 197). Slash each piece from outer to inner edges on crosswise grain. Staystitch ½" (1.3 cm) from inner edge.

2) Stitch circles together in a long strip, right sides together; finish seam allowances. Clip up to the staystitching at 2" (5 cm) intervals; space the clips evenly so bed skirt will hang in even folds.

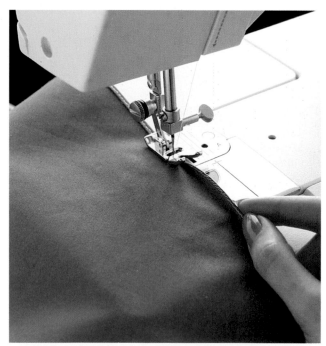

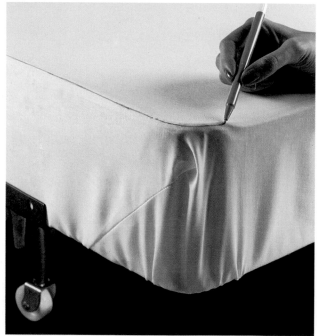

3) Machine-stitch ¼" (6 mm) from hem edge. Turn edge to wrong side on stitching line; press fold. Stitch close to fold. Trim excess fabric close to stitching. Turn hem edge to wrong side a scant ¼" (6 mm), enclosing raw edge. Edgestitch.

4) Place fitted sheet over box spring; mark sheet along upper edge of box spring, using water-soluble marking pen or chalk.

5) Lay circular ruffle on top of box spring; pin ruffle to sheet, right sides together, matching staystitching to marked line. Ruffle may extend around corners at head of bed, if desired; extend raw edge ½" (1.3 cm) beyond desired endpoint to allow for side hem.

6) Mark side hems at head of bed perpendicular to floor, allowing ½" (1.3 cm) for double ¼" (6 mm) hem.

7) Remove fitted sheet and ruffle from bed. Cut off any excess ruffle at sides; stitch side hems. Stitch ruffle to fitted sheet, stitching just beyond staystitching.

Split corners. Follow steps 1 to 4. Cut ruffle into three sections, each section long enough to fit on one side of the bed plus 1" (2.5 cm) for side hems. Lay section for foot of bed on top of box spring; pin to sheet, right sides together, matching staystitching to marked line. Mark side hems at corner, as in step 6. Pin side sections to sheet, overlapping hem allowances at corners. Complete bed skirt, as in steps 6 and 7.

Swag Bed Skirt

The swag bed skirt has soft drapes of fabric that are layered over a gathered underskirt. This treatment complements swag window treatments and works well for bedrooms with romantic, feminine styling. To show off the bed skirt to its best advantage, select a duvet cover with a drop length that is only 1" to 2" (2.5 to 5 cm) below the mattress.

For easier draping of the swags, two-cord shirring tape is used. For a more finished look, matching or contrasting straps are added to cover the shirring tape. The entire bed skirt is attached to a fitted sheet, which prevents the skirt from shifting out of position.

For a bed with a footboard, a split-corner underskirt can be sewn by attaching three sections to the fitted sheet. For this style, the three sections are hemmed at both sides, and the sections are butted together at the corner. If the bed does not have a footboard, the underskirt is sewn in one continuous strip.

✂ Cutting Directions

Determine the number of swags you will need for the bed skirt, according to the chart, opposite. The size of the swags will vary, depending on the size of the bed. Also, the swags will be a slightly different size on the foot of the bed than on the sides, but this difference is unnoticeable.

Cut a rectangle of fabric for each swag; railroad the fabric to avoid seaming, or piece the rectangles, as necessary. Cut the rectangles 27" (68.5 cm) long and 5" (12.5 cm) wider than the distance between the markings on page 202. If you are using a patterned fabric with large motifs, you may want to center a motif on each rectangle.

Cut 3" × 11" (7.5 × 28 cm) straps from matching or contrasting fabric. You will need one strap for each swag plus one extra strap.

For a bed without a footboard, the cut width of the gathered underskirt is two and one-half to three times the distance around the sides and foot of the bed; the fabric may be railroaded or fabric widths may be pieced together, as necessary. The cut length of the underskirt is equal to the distance from the top of the box spring to the floor plus 2" (5 cm). This allows for the hem and seam allowances and for ½" (1.3 cm) clearance at the floor.

For a bed with a footboard, make a split-corner underskirt. The cut width for each of the two side sections is two and one-half to three times the length of the bed, and the cut width for the foot section is two and one-half to three times the width of the bed. The cut length of the sections is equal to the distance from the top of the box spring to the floor plus 2" (5 cm).

YOU WILL NEED

Decorator fabric.

Fitted sheet.

Two-cord shirring tape, 23½" (59.8 cm) for each swag plus an extra 23½" (59.8 cm).

Determining the Number of Swags Needed

No. of Swags	Twin	Full	Queen	King
At foot	1	2	2	3
Each side	2	3	3	3
Total swags	5	8	8	9

How to Sew a Swag Bed Skirt

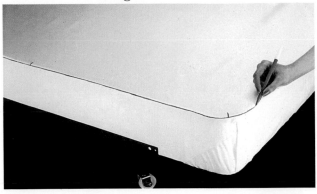

1) Place fitted sheet over box spring; mark sheet along upper edge of box spring, using water-soluble marking pen or chalk. Mark corners at upper edge of box spring on sheet at center of curve. Divide each side of bed into equal parts according to the number of swags.

2) Fold each rectangle in half crosswise; measure and mark 2" (5 cm) in from corner along upper edge. Draw line diagonally to opposite corner. Cut on marked line through both layers.

3) Press and stitch 1" (2.5 cm) double-fold hem at lower edge of each swag piece. Stitch swag pieces together; press seams open. Press under ½" (1.3 cm) at the sides.

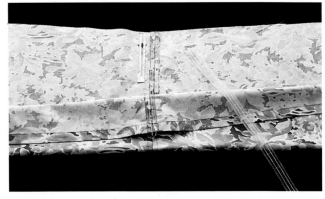

4) Fold under ½" (1.3 cm) on both ends of shirring tape. Center tape over one seam on wrong side, starting above hem; pin in place. Stitch three rows of stitching on tape; stitch along center first, then along outer edges. Repeat for remaining seams and at sides.

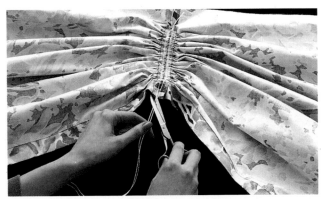

5) Knot cords at upper end of tape. Pull cords from lower end, gathering fabric as tightly as possible; knot ends securely. Trim tails.

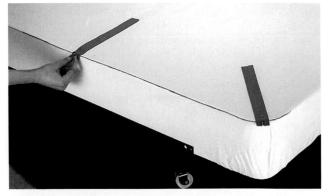

6) Fold strap pieces in half lengthwise, right sides together; stitch ¼" (6 mm) seam. Turn straps right side out; press. Pin straps to fitted sheet, centering them over markings; extend ½" (1.3 cm) at end of each strap beyond marked line, as shown.

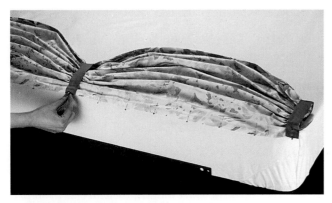

7) Lay swags on top of box spring; pin upper edge to sheet, right sides together, extending ½" (1.3 cm) seam allowance beyond marked line. Wrap straps around swags; pin in place, matching ends. If desired, remove sheet from bed and machine-baste upper edge of swags in place, stitching scant ½" (1.3 cm) from raw edge.

8) Seam underskirt panels together; for bed without footboard, stitch panels in one continuous strip, or for bed with footboard, stitch panels in three sections. Finish seam allowances. Press and stitch 1" (2.5 cm) double-fold hem at lower edge of underskirt. Stitch ½" (1.3 cm) double-fold side hems.

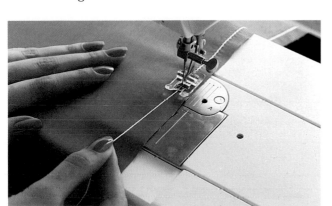

9) Zigzag over a cord at upper edge of underskirt, within seam allowance, just beyond seamline. Zigzag over second cord ¼" (6 mm) from first cord, if desired, for more control when adjusting gathers.

10) Divide marked line on fitted sheet and upper edge of underskirt into fourths or eighths. Lay underskirt, right side down, over swags; match and pin together at markings. Pull on gathering cords, and gather underskirt evenly to fit; pin.

11) Remove bed skirt and sheet from bed. Stitch bed skirt to sheet, stitching ½" (1.3 cm) from raw edge.

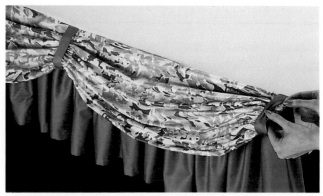

12) Place bed skirt on box spring. Hand-stitch straps to swags at head of bed. Arrange folds of swags.

Daybed Dust Skirt & Tufted Cover

This tailored daybed set combines a fitted, tufted cover with a gathered dust skirt. The daybed cover is shaped at the corners to fit smoothly around the frame of the bed.

Most daybed frames have rims on either two or four sides to keep the mattress from shifting; other frames have no rims. Make adjustments accordingly so the dust skirt hangs from the top of the frame or rim, is open at the corners, and hangs evenly ¼" (6 mm) from the floor. For some daybed frames, it may be necessary to attach the dust skirt 1½" to 2" (3.8 to 5 cm) from the corners of the deck, so the gathers will not bunch at the corners. The drop of the cover will overlap the skirt to conceal the frame at the corners.

✂ Cutting Directions (Cover)

Cut center panel 60" (150 cm) long from full width of fabric. Divide another width in half for the side panels; join side panels to center panel, matching design at seams. Trim excess fabric from each side panel so width measures 96" (244 cm).

Cut and seam lining 1" (2.5 cm) longer and 1" (2.5 cm) wider than top.

Cut strips of fabric for welting (page 40). Join ends to make a strip 9 yd. (8.25 m) long.

✂ Cutting Directions (Deck & Skirt)

Cut dust skirt deck the length and width of the frame plus 1" (2.5 cm) for seam allowances. For daybeds with rims, cut a strip of decorator fabric for each rim the height of the rim plus 1" (2.5 cm) for seam allowances, and the length or width of the frame plus 2" (5 cm) for hem allowances.

Cut two skirt sections each 2 times the length of the deck plus 2" (5 cm) for hems. Cut two skirt sections each 2 times the width of deck plus 2" (5 cm) for hem. To determine skirt length, measure as in step 1, opposite.

YOU WILL NEED

For dust skirt, 6¼ yd. (5.75 m) of 54" (140 cm) decorator fabric and one twin flat sheet for deck.

For cover top and lining, 3⅜ yd. (3.10 m) of 54" (140 cm) fabric, plus extra for matching and welting.

Extra lofty polyester batting, 60" × 96" (150 × 244 cm).

Cording, 9 yd. (8.25 m).

Narrow ribbon for ties, 18 yd. (17.5 m) of ⅛" (3 mm) ribbon; crewel needle; about 13 dozen safety pins.

How to Sew a Daybed Dust Skirt

1) Measure frame to determine finished length **(a)** and width **(b)**. To determine skirt length, measure from frame **(c)** to floor and add 2½" (6.5 cm). For sides with rims, measure from top of rim **(d)** to floor and add 2½" (6.5 cm).

2) Press under and stitch double 1" (2.5 cm) hem on lower edge of each skirt section. Zigzag over a cord (as on page 203, step 9) to gather upper edge. For sides with rims, match skirt section to fabric strip, right sides together; stitch ½" (1.3 cm) seam. On all skirt sections, press under and stitch double ½" (1.3 cm) side hems.

3a) For bed without rims. Pin skirt sections to sides of deck, right sides together, with edges of ruffle meeting at each corner. Stitch ½" (1.3 cm) seam. Finish seams with zigzag or overlock stitch.

3b) For bed with two rims. For sides that do not have rims, attach to deck as in step 3a. For sides that have rims, stitch strips to edges of deck in ½" (1.3 cm) seam.

3c) For bed with four rims. Stitch strips to edges of deck, right sides together, in ½" (1.3 cm) seam; finish seams with zigzag or overlock stitch.

4) Place dust skirt over frame of daybed, adjusting ruffles so the deck seam is on the upper edge of rim or even with the edge of the frame. Replace mattress on frame.

How to Sew a Tufted Daybed Cover

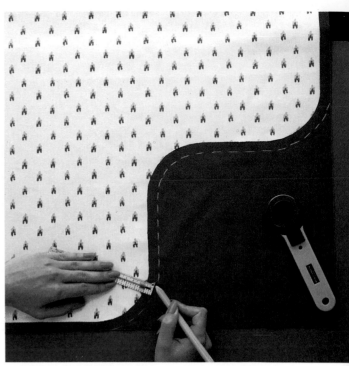

1) Fold top in half lengthwise, then crosswise, with right sides together and corners matching. Draw a 9½" (24 cm) square at matched corner. (This is the corner *without* any folds.) Using a saucer as a pattern, draw three curves as shown. Cut on curved line.

2) Place top over lining so ½" (1.3 cm) seam allowance extends beyond top at straight edges. Following curved corners on top, add ½" (1.3 cm) seam allowance and trim lining corners. Trim polyester batting to match lining.

5) Place lining, *wrong* side up, on large, flat surface. Place batting on lining; place top, *right* side up, on batting. Pin through all layers at each tufting location.

6) Thread needle with ribbon. At each tuft marker, insert needle from right side through all layers. Pull through bottom layer, leaving 4" (10 cm) tail at top for tying. Bring needle to the top ¼" (6 mm) away. Cut ribbon, leaving 4" (10 cm) tail; tie a square knot.

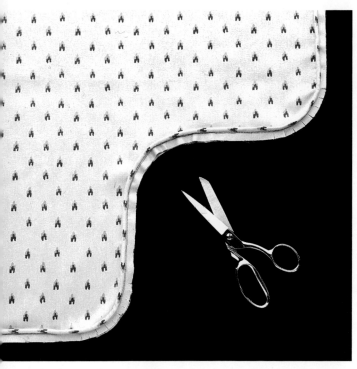

3) Cut and sew welting strips (page 40). Stitch welting to cover top in ½" (1.3 cm) seam, raw edges even. Clip seam allowances on inner curves; be careful not to stretch welting on outer curves.

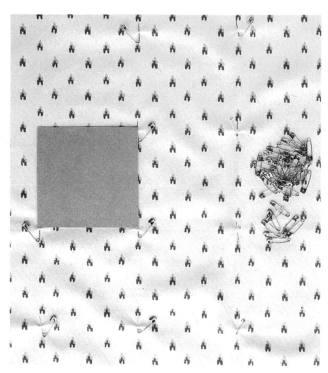

4) Fold top in half lengthwise, then crosswise, to mark center. Mark tufting locations on right side of top, beginning at center and spacing tufts about 6" (15 cm) apart. Or use the fabric design to space tufts evenly.

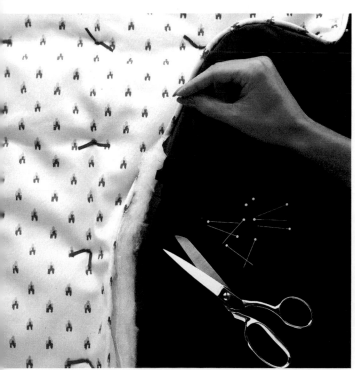

7) Clip lining seam allowances on curves. Turn under ½" (1.3 cm) on outer edges of top and lining layers, enclosing seams. Pin so folded edge of lining butts welting.

8) Slipstitch lining to welting seam by hand. Or edgestitch by machine, using zipper foot; stitch from lining side close to welting.

Padded Headboard

As a finishing touch, a fabric headboard can be coordinated with the bedcover. This is a custom project requiring simple upholstery techniques.

Make a paper pattern template to determine the size and shape of the headboard that will be appropriate to the size of the bed. The headboard should be cut as wide as the bed frame plus allowance for bedding, and 20" to 24" (51 to 61 cm) high plus approximately 20" (51 cm) for legs. Tack the headboard template on the wall behind the bed to check the size and shape. Adjust as necessary.

A shirred border frames the gentle curve of the headboard shown here. Determine the width of the border, approximately 4" (10 cm), and mark template for inner curve.

✂ Cutting Directions
Cut decorator fabric 5" to 6" (12.5 to 15 cm) larger than inner curved section. Cut shirring strip 3 times the measurement of the outer curve and 6" (15 cm) wider than width of shirred border.

For legs, cut fabric the length of leg plus 1" (2.5 cm), and twice the width plus 3" (7.5 cm).

For double welting, cut 3" (7.5 cm) bias strips the length of inner curve, plus extra for finishing.

Use the paper headboard template to cut lining for back of headboard.

YOU WILL NEED

Decorator fabric for front of headboard, for shirred border, and for legs.

Lining for back.

Polyester batting to pad shirred border.

5/32" cording, 2 times the measurement of inner curve.

½" (1.3 cm) plywood, cut to shape; 2" (5 cm) foam to cover headboard; staple gun with ½" (1.3 cm) heavy-duty staples; cardboard stripping the length of inner curve; foam adhesive; white glue.

How to Make a Padded Headboard

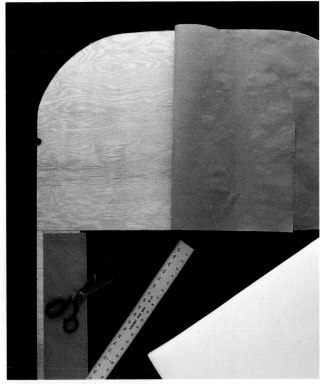

1) Cut ½" (1.3 cm) plywood from paper headboard template. Mark template for inner curved section 4" (10 cm) smaller than outer curve.

2) Cut 2" (5 cm) foam even with lower edge and 1" (2.5 cm) larger than headboard curve. Glue to headboard using foam adhesive. To soften edge, pull excess foam to back and staple to edge of plywood.

(Continued on next page)

3) Mark inner curve on foam. Staple cardboard stripping on marked line to establish smooth curve. If staples do not penetrate plywood easily, use hammer to tap them in place.

4) Place decorator fabric, right side up, over inner section. Starting at center, smooth fabric taut over foam and staple to cardboard stripping in order shown; then staple every 2" (5 cm). At bottom edge, fold fabric to back; staple. Trim excess fabric.

7) Staple shirring strip to back, easing fabric evenly around curve and forming small tucks as you staple. Keep shirred area an even width on the front.

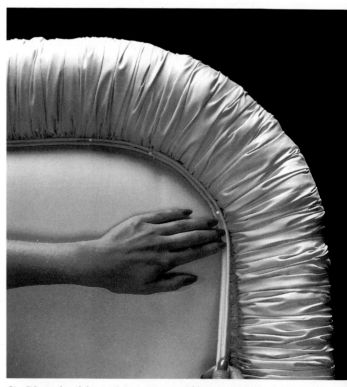

8) Glue double welting (page 41) over stapled area to cover raw edges, stretching welting as you attach it. Secure with pins to hold in place until glue dries.

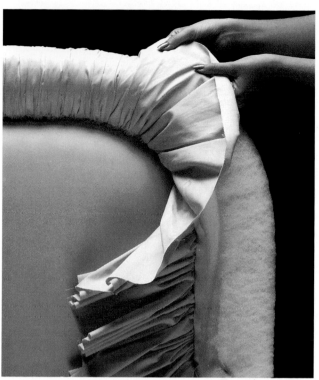

5) Zigzag over cord to gather one long edge of shirring strip. Divide curve and shirring strip into quarters, and mark. Working from right side, staple gathered edge of shirring to curve, matching marks and adjusting gathers evenly.

6) Pad border lightly with polyester batting to puff and shape curve. Pull shirred strip to the back.

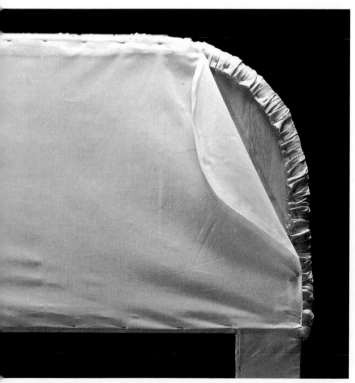

9) Staple or glue fabric to legs. Press edges of lining under ½" (1.3 cm). Finish back by stapling lining fabric over raw edges.

10) Drill holes in headboard to match screws in bed frame. Attach headboard to frame.

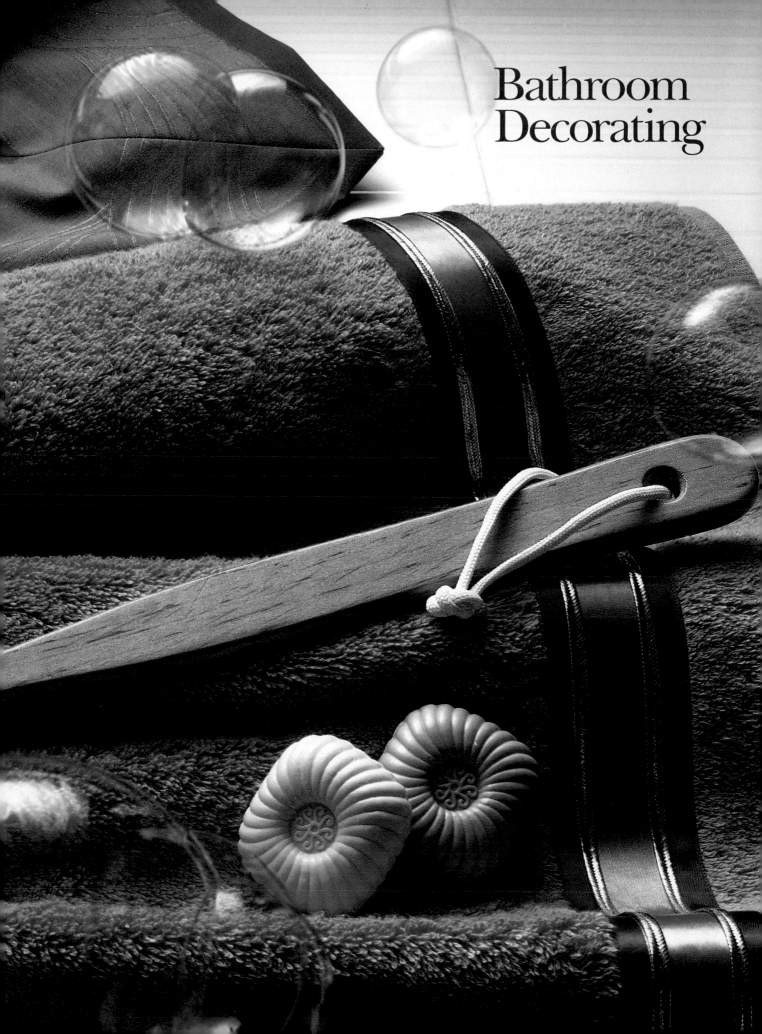

Bathroom
Decorating

Basic Shower Curtains

A shower curtain is one of the simplest curtains to sew. Valances and tiebacks can be used with the standard shower curtain. Because of its size, the shower curtain is a good place to use bold colors and prints. The instructions for sewing a shower curtain can also be used for cafe curtains or straight curtains hung with rings or hooks on decorative poles.

✂ Cutting Directions

Measure the distance from the bottom of the shower rod to the desired length. Add 10" (25.5 cm) for upper and lower hems. Measure the width of the area to be covered by the curtain and add 4" (10 cm) for side hems. Standard shower curtain liners are 72" × 72" (183 × 183 cm), so the curtain should be cut 76" (193 cm) wide if using a standard liner. Seam fabric together as needed, using French seams.

YOU WILL NEED

Decorator fabric for shower curtain.

Fusible interfacing.

Plastic shower curtain liner.

Eyelets or grommets (not necessary if buttonholes are used), equal to number of holes in plastic liner.

Shower curtain hooks, equal to number of eyelets or buttonholes.

The fabric curtain and plastic liner can hang together on the same rings or hooks, or separately on a shower rod and a spring tension rod. When they hang together, the shower curtain and the liner should be the same width.

How to Sew a Shower Curtain

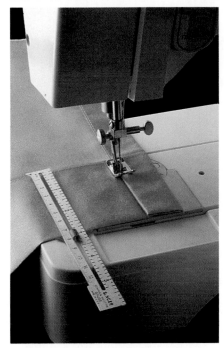

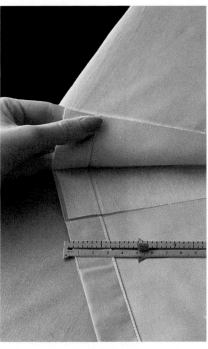

1) Turn under and stitch a 3" (7.5 cm) double-fold hem on lower edge of curtain. Turn under and stitch 1" (2.5 cm) double-fold hem on each side of the curtain.

2) Press under 2" (5 cm) double-fold hem at upper edge of curtain. Open out fold and fuse a 2" (5 cm) strip of fusible interfacing along foldline. Fold again to form a double-fold hem.

3) Edgestitch upper hem in place. Or apply fusible web, following the manufacturer's directions. Fusing adds more stability to upper edge of curtain.

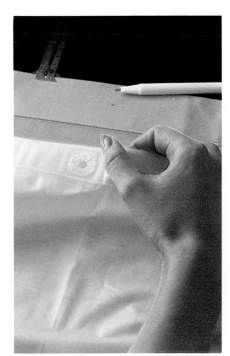

4) Mark positions for eyelets, grommets or buttonholes across upper hem, using the plastic liner as the guide for spacing holes. Position liner ¼" (6 mm) down from upper edge of curtain.

5a) Fasten eyelets securely using eyelet set and hammer or eyelet pliers. If using eyelet set, work on a piece of scrap wood or a hard surface that will not be damaged when pounding eyelets.

5b) Make vertical buttonholes, ¼" to ½" (6 mm to 1.3 cm) long. To prevent buttonholes from raveling, apply liquid fray preventer to cut edges. Insert rings or hooks.

Shower Curtains & Valances

A simple shower curtain can instantly change and refresh a bathroom. Use the shower curtain as a bold splash of color. Coordinate window treatments, towels, and other accessories with your new shower curtain.

The shower curtain pictured , used with a plastic liner, is especially easy to sew because it does not require grommets or eyelets in the heading. Instead, use a drapery folding or pleating tape, and insert metal shower curtain hooks in the loops that are woven right into the tape. These self-styling drapery tapes can also be used for valances and attached to a flat tension rod with standard drapery hooks.

A valance is a special finishing touch on a shower curtain. It helps to enclose the space and coordinate the room. Most of the valance top treatments used for windows are appropriate shower curtain headings as well. The cloud, pouf, and smocked valances are soft, light treatments; the straight lines of pleated and flat valances are more tailored.

Trim a shower curtain with lace, eyelet, ruffling, or grosgrain or satin ribbon.

✂ Cutting Directions

Cut two 81" (206 cm) lengths of fabric (extra fabric will be needed for matching prints); stitch lengths together. Cut shower curtain 6" (15 cm) wider and 9" (23 cm) longer than vinyl liner.

Cut valance width 2½ times the length of rod, and the desired length plus 6½" (16.3 cm) for heading and hems. Seam together as necessary for desired width. Cut smocking tape the cut width of the valance, plus a little extra for aligning and finishing ends.

YOU WILL NEED

Shower curtain fabric, 4½ yd. (4.15 m) for standard liner; extra needed for matching prints.

Drapery folding tape, 2⅛ yd. (1.95 m) for shower curtain; smocking tape for valance, 2½ times the length of the rod.

Vinyl shower curtain liner, 70" × 72" (178 × 183 cm); 12 metal shower curtain rings; flat tension rod for valance.

Drapery hooks.

How to Sew a Shower Curtain

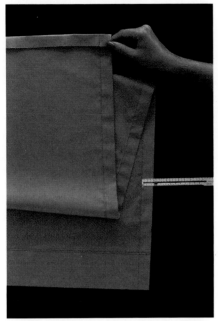

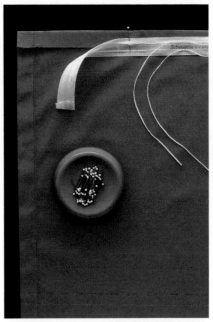

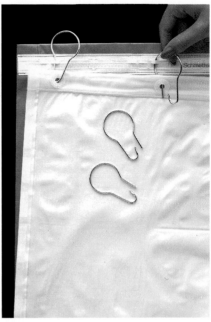

1) Turn under and stitch double 1" (2.5 cm) side hems. At bottom edge, make a double 3" (7.5 cm) hem. At top, press under 1" (2.5 cm). Do not stitch.

2) Remove pull-cords from folding tape. You will use hook loops only. With loop side facing you and toward the top, pin tape on wrong side of fabric ½" (1.3 cm) from upper edge. Turn under raw edge at ends of tape; stitch in place.

3) Insert shower curtain rings into holes of vinyl liner and into hook loops of folding tape. Hang on shower curtain rod.

How to Sew a Smocked Shower Curtain Valance

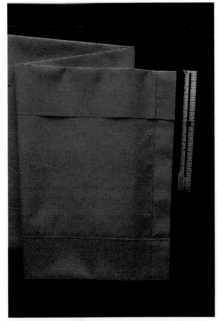

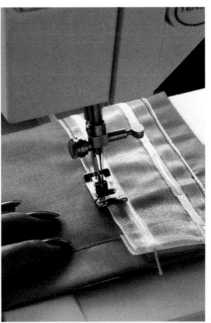

1) Stitch double 1" (2.5 cm) side hems; stitch double 2" (5 cm) bottom hem; turn upper edge under 2½" (6.5 cm), and press.

2) Pin smocking tape ½" (1.3 cm) from upper folded edge with loops on top. Turn under 1" (2.5 cm) of tape at each end, and lift out strings. Stitch both sides of tape.

3) Knot strings securely to prevent them from being pulled out. Pull up strings to smock, adjusting fullness to fit rod. Insert drapery hooks every 3" to 4" (7.5 to 10 cm). Mount flat tension rod; hang valance from rod.

Shower Curtain Ideas

Eyelet-trimmed curtain. Stitch flat eyelet to curtain in ½" (1.3 cm) seam. Press. Turn under seam allowance; stitch narrow hem.

Puff valance. Make valance (page 116). Mount valance on tension rod. The valance may be mounted at ceiling or just above shower curtain rod.

Box-pleated valance. To make this box-pleated valance, use self-styling tape. Attach separate rod pocket, and cover stitching line with satin or grosgrain ribbon. Mount valance on tension rod.

Balloon valance. Make valance (page 116). Make two shower curtain panels (page 216) to tie back at sides. Mount curtain panels on shower curtain rod with plastic liner. Mount valance on separate tension rod above shower curtain.

How to Sew a Sink or Vanity Skirt

1) Turn under and stitch double 1" (2.5 cm) hem on bottom edge. Turn under double 1" (2.5 cm) hem on center front edges. For 2-piece skirt, stitch narrow hem on back edges.

2) Press under 1" (2.5 cm) on upper edge of panels. Turn under raw edges on ends of shirring tape; pull out shirring cords. Place tape, right side up, over raw edge, with upper edge of tape ¼" (6 mm) from fold. Stitch both sides of tape.

3) Tie cords at both ends of shirring tape. From wrong side of skirt, pull up cords in shirring tape to the finished width. Knot cords; wrap and tuck under skirt. Adjust the gathers evenly.

Sink & Vanity Skirts

For covering up an outdated sink or bringing more fabric coordination into the bathroom, the sink skirt is a perennial favorite. It conceals the plumbing and provides a hidden storage area.

Vanity skirts are sewn the same way as the sink skirt. They can transform an unsightly table into a charming bedroom or bath accessory.

Self-styling shirring tapes, available in a variety of styles, make the sewing quick and easy and add a dimensional interest to the top of the skirt. For a more traditional approach, gather the upper edge (page 31). Attach the skirt to the sink or vanity with hook and loop tape so the skirt can easily be removed for laundering or a quick change. To make the skirt washable, hand-sew the tape in place.

If the sink skirt is attached on the outside porcelain, make two side panels; each panel of the skirt will extend from the center front to the wall. If the skirt is attached underneath the apron of the sink, it can be made in one piece with a center front opening.

✂ Cutting Directions

To finished length, add 3" (7.5 cm) for a double 1" (2.5 cm) bottom hem and 1" (2.5 cm) to turn under at the top. To determine cut width, measure the distance around the sink or vanity where the skirt will be attached; multiply by 2½ times the fullness. Add 4" (10 cm) for front opening hems.

Cut the number of panels as figured above, and seam together for width as needed. If necessary to seam extra widths, place seams toward back.

YOU WILL NEED

Decorator fabric for skirt.

Shirring tape the cut width of the upper edge of the flat panels before gathering.

Adhesive-backed hook and loop tape to go around the sink or vanity.

4) Finger press loop side of self-adhesive hook and loop tape to the wrong side of the skirt, over the shirring tape.

5) Attach the hook side of self-adhesive tape to the outside of the sink or vanity table. Attach skirt to tape.

Alternative mounting. To hang skirt under apron of sink, attach loop side of tape on right side of skirt ½" (1.3 cm) from upper edge; adhere the hook side of tape to underside of the sink. Attach skirt.

Terry Cloth Bath Mats

Comfortable, absorbent bath mats can be made from two layers of terry cloth, sewn together with cotton fringe at each end. For a decorative quilted effect, cotton cording or soutache braid is applied to the top of the mat by stitching through both layers, in a technique called *couching*. This technique uses wide zigzag or blanket stitches to secure the cording or soutache on each side of the trim.

Cording may be easily couched to the bath mat with the help of a cording foot. The trim is threaded through a hole in the foot and is guided automatically as you sew, leaving your hands free to turn the fabric. If a cording foot is not available, the trim can be stitched to the mat using a general-purpose foot and the zigzag stitch.

The bath mat can be made from either a loop or cut pile terry cloth. Choose fringe and cording or soutache braid that are colorfast. To prevent shrinkage, prewash the fabric and all trims.

✄ Cutting Directions

For the bath mat top and bottom, cut two rectangles of fabric 1" (2.5 cm) longer and wider than the desired finished length and width of the bath mat, excluding the length of the fringe. Cut each piece separately, rather than layered, for accuracy. Cut two lengths of fringe equal to the finished length of the short sides plus 1½" (3.8 cm).

YOU WILL NEED

Woven terry cloth fabric; knit or stretch fabric is not suitable.

Cotton fringe.

Cotton cording or soutache braid.

How to Sew a Terry Cloth Bath Mat

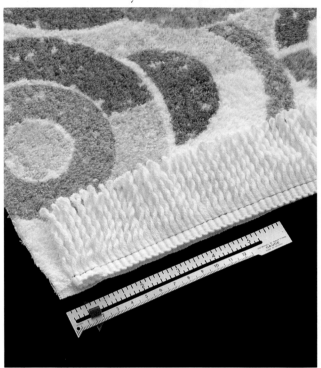

1) Pin fringe to right side of bath mat top on each short side, aligning upper edge of fringe tape with raw edge of fabric; fold up ¾" (2 cm) at the ends of fringe, and position folded ends ½" (1.3 cm) from the long edges of fabric. Baste in place.

2) Pin the bath mat top to the bath mat back, right sides together. Stitch ½" (1.3 cm) seam around mat, pivoting at corners; leave an opening for turning on one side. Avoid catching fringe in stitching.

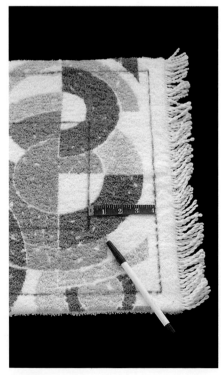

3) Clip corners diagonally. Turn bath mat right side out. Slipstitch opening closed.

4) Mark a line 1" (2.5 cm) from each edge of mat. Mark a second set of lines 4" (10 cm) from the first set.

5) Hand-baste top to back within ¼" (6 mm) of each line, to prevent layers from shifting when you are couching.

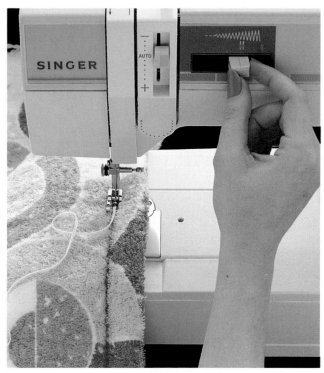

6) Align cording foot with first line on mat. Place the cording or soutache braid from front to back through the hole in the foot. Set the machine for zigzag stitch, and set stitch width so stitches will catch fabric on both sides of cording or braid.

7) Stitch over cording, guiding fabric so the stitching follows marked line; cording will feed by itself. Pivot at corners, keeping needle down in fabric on the left side of the cording as you turn fabric. (Contrasting thread was used to show detail.)

8) Stop stitching about 2" (5 cm) from the starting point. Cut cording so end overlaps starting point about ½" (1.3 cm). Continue stitching, overlapping cording and stitching over both ends to secure.

9) Repeat steps 6 through 8 to couch the cording or soutache braid on second set of lines.

Embellished Towels

Perk up the bath with designer touches added to inexpensive, plain towels. Laces, ribbons, or monograms can be added to coordinate with bedroom sheets and trims, window treatments, and shower curtains.

Preshrink or steam-shrink woven ribbon trims, particularly all-cotton trims; polyester laces will not need preshrinking. Mark trimming placement on towel with water-soluble marking pen.

When applying trims to terry towels, loosen the tension and use a long stitch length. Ease the trimming slightly as you stitch; when the towel is folded on the rack, the trim will lie smooth.

Lace and ribbon. Trim towels with prefinished lace beading (**1**), lace edging (**2**), or galloon lace (**3**). For lace beading, insert ribbon into beading, position beading on towel, and straight-stitch upper edge. For lace edging, position so lower edge of lace covers towel fringe or hem. Cover upper edge of lace with ribbon trim; straight-stitch along both edges of ribbon. For galloon lace, position trim on towel, and straight-stitch near edges of lace.

Machine monogram. On electronic sewing machine, insert monogram cassette and program desired lettering. Cover monogram area with dissolvable plastic film protector to prevent snagging terry loops. Stitch; tear away plastic film. Laundering dissolves any remaining film.

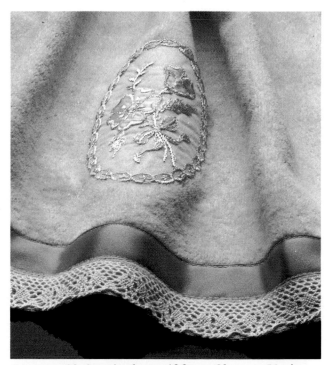

Lace motif. Cut single motif from Cluny or Venice lace, or use purchased appliqué. Fusible web may be used to hold appliqué in place; stitch with narrow zigzag. Coordinating trims may be stitched at lower edge of towel.

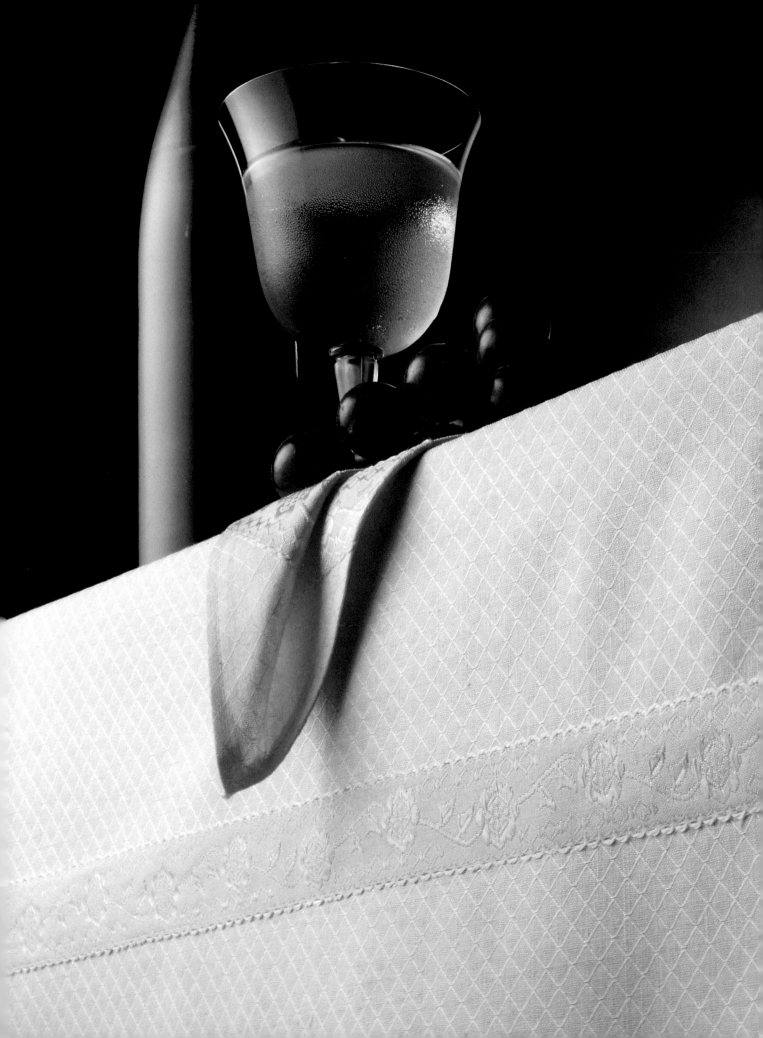

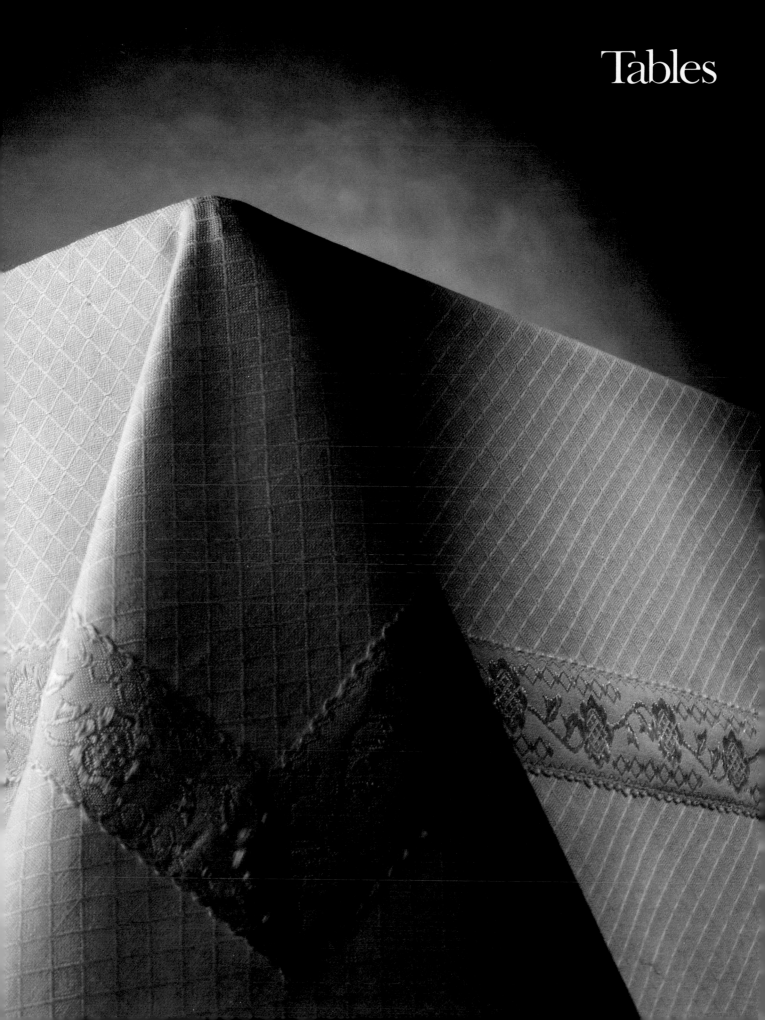

Tables

Placemats & Table Runners

Placemats, table runners and table mats protect tabletops and add color and style to table settings. Use them over tablecloths, or alone to show off the beauty of wood and glass tables. The sewing techniques for placemats, table runners and table mats are very similar.

Select fabric for mats and runners according to the general guidelines for choosing tablecloth fabrics.

Finish edges of tabletop projects with wide banding (pages 37 and 38) or bias binding. To make bias binding, cut and join bias strips (page 40). Fold strip in half lengthwise, wrong sides together, and press. Open binding and press cut edges toward center.

Tips for Binding Placemat Edges

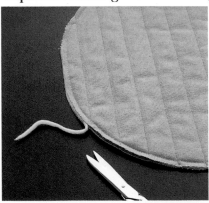

Quilted fabrics. Before applying binding, stitch placemat ¼" (6 mm) from edge. Trim batting from hem area to reduce bulk in bound edge.

Slipstitched edges. Open out bias binding. Pin right side of binding to front of mat, raw edges even. Stitch on foldline. Turn binding to back of mat and slipstitch.

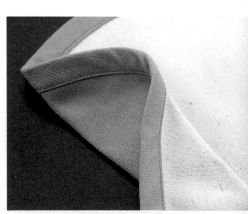

Topstitched edges. Open out bias binding. Pin right side of binding to back of mat, raw edges even. Stitch on foldline. Turn binding to front of mat and topstitch.

Placemats can be lined, underlined with fusible interfacing, made of quilted fabric, or sewn double for extra body. Two common finished sizes of placemats are 18" × 12" (46 × 30.5 cm) and 16" × 14" (40.5 × 35.5 cm). Choose the best size for your table and place settings.

Table runners are usually 12" to 18" (30.5 to 46 cm) wide; make them wider if they will be used as placemats. Drop lengths vary from 8" to 12" (20.5 to 30.5 cm). Table runners may be cut on either the lengthwise or the crosswise grain of the fabric, but less piecing of fabric is required if they are cut on lengthwise grain.

Table mats protect the surface of a table without hiding the legs or base. Cut and sew a mat to the exact size of the tabletop and finish the edges.

Corners. Sandwich the fabric in binding, starting binding at center of one side. Baste binding and topstitch to corner, catching all layers. At corner, fold diagonally; baste and topstitch next side. Finish ends, right.

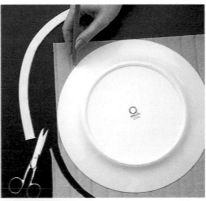

Oval mats. Shape corners of mat using a dinner plate as a guide. Before applying bias binding, shape binding to curves with a steam iron.

Finishing ends. Cut bias binding 1" (2.5 cm) beyond the end. Turn under ½" (1.3 cm); finish stitching to end of binding. Slipstitch.

Fagoted Placemats

Fagoting is used to create an open, lacelike effect. Placemats and table linens are ideal places to feature fagoting. There are two methods for fagoting, each giving a different appearance. In the first method, curved or straight seamlines are stitched with an open-toe presser foot, using the fagoting stitch or three-step zigzag stitch. The placemat shown above left, made using this method, is oval-shaped and bound with bias strips (page 231).

In the second method, a tacking or fringe presser foot and the zigzag stitch are used for straight seamlines only. The width of the fagoting varies from ⅛" to ⅜" (3 mm to 1 cm), depending on the tacking foot; ⅜" (1 cm) fagoting may increase the finished size of the placemat slightly. If the bar on the tacking foot is not centered on the foot, use a zigzag stitch with a right-needle position to center the stitches over the bar. The placemat shown above right, made using the second method, is square, with satin-stitched edges.

Select the thread and needle according to the weight of the fabric. Cotton machine embroidery thread

and a size 70/9 or 80/11 needle will work well for lightweight to mediumweight fabric; rayon thread and a size 80/11 needle may be used if extra sheen is desired. Topstitching thread or buttonhole twist and a size 90/14 needle are recommended for fagoting on mediumweight to heavyweight fabric.

Loosen the needle thread tension, if necessary, so the bobbin thread does not show on the right side of the fabric. Experiment with the stitches on your sewing machine and make a test sample, checking the tension adjustments and stitch length; the shorter the stitch length, the more filled-in the fagoting space.

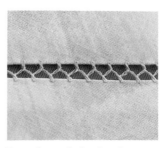

Fagoting stitched using open-toe presser foot.

Fagoting stitched using tacking presser foot.

How to Stitch Fagoted Seams Using the Open-toe Foot

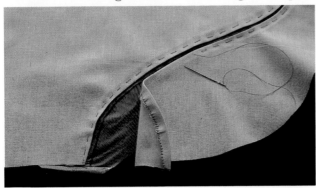

1) Trim seam allowances to ¼" (6 mm); finish edges. Press under the seam allowance plus ¹⁄₁₆" (1.5 mm). Baste one folded edge, right side up, to water-soluble stabilizer. Mark a line on stabilizer ⅛" (3 mm) beyond fold. Baste adjoining folded edge to stabilizer at marked line.

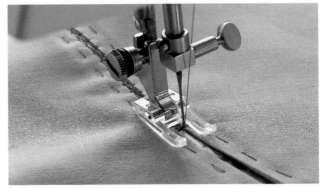

2) Center open area under open-toe presser foot. Stitch edges together, using fagoting stitch or 3-step zigzag, barely catching alternate edges as you stitch. Remove stabilizer; press.

How to Stitch Fagoted Seams Using the Tacking Foot

1) Attach tacking foot; place needle thread to back of foot. Set zigzag stitch width so needle barely stitches over bar on foot. If bar is not centered on foot, set machine for zigzag stitch with a right-needle position so stitches are centered over bar. Set stitch length and loosen needle thread tension.

2) Stitch seam, right sides together, so center of zigzag stitches is ⅝" (1.5 cm) from raw edge.

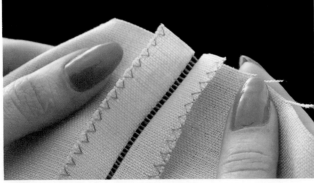

3) Remove fabric from machine carefully to prevent threads from drawing up. Finish seam allowances. Pull layers apart firmly. Press seam open.

4) Attach open-toe presser foot. Set the machine to balanced tension. Stitch on each side of fagoting, from right side, using satin stitch or other decorative stitch; pull fabric flat as you stitch. If short stitch length is used, the seam allowances may be trimmed close to the stitching.

Table Linens with Mitered Corners

Table linens with wide hems and mitered corners are elegant and easy to make. Use the same hemming technique for tablecloths, placemats, and napkins. Any of these items can be customized with transparent appliqués (page 306), cutwork (page 308), or other surface embellishments such as fabric painting.

Make tablecloths the desired width by joining fabric widths as necessary, using full widths in the center and partial widths on the lengthwise edges. Straighten the crosswise ends of the fabric to square the corners. Use French or overedge seams (page 32), or use selvage edges to eliminate seam finishing, if seaming is necessary.

Select the width and finish of the hem to complement the weight and texture of the fabric. Mitering is the neatest way to square corners, because it covers the raw edges and eliminates bulk.

Determine the amount of fabric needed for the tablecloth by dividing the total width of the tablecloth by the width of your fabric less 1" (2.5 cm). Multiply this figure, which is the number of panels needed, by the total length of the tablecloth. Divide this number by 36" (91.5 cm) to get the total yards (meters) required. Allow for about 1" (2.5 cm) hems, depending on the size of the project.

Determine the size of placemats as on page 231; add about 1" (2.5 cm) hems. You will need 1 yd. (0.95 m) of 36" (91.5 cm) fabric to make four 17" (43 cm) napkins. You may wish to vary the size of napkins.

How to Make Mitered Corners

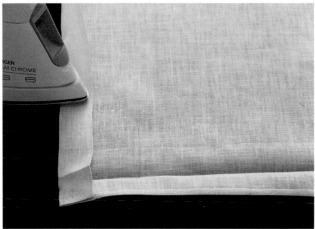

1) **Stitch** a scant ¼" (6 mm) from edges of fabric. Fold the edges to wrong side; press just beyond the stitching line. Press under desired hem depth on each side of fabric.

2) **Open** out corner; fold diagonally so pressed folds match. Press diagonal fold.

3) **Open** out corner. Fold through center of corner, right sides together. Stitch on diagonal foldline from step 2. Trim fabric from corner to ¼" (6 mm) from stitching. Press seam open.

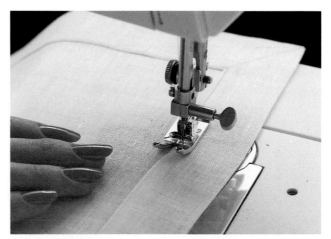

4) **Press** the hem in place, turning corners right side out. Stitch hem, pivoting at corners; use decorative thread, such as rayon or metallic thread, if desired.

Satin-stitched Tablecloth

Satin stitching can be used to apply appliqués, outline cutwork, stitch decorative design lines, or finish edges. The tablecloth below utilizes all of these applications. Choose a mediumweight linen for this square tablecloth with satin-stitched hem. Choose designs from appliqué, cutwork, and embroidery patterns.

To sew the satin stitch, set the machine for a zigzag stitch and a short stitch length, so the stitches lie close to each other, concealing all the fabric under the stitches. Satin stitches can be any stitch width desired; generally, the smaller the design, the narrower the stitch width.

Adjust the tension so the bobbin thread does not show on the upper side of the fabric. Use an open-toe presser foot or special-purpose presser foot for sewing satin stitching. The groove on the bottom of the foot provides space for the stitches, so the fabric feeds through the sewing machine evenly.

Machine embroidery thread is recommended for satin stitching. Cotton embroidery thread has a subtle sheen, rayon embroidery thread, a more pronounced sheen.

Satin stitching may be corded, using one to three strands of pearl cotton or topstitching thread. A cording foot is helpful, because it guides the cord under the stitches automatically. However, if a cording foot is not available for your sewing machine, the cord can be guided by hand.

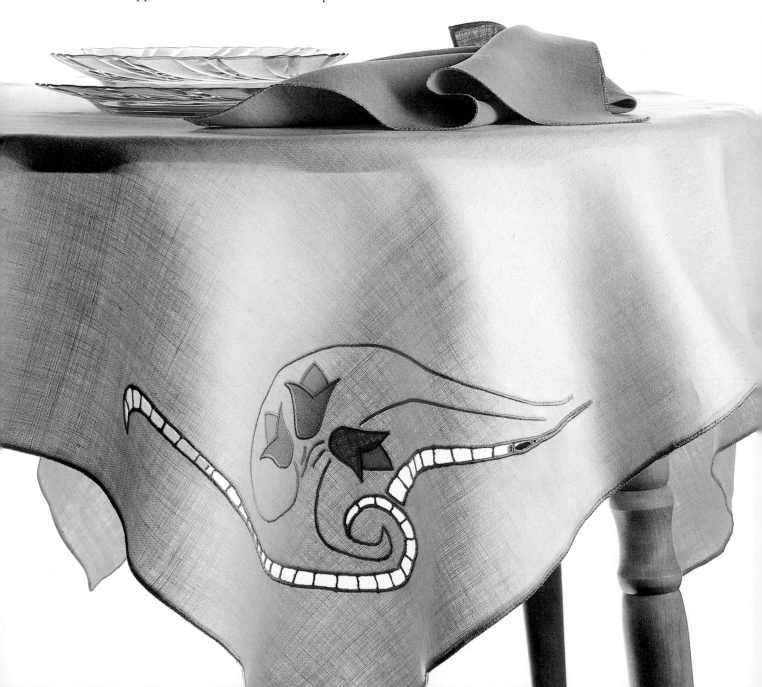

Setting the Stitch Length

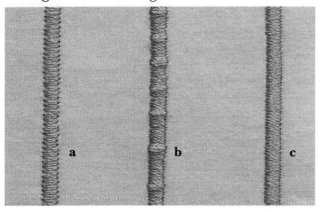

Set the stitch length for short stitches. Place a stabilizer under a fabric scrap, and stitch to check stitch length. If stitches are too long **(a)**, the fabric shows between the stitches. If stitches are too short **(b)**, the stitches pile up or overlap, and the fabric does not feed smoothly. Perfect satin stitches **(c)** are evenly spaced and lie next to each other without overlapping.

Two Ways to Sew an Edge Finish Using Satin Stitching

Folded edge. Press the edge under ½" (1.3 cm). If using a lightweight fabric, place tear-away stabilizer under fabric, aligning it with fold. Stitch along the folded edge so needle stitches just over fold. Turn corners or curves, and remove stabilizer. Trim excess fabric close to stitches.

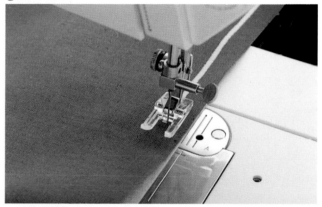

Single layer. Place 1" (2.5 cm) strip of tear-away or water-soluble stabilizer under edge. Satin stitch ½" (1.3 cm) from raw edge to prevent stretching at edge. Turn corners or curves, and remove stabilizer. Trim fabric at edge, close to stitches.

How to Sew Corded Satin Stitching

1) Satin stitch, above. Place pearl cotton in hole of cording foot. Stitch over cord along outer edge, using narrow zigzag stitch. Stop one stitch width away from corner, with needle down at inner edge; stitch in place for a few stitches.

2) Pivot fabric. Make a loop in cord and stitch in place for a few stitches. Continue zigzag stitching over cord for a few inches (2.5 cm). Pull on ends of cord to eliminate the loop.

3) Trim end of cord at starting point so cord ends meet. Overlap stitching ½" (1.3 cm).

Six Ways to Make and Hem Napkins

Satin stitch. Turn under ¾" (2 cm) on all sides. Miter corners (page 235). Use wide, closely spaced zigzag to stitch from right side over edgestitching; use edgestitching as guideline.

Zigzag overedge. Trim loose threads from napkin edges. Stitch over raw edge, using wide, closely spaced zigzag. Use overedge foot or special-purpose foot to maintain zigzag width. See page 237.

Decorative stitch. Press under ¼" (6 mm) and stitch. From right side, stitch with a decorative stitch, using straight stitching as the guideline. Blanket stitch (shown above) gives a hemstitched look.

Napkins

Coordinating napkins are the finishing touch to your tabletop fashions. Standard finished napkins are 14" or 17" (35.5 or 43 cm) square. Before cutting the fabric, square the ends, using a carpenter's square. For fringed napkins, square the fabric by pulling threads at desired intervals.

Napkin hems can be decorative. Experiment with some of the decorative stitches on your sewing machine. The hemming techniques shown here can also be used on tablecloths and placemats.

✂ Cutting Directions

Cut napkins 1" (2.5 cm) larger than finished size. One yard (meter) of 36" (91.5 cm) wide fabric yields four 17" (43 cm) napkins. A piece of fabric 45" (115 cm) square yields nine 14" (35.5 cm) napkins.

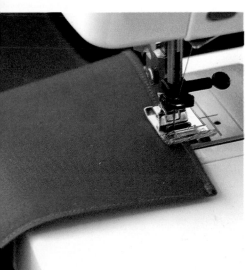

Narrow hem. Press under ¼" (6 mm) double-fold hem on opposite sides of all napkins. Edgestitch from one napkin to the next using continuous stitching. Repeat for remaining sides.

Double-fold hem. Turn under ¼" (6 mm) on all edges and press. Turn under another ¼" (6 mm). Miter corners (page 235).

Fringe. Cut napkins on a pulled thread to straighten edges. Stitch ½" (1.3 cm) from raw edges with short straight stitches or narrow, closely spaced zigzag. Pull out threads up to the stitching line.

Seating

Reversible Seat Covers

Freshen the look of dining-room and kitchen chairs with simple seat covers. The lined cover is shaped at the front of the chair and secured to the chair with fabric ties at the back legs. To make the seat cover reversible, use a coordinating decorator fabric for the lining. For best results, choose firmly woven, mediumweight decorator fabrics. These fabrics wear well and are easy to work with. When working with heavier fabrics, select a lighter-weight fabric for the lining. To add a decorative touch to the cover, embellish the lower edge with a contrasting trim, such as ribbon or braid. This seat cover is suitable for armless chairs that have open backs and smooth, flat seats.

✂ Cutting Directions

Make the seat cover pattern as on page 244. Cut one piece each from fabric and lining. Cut four fabric strips, 2" (5 cm) wide and 10" to 16" (25.5 to 40.5 cm) long, for ties.

YOU WILL NEED

Muslin, for pattern.
Decorator fabric.
Lining fabric.
Decorative trim, optional.

Seat covers can give an updated look to dining-room and kitchen chairs. Make the covers reversible by using a decorator fabric for the lining, and, for added interest, embellish the lower edge with a decorative trim.

How to Make a Seat Cover Pattern

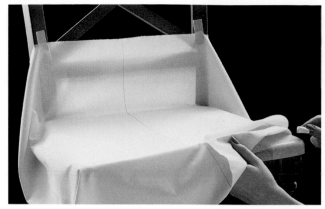

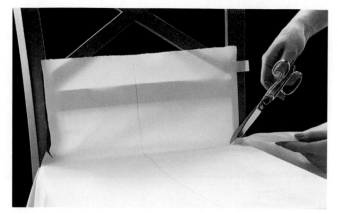

1) Measure chair seat, and add 3" to 4" (7.5 to 10 cm) on all sides for drop length; cut a piece of muslin about 4" (10 cm) larger than measurements. Mark center line, following lengthwise grain. Center muslin on seat; pin or tape in place.

2) Clip fabric diagonally at back corners, so fabric fits around the back posts; make additional clips as necessary for smooth fit.

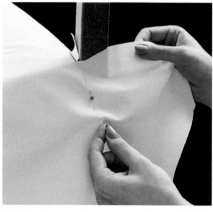

3) Smooth fabric around sides and front of chair; pin out excess fabric at front corners. Mark seamline at front corners, using pencil.

4) Mark seamline around the back posts, using pencil. Pin-mark ends of seat cover on drop, at sides of chair; repeat for drop at chair back.

5) Pin-mark the lower edge of cover at the desired length around front, sides, and back; drop length on sides and back should align. Mark the seamlines.

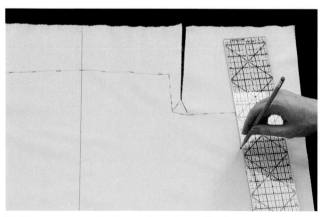

6) Remove muslin from the chair. Redraw seamlines as necessary, using straightedge; redraw any curved lines, drawing smooth curves. Reposition muslin on chair; make corrections, if necessary.

7) Add ½" (1.3 cm) seam allowances. Cut pattern on the marked lines.

How to Sew a Seat Cover

1) Press under ½" (1.3 cm) on one short end of the fabric strip for tie. Press the strip in half lengthwise, wrong sides together. Open, and press raw edges to the center crease, wrong sides together; refold at the original crease. Repeat for remaining fabric strips.

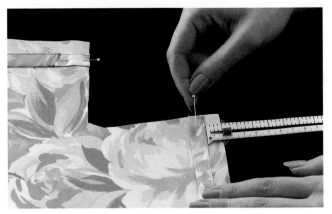

2) Stitch close to folded edges of strips. Pin one tie to right side of seat cover at lower back corner, with raw edges even and long stitched edge of tie ½" (1.3 cm) from lower edge of cover. Baste tie in place. Repeat for remaining ties.

3) Pin seam at front corners of seat cover; stitch. Repeat for lining. Press seams to one side, pressing seams of the seat cover and the lining in opposite directions.

4) Pin lining to the seat cover, right sides together and raw edges even. Stitch ½" (1.3 cm) seam, leaving 6" (15 cm) opening, centered on back of seat cover.

5) Trim outside corners diagonally; clip any curves and inside corners. Press seam allowances open.

6) Turn cover right side out; press. Slipstitch opening closed. Position trim, if desired, at the lower edge of the cover or lining, using glue stick. Turn under ½" (1.3 cm) at ends. Topstitch trim in place; stitch both sides in same direction to prevent diagonal wrinkles.

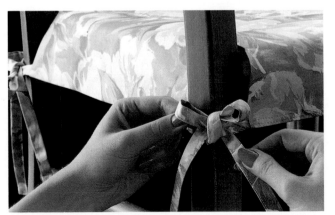

7) Position seat cover on chair; secure ties in bow or square knot.

Slipcovers for Folding Chairs

Slipcovers for folding chairs are an easy and affordable way to dress up an old steel folding chair. For special occasions, for a change of seasons, or simply for some fun in home decorating, folding-chair slipcovers are attractive and versatile. They can work with any decorating scheme from contemporary to country, depending upon fabric choice and styling options. And they offer a practical solution to the age-old problem posed by large gatherings: attractive yet portable and stowable temporary seating.

Folding chairs come in a variety of shapes and sizes, quite similar but not exactly the same. To make a well-fitting slipcover, make a custom-fitted pattern out of muslin. Start with four rectangles of fabric cut approximately to size, then drape and pin them to the chair to fine-tune the shape. Once this muslin has been fitted, use it as a pattern for cutting the slipcover.

When you make the actual slipcover, add a decorative bow tied across the back, or add contrasting piping or ruffles or creative touches of your own.

YOU WILL NEED

3 yd. (2.75 m) unbleached muslin, 42" (107 cm) wide, for pattern.

Folding chair.

Marker or pencil, pins, shears, double-stick tape.

Heavy weight, such as books or gallon (3.78 L) bottle of water.

Decorator fabric.

Muslin pattern layout. Mark muslin for rough pattern pieces; cut on solid lines. Mark dotted center lines. Mark arrows on skirt pattern piece, 6" (15 cm) and 12" (30.5 cm) on each side of center line.

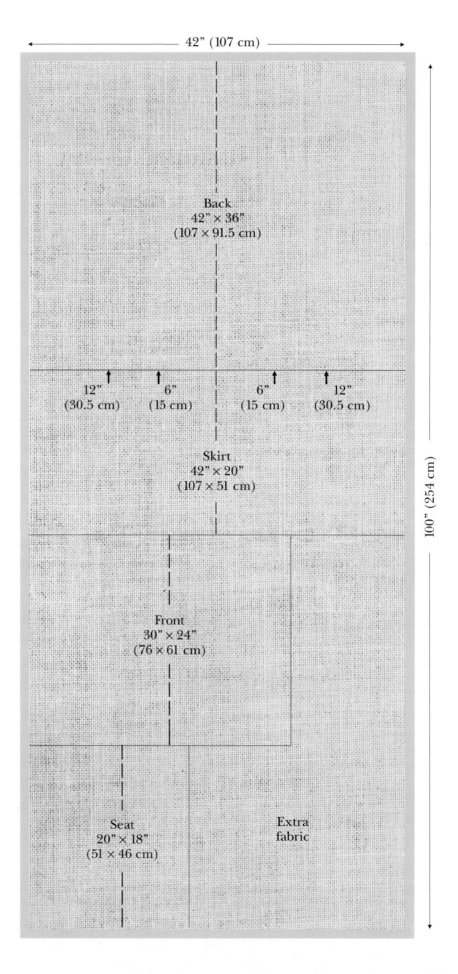

42" (107 cm)

Back
42" × 36"
(107 × 91.5 cm)

12"
(30.5 cm)   6"
(15 cm)   6"
(15 cm)   12"
(30.5 cm)

Skirt
42" × 20"
(107 × 51 cm)

Front
30" × 24"
(76 × 61 cm)

Seat
20" × 18"
(51 × 46 cm)

Extra
fabric

100" (254 cm)

How to Make a Folding Chair Slipcover

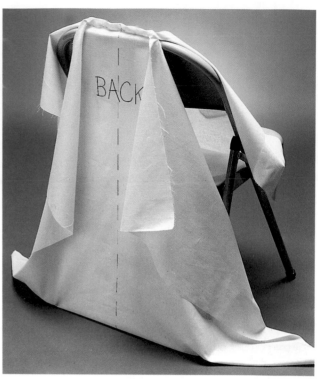

1) Pin back and front pattern pieces together for 4" (10 cm) on either side of the center marks. Pin horizontally from center toward sides, using a ½" (1.3 cm) seam allowance.

2) Drape pinned pattern over chair, matching center lines to center of chair back. Secure pattern at top of chair back with double-stick tape. Tuck pattern under back legs; keep grainline straight.

3) Push front pattern piece toward back edge of seat at bottom to allow enough ease for sitting. Secure pattern to chair with double-stick tape at center of seat and both corners.

4) Drape back pattern around curve of chair. Drape smoothly, keeping grainline perpendicular to floor. Pin along edge of chair to indicate seamline. Repeat for other side.

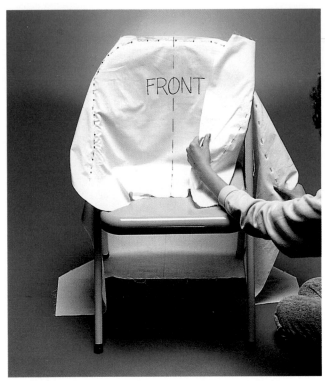

5) Drape front pattern around curve of chair. Pin along edge of chair to indicate seamline. Pin back pattern to front pattern along seamlines, adjusting to fit chair smoothly and maintain grainline.

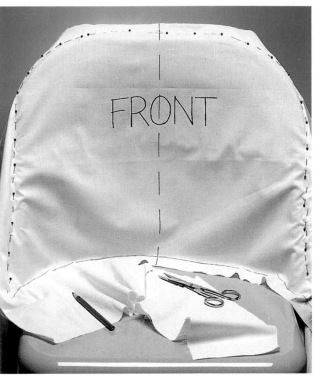

6) Trace edge of the chair seat at bottom of front pattern. Trim to 1" (2.5 cm) beyond traced outline.

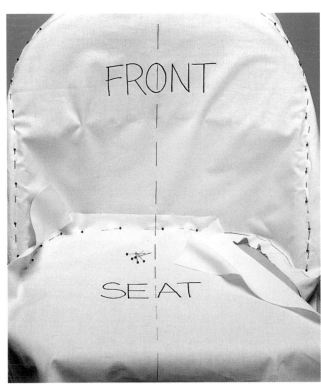

7) Secure seat pattern to chair at center front with double-stick tape. Pin back of seat pattern to bottom of front pattern, stopping where the front and back pieces meet.

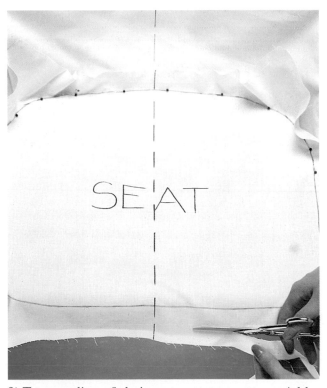

8) Trace outline of chair seat onto seat pattern. Add ¼" (6 mm) to front edge of seat pattern to allow for the rounded front edge of chair. Trim to 1" (2.5 cm) beyond outline.

(Continued on next page)

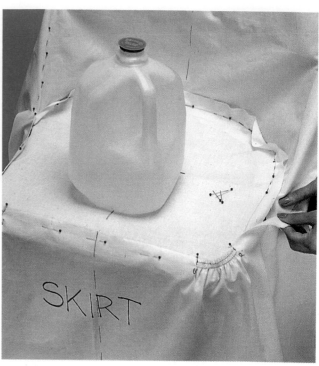

9) Gather or pleat skirt pattern between 6" and 12" (15 and 30.5 cm) marks on each side of center line. Draw up each set of gathers to 3" (7.5 cm).

10) Weight pattern pieces on chair so they do not move; a gallon (3.78 L) of water or stack of books works well. Match center lines of seat and skirt patterns. Pin skirt to seat ending where all four pieces meet.

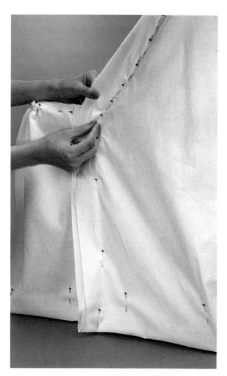

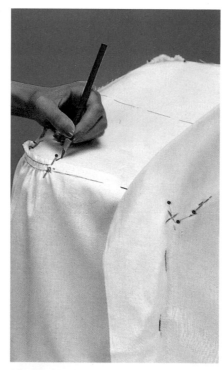

11) Turn up and pin hem to the desired length. Pin skirt to back pattern at sides. Examine fit of muslin on chair and make any necessary adjustments. Pattern should fit snugly, without pulling.

12) Mark seamlines between pins on all pieces. Mark placement for gathers on seat and skirt patterns. Mark all pieces with an "X" at point where all four pattern pieces meet at sides.

13) Remove pins and release gathers. Lay pieces flat. Mark seamlines. Fold pieces along centers. Compare markings on each half. Make any necessary adjustments so pattern is symmetrical.

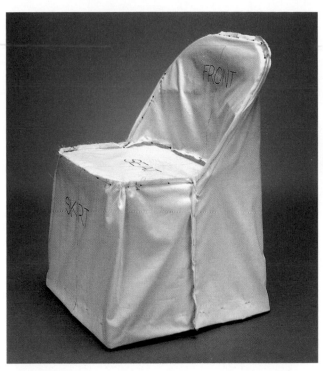

14) Trim hem allowance on skirt to 2" (5 cm) for a finished 1" (2.5 cm) double-fold hem.

15) Repin, and try pattern on chair. Adjust the fit, seamlines, and placement marks, as necessary. Add ½" (1.3 cm) seam allowances; trim excess fabric. Try pattern on chair again, if desired.

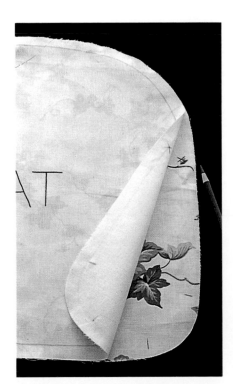

16) Cut chair cover from decorator fabric, using the muslin pieces as a pattern. Transfer markings.

17) Cut two pieces for ties, each 7" (18 cm) wide and 42" (107 cm) long. Fold in half lengthwise, right sides together. Fold one end to form triangle; cut on fold. Stitch cut side and bias end; turn and press.

18) Stitch front to seat along back edge of seat between Xs **(a).** Stitch back to skirt at side seams, inserting tie in seam **(b).** Gather skirt between markings; stitch front/seat to back/skirt **(c).** Stitch hem.

Slipcovers

Slipcovers are removable covers, positioned over the existing fabric of the furniture. They can extend the life of a piece of furniture and update the decor at the same time. You can even change the look in a room from season to season by changing slipcovers. Because the pattern is developed when the first slipcover is made for the piece of furniture, a second slipcover can be made in less time.

A frequent concern about a slipcover is whether it will stay in place. To help secure the slipcover, an attached fabric strip, concealed under the skirt, is pinned to the existing fabric. Also, polyurethane foam pieces are tucked along the sides of the deck to provide a tight fit.

Sewing slipcovers is an alternative to upholstering. However, upholstering is required when the furniture needs structural repair, such as springing. It is easier to sew slipcovers for furniture that is fairly square, with straight lines, than it is for furniture with more details. Furniture with exposed wood usually requires upholstering, but furniture with wood strips on the arm can be slipcovered if the arms are first wrapped with upholstery batting. Recliners should be upholstered because of the movable parts.

Furniture with a concave back design, such as a channel back or barrel back, is difficult to slipcover, and the slipcover may not fit well. For best results, a concave back should be wrapped or covered in a thick upholstery batting before it is slipcovered. Furniture with a tufted back or button back can be slipcovered, but the tufting and buttons are eliminated in the slipcover. The back is wrapped with upholstery batting to fill it out for a smooth-fitting slipcover.

Selecting the Slipcover Fabric

Decorator fabrics are recommended for slipcovers. Heavy upholstery fabrics should be avoided, because they are difficult to sew on most home sewing machines and do not shape easily around curves. Regardless of the fabric selection, dry cleaning is recommended instead of washing to keep the slipcover looking its best.

It may be necessary to underline the slipcover if the fabric on the furniture is heavily textured and the slipcover fabric is smooth, or if the fabric on the furniture is dark or bright and the slipcover fabric is light-colored.

For faster and easier sewing, select a fabric that does not require matching, such as solid-colored fabrics or all-over prints. Striped fabrics require matching in one direction, and plaids require matching in both directions. Many print fabrics have a 27" (68.5 cm) pattern repeat, which fits perfectly on most cushions.

The amount of fabric required depends on the size of the furniture, pattern pieces, fabric width, and pattern repeat. Depending on how close together the pattern pieces can be cut, there may be a lot of scraps. Frequently these scraps can be used for room accessories, such as pillows and bow picture hangers.

As a general rule, a chair requires about 7 to 8 yd. (6.4 to 7.35 m); a love seat, 10 to 12 yd. (9.15 to 11 m); and a sofa, 16 to 20 yd. (14.7 to 19.4 m). These amounts include matching welting and a skirt with pleats at the corners. Allow additional fabric for cushions and ruffled or box-pleated skirts. Each cushion requires 1 to 1½ yd. (0.95 to 1.4 m) of fabric. For a ruffled or box-pleated skirt, allow 1 yd. (0.95 m) extra for a chair, 2 to 3 yd. (1.85 to 2.75 m) for a love seat, and 4 yd. (3.7 m) for a sofa.

YOU WILL NEED

Muslin for pin-fitting the pieces.

Decorator fabric.

Cording for welting; select soft, pliable cording with a cotton core.

Zippers; one for chairs, two for sofas and love seats. The length of each zipper is 1" to 2" (2.5 to 5 cm) shorter than the length of the vertical seam at the side of the outside back. Additional zippers are needed for cushions (page 268).

Upholstery batting, if necessary, to pad the existing furniture.

Polyurethane foam, 2" (5 cm) strips, to insert at sides and back of deck.

T-pins, tacks, or heavy-duty stapler and staples, for securing tacking strip to furniture.

Pin-fitting

The easiest way to make a slipcover pattern is by pin-fitting muslin on the chair or sofa. Before you start, look carefully at the furniture. Usually the seams in the slipcover will be in the same locations as the seams on the existing cover, but you may be able to add or eliminate some details, provided it will not affect the fit of the slipcover. For example, if the existing cushions are wrap-style, you may want to slipcover them as box cushions with welting. Or a chair with a pleated front arm may be slipcovered with a separate front arm piece.

The style of the skirt can also be changed. You may want to gather a skirt all the way around the furniture, allowing double fullness. Or you may want bunched gathers at the corners of a chair, or at the corners and center front of a sofa. For a more tailored look, the skirt may have box pleats instead of gathers.

A chair with rolled arms and loose back and seat cushions is used in the instructions that follow. This example includes the details that are common to most furniture. Although your furniture style may be somewhat different, use these basic steps as a guide.

How to Pin-fit the Pattern for the Inside Back and Outside Back

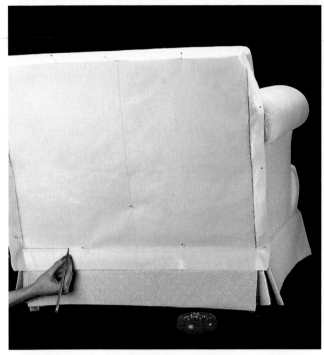

1) **Remove** cushions. Measure outside back of chair or sofa between seamlines; cut muslin 3" to 4" (7.5 to 10 cm) larger than measurements. Mark center line on outside back piece, following lengthwise grain. Pin to chair, smoothing fabric; mark seamlines.

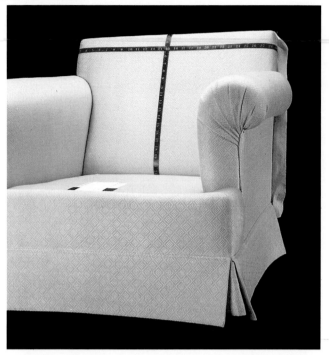

2) **Measure** inside back between seamlines; cut muslin 15" (38 cm) wider and about 10" (25.5 cm) longer than measurements. This allows for 6" (15 cm) at the lower edge to tuck into the deck and hold the slipcover in place. Mark center line on inside back piece, following lengthwise grain.

3) **Pin** outside back and inside back together along top of chair or sofa, matching center lines. Fold out excess fabric on inside back piece at upper corner, forming a dart. Pin muslin snugly, but do not pull fabric tight.

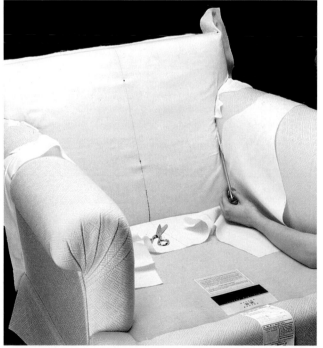

4) **Trim** excess fabric on sides of inside back to 2" (5 cm); clip along arms as necessary for smooth curve. Push about ½" (1.3 cm) of fabric into crevices on sides and lower edge of inside back; mark seamlines by pushing pencil into crevices.

How to Pin-fit the Pattern for a Pleated Arm

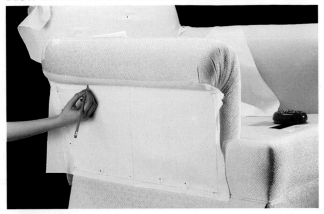

1) Measure outside arm between seamlines; cut muslin 3" (7.5 cm) larger than measurements. Mark lengthwise grainline on muslin. Pin outside arm in place, with grainline perpendicular to floor and with lower edge extending ½" (1.3 cm) beyond seamline at upper edge of skirt. Smooth fabric upward; pin. Pin outside arm to outside back. Mark seamlines.

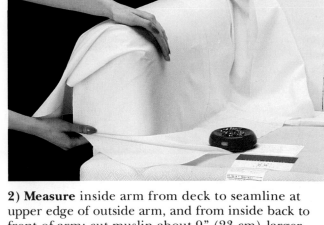

2) Measure inside arm from deck to seamline at upper edge of outside arm, and from inside back to front of arm; cut muslin about 9" (23 cm) larger than measurements. Mark lengthwise grainline on muslin. Pin inside arm piece in place, with 7" (18 cm) extending at inside back and grainline straight across arm, smoothing fabric up and around arm.

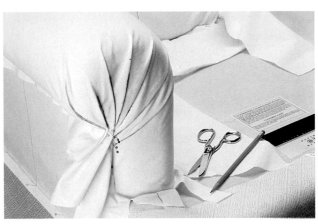

3) Pin inside arm to outside arm at front; clip and trim fabric at front lower edge as necessary for smooth fit. Pleat out fabric for rolled arm to duplicate pleats in existing fabric. Mark radiating foldlines of pleats.

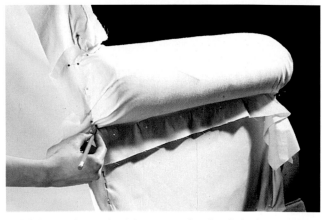

4) Make tucks on inside arm at back of chair, to fold out excess fabric; clip inside arm as necessary for smooth fit. Mark seamline at beginning and end of tucks on inside arm and outside back.

5) Mark inside arm and inside back with large dots, about halfway up the arm. Push about ½" (1.3 cm) of fabric on inside arm into crevices at deck and back.

6) Mark all seamlines on muslin, smoothing the fabric as you go.

How to Pin-fit the Pattern for an Arm with a Front Section

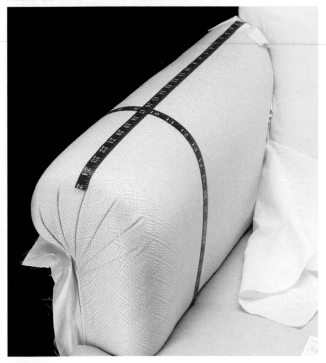

1) **Follow** step 1, opposite, for outside arm. Measure inside arm from deck to seamline at upper edge of outside arm, and from inside back to front edge of arm; cut muslin about 9" (23 cm) larger than these measurements. Mark lengthwise grainline on muslin.

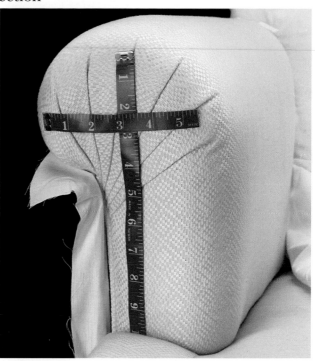

2) **Measure** front of the arm; cut muslin 2" to 3" (5 to 7.5 cm) larger than measurements. Mark lengthwise grainline on muslin.

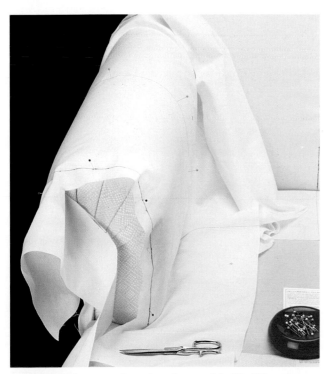

3) **Pin** inside arm piece in place, with 7" (18 cm) extending at inside back and grainline straight across arm, smoothing fabric up and around arm. Mark seamline at front edge of arm; trim away excess fabric not needed for seam allowances.

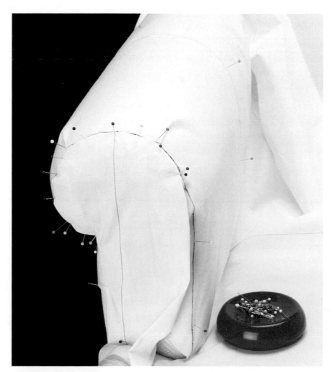

4) **Pin** front arm piece in place. Fold out excess fabric on inside arm as necessary to fit front arm piece, making two pleats. Mark seamline for curve of arm, following existing seamline on chair. Complete pattern as in steps 4, 5, and 6, opposite.

How to Pin-fit the Pattern for the Deck

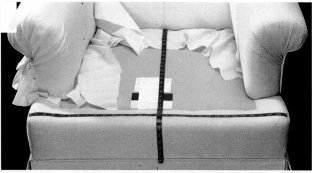

1) Measure width at front of deck; measure length of deck, down front of chair to skirt seam; cut muslin 15" (38 cm) wider and 9" (23 cm) longer than the measurements. Mark center line on muslin, following grainline. Mark seamline on muslin at front edge on straight of grain, ½" (1.3 cm) from raw edge.

2) Pin marked line on muslin to welting of skirt seam, with center line centered on skirt; this positions muslin on straight of grain. Smooth muslin over front edge and deck, and match center lines of deck and back.

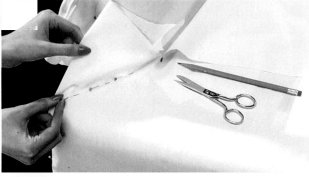

3) Mark deck and inside arm pieces with large dots, at point where deck meets front of inside arm. For furniture with T-cushion, clip excess deck fabric to dot. Fold out excess fabric on deck at front corner, forming a dart; pin and mark.

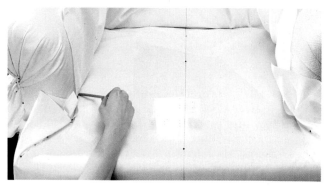

4) Pin deck to outside arm piece at side of chair; mark seamline. Do not fit deck snug. Push about ½" (1.3 cm) of fabric into crevices at sides and back of deck; mark seamlines by pushing pencil into crevices.

How to Pin-fit the Skirt

1) Measure for skirt around sides, front, and back to determine cut width of skirt; allow for gathers or pleats. Plan seam placement, based on width of fabric and size of furniture, so seams are concealed in gathers or pleats whenever possible; plan a seam at back corner where zipper will be inserted. Cut number of fabric widths needed; cut muslin pieces 1" (2.5 cm) longer than length of skirt.

2) Place raw edge of muslin just below lower edge of skirt; pin at upper edge of skirt, keeping muslin straight and even. Pin seams as you come to them; pin out fullness for pleats or gathers. Pin vertical tucks in skirt, pinning ⅛" (3 mm) tuck near back corner on each side of chair and ¼" (6 mm) tuck near each corner on back of chair; tucks will be released in step 3, opposite, adding ease to skirt. Mark seams and placement of pleats or gathers.

How to Prepare the Pattern for Cutting

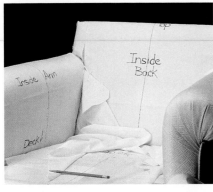

1) Mark upper edge of all muslin pieces; label pieces. Check that all seamlines, darts, gathers, and pleats are marked. Mark dots at intersecting seams; label.

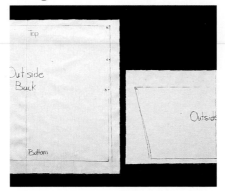

2) Remove muslin. Add ¼" (6 mm) ease to back edge of outside arm at lower corner. Add ½" (1.3 cm) ease to sides of outside back at lower corners. Taper to marked seamlines at upper corners.

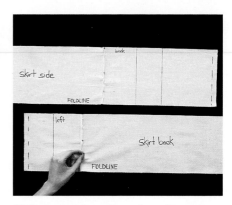

3) Remove the pinned tucks near back corners of skirt pieces. Mark "foldline" at lower edge of muslin for self-lined skirt.

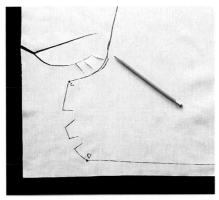

4) True straight seamlines, using straightedge; true curved seamlines, drawing smooth curves. Do not mark seamlines in pleated areas.

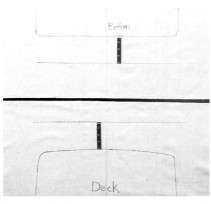

5) Add 4" (10 cm) to lower edge of inside back and back edge of deck.

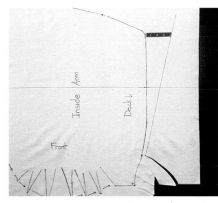

6) Mark the lower edge of inside arm from a point 4" (10 cm) away from seamline at back edge to ½" (1.3 cm) from large dot at front edge; repeat for sides of deck.

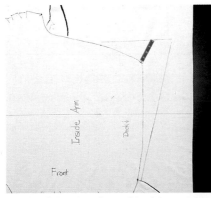

7) Mark back edge of inside arm from a point 4" (10 cm) away from seamline at the lower edge to ½" (1.3 cm) from large dot; repeat for sides of inside back.

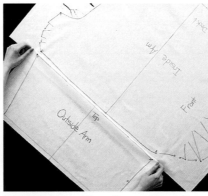

8) Check lengths of seamlines for adjoining seams; adjust as necessary to ensure that seamlines match.

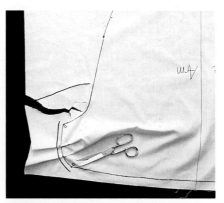

9) Fold pleats on marked lines. Mark seamlines in pleated area; add ½" (1.3 cm) seam allowances. Trim on cutting line through all layers of pleats. Add ½" (1.3 cm) seam allowances to any remaining seams. Cut pieces on marked lines.

259

Laying Out & Cutting the Fabric

Whenever possible, lay out all the pattern pieces on the fabric before you start to cut. This allows you to rearrange the pieces as necessary to make the best use of the fabric. For boxed cushions, follow the cutting directions on pages 268 and 269.

When a patterned fabric with an all-over design is used for slipcovers, little or no matching is required. If a patterned fabric with a one-way design is used, be careful to lay the pieces in the correct direction on the fabric. Patterned fabrics may be matched at the seamline on the upper edge of the skirt, if desired, following the technique for boxed cushions (page 273).

Center large motifs in a print fabric on the top and the bottom of the cushion. For best results, also align the design so it continues down the back of the furniture, onto the cushion, and down the skirt.

In addition to the pieces cut from the muslin pattern, you will need a 3" (7.5 cm) tacking strip cut on the straight of grain. This strip is used to secure the slipcover to the furniture with T-pins, tacks, or staples. Cut the length of the tacking strip equal to the distance around the furniture at the upper edge of the skirt.

Cut fabric strips for the welting as on page 40. Measure the seamlines that will have welting to determine the total length of the bias strips you will need to cut.

Tips for Laying Out and Cutting the Slipcover Fabric

Center large motifs, such as floral clusters, on the back, sides, cushions, and on the top of the arms.

Center the prominent stripe of a striped fabric on the center placement line of the outside and inside back pieces and on the cushion pieces. Decide in which direction the stripes will run on the arms; usually it is preferable to have the stripes run in the same direction as the stripes on the skirt.

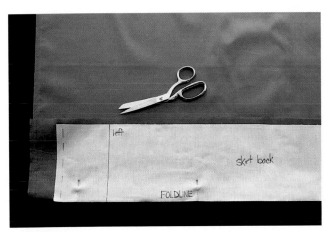

Cut the skirt pieces for a self-lined skirt, placing the foldline at lower edge of skirt on a crosswise fold of the fabric. Self-lined skirts hang better than single-layer skirts with a hem.

Cut arm pieces, right sides together, using the first piece as the pattern for cutting the second piece.

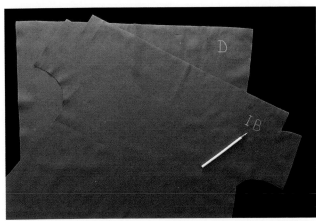

Mark names of pieces on wrong side of fabric, using chalk. Abbreviations like "D" for deck, "IB" for inside back, and "OA" for outside arm may be used.

Transfer all markings, including notches and dots, from the muslin pieces to the slipcover fabric.

Sewing the Slipcover

Although the slipcover for your piece of furniture may be somewhat different from the style shown, many of the construction steps will be the same. It will be helpful for you to lay out the pieces and think through the sequence for sewing the seams of your slipcover. The labeled notches on adjoining seams will help you see how the pieces are to be joined together. To minimize the handling of bulky quantities of fabric, stitch any small details, such as darts, before assembling the large pieces.

For durable seams, use a strong thread, such as long-staple polyester, and a medium stitch length of about 10 stitches per inch (2.5 cm). Because slipcovers have several thicknesses of fabric at intersecting seams with welting, use a size 90/14 or 100/16 sewing machine needle.

Add welting to any seams that will be subjected to stress and wear, because welted seams are stronger than plain seams. For decorative detailing, welting can also be added to seams such as around the outside back and at the upper edge of the skirt. On furniture with front arm pieces, welting is usually applied around the front arm as a design detail. To prevent welted seams from puckering, take care not to stretch either the welting or the fabric as the seam is stitched. When a welted seam will be intersected by another seam, remove ½" (1.3 cm) of cording from the end of the welting to prevent bulk at the seamline.

For a chair, apply a zipper to one of the back seams of the slipcover. For a sofa, apply zippers to both back seams.

How to Sew a Slipcover with a Pleated Front Arm

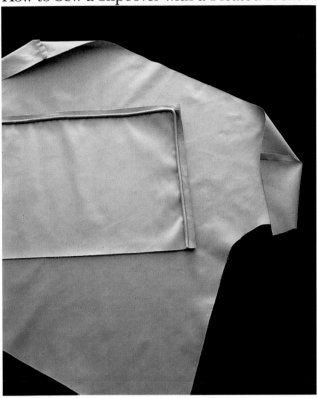

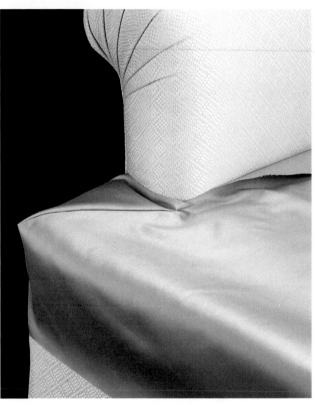

1) Stitch darts at upper corners of inside back. If welting is desired, apply it to upper and front edges of outside arm, pivoting at corner.

2) Stitch darts at outer front corners of deck; stop stitching ½" (1.3 cm) from raw edge at inner corner.

3) Stitch deck to front of arm and inside arm; this can be stitched as two separate seams.

4) Pin pleats in place at front and back of arm. Check the fit over arm of chair. Baste in place on seamline.

(Continued on next page)

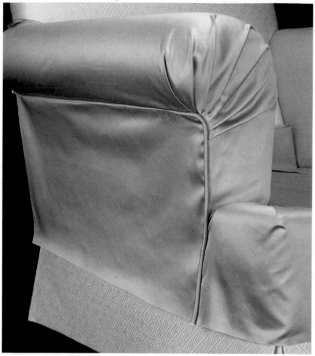

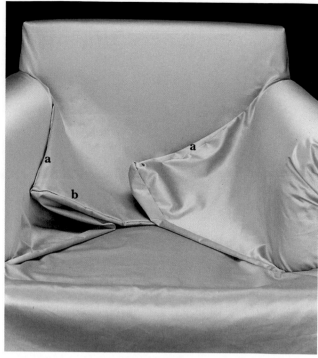

5) Stitch the horizontal and vertical seams, joining outside arm to inside arm; pivot at corner.

6) Pin inside arms to inside back on both sides **(a)**. Pin lower edge of inside back to back edge of deck **(b)**. Make tucks in seams at corners, if necessary, so pieces fit together. Stitch seams.

7) Apply welting around sides and upper edge of slipcover unit (page 40); curve ends of welting into seam allowance ½" (1.3 cm) from the lower edges (arrow). Join slipcover unit to outside back, leaving seam open for zipper application. Apply welting to lower edge.

8) Stitch skirt pieces together, leaving seam at back corner unstitched for zipper insertion; press seams open. Fold skirt in half lengthwise, wrong sides together; press.

9) **Press** pleats for pleated skirt. Or for gathered skirt, stitch gathering stitches by zigzagging over a cord as on page 31; for skirt with bunched gathers, stitch gathering stitches between the markings.

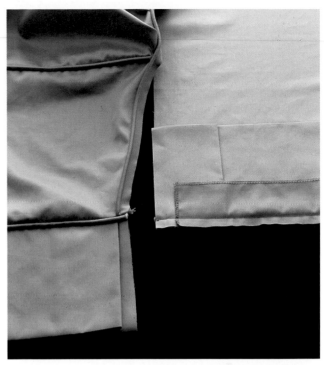

10) **Pin** tacking strip to upper edge of skirt on wrong side. Join the skirt to adjoining pieces; for gathered skirt, pull up gathers to fit. Apply zipper (page 267). Sew cushions (pages 269 to 271).

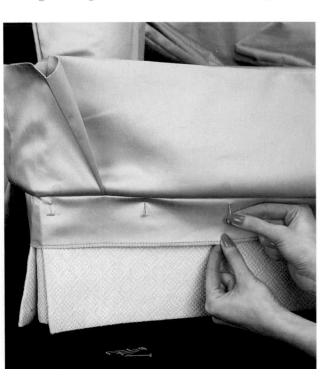

11) **Apply** slipcover to furniture. Secure tacking strip to furniture by pinning into upholstery with T-pins.

12) **Push** extra fabric allowance into crevices around the deck and inside back. Stuff 2" (5 cm) strips of polyurethane foam into crevices around deck to keep fabric from pulling out. Insert cushions.

How to Sew a Slipcover with Front Arm Piece

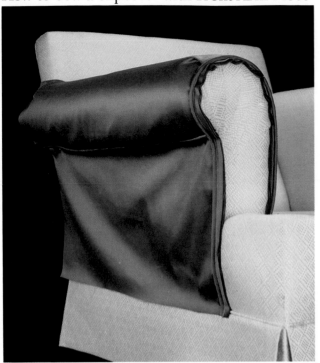

1) Stitch darts at upper corners of inside back. Apply welting to the upper edge of inside arm, if desired. Stitch horizontal seam, joining the outside arm to the inside arm. Pin and baste tucks at front edge of inside/outside arm. Apply welting to front edge of inside/outside arm.

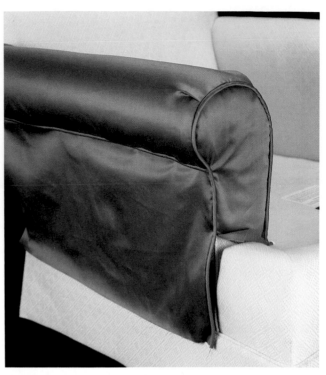

2) Stitch the front arm piece to the front edge of inside/outside arm; stop stitching 2" (5 cm) from outer end of front arm piece.

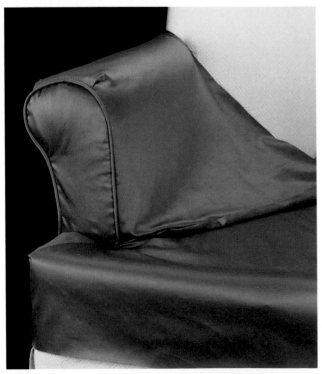

3) Follow steps 2 and 3 on page 263. Pin pleats in place at back of arm; baste in place on seamline.

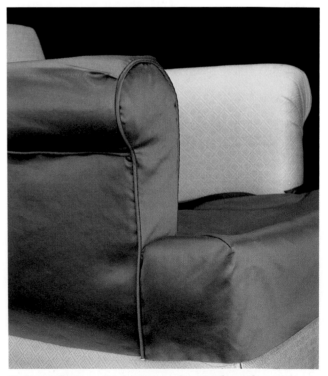

4) Complete vertical seam at front edge of outside arm. Finish the slipcover as on pages 264 and 265.

How to Apply the Zipper

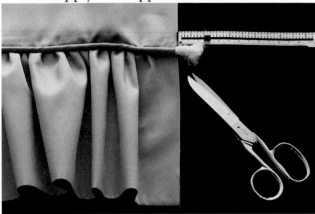

1) Pull the cording out slightly from ends of skirt opening; trim off ends 1" (2.5 cm). Pull seam to return cording to original position.

2) Press under seam allowances on zipper opening. Place open zipper on welted side of seam, so welting just covers zipper teeth and with zipper tab at lower edge. Pin in place; fold in seam allowance at lower edge of skirt to miter. Fold up end of zipper tape.

3) Edgestitch on skirt, using zipper foot, with zipper teeth positioned close to folded edge. Stitch in the ditch of the welted seam.

4) Close zipper. Place remaining side of zipper under seam allowance, with folded edge at welted seamline. Pin in place; fold in seam allowance at lower edge of skirt to miter. Fold up end of zipper tape.

5) Open zipper. Stitch ⅜" (1 cm) from folded edge, pivoting at top of zipper.

Pleated skirt. Follow steps 1 to 5, above, except break stitching at upper edge of the skirt. On skirt, stitch through lower layer of box pleat; stitch as close as possible to seam at upper edge of skirt.

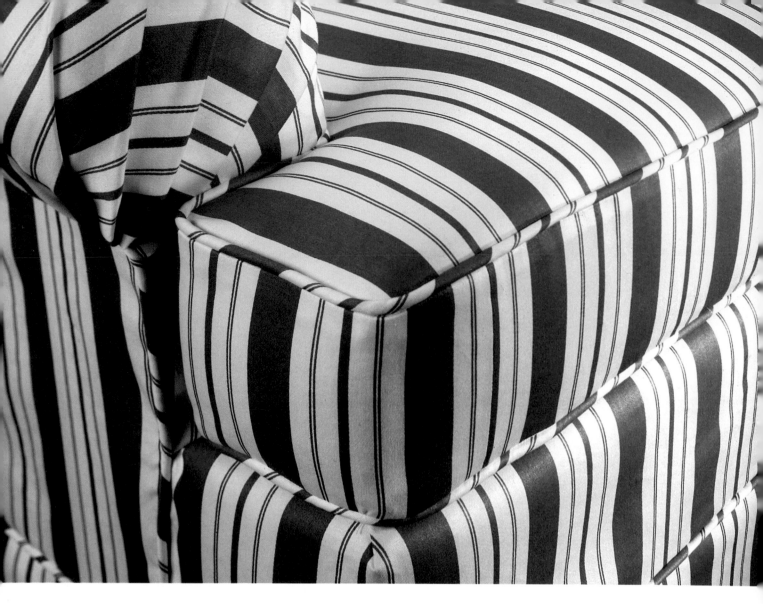

Slipcovers for Cushions

You can make slipcovers for cushions on benches or window seats, as well as on sofas or chairs. Often cushions have welting at the edges, which adds strength to the seams. Plain welting (pages 39 and 145) is most commonly used, but shirred cording (page 147) or twisted welting (page 148) may also be used.

To make it easier to insert the cushion, install a zipper across the back of the slipcover, extending around about 4" (10 cm) on each side. For cushions that are exposed on three sides, install a zipper across the back of the slipcover only. Use upholstery zippers, which are available in longer lengths than dressmaker zippers. The tab of the zipper will be concealed in a pocket at the end of the zipper opening. This is an upholsterer's technique that gives a professional finish.

✂ Cutting Directions

For a boxed cushion, cut the top and bottom pieces 1" (2.5 cm) larger than the cushion size to allow for seam allowances. T-cushions are pin-fitted, using muslin, to ensure accurate cutting. Cut two zipper strips, each the length of the zipper tape; the width of each zipper strip is equal to one-half the thickness of the cushion plus 1" (2.5 cm) for seam allowances. Cut a boxing strip the length of the cushion front plus twice the length of the cushion side; the width of the boxing strip is equal to the thickness of the cushion plus 1" (2.5 cm) for seam allowances. Seam boxing strips together as necessary. Cut and seam bias strips for welting (page 40). To match patterns on cushion, see page 273.

YOU WILL NEED

Decorator fabric.

Zipper, about 8" (20.5 cm) longer than back edge of cushion.

Fabric and cording for fabric-covered welting; or twisted welting.

How to Cut the Fabric for a T-cushion

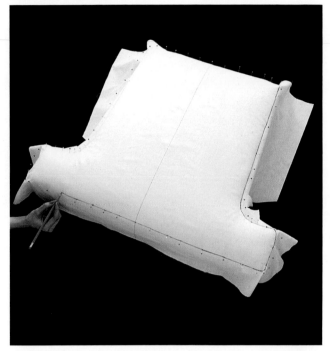

1) Cut muslin about 4" (10 cm) larger than top of cushion; mark grainline at center of fabric. Place muslin over cushion; pin along seamlines, smoothing out fabric. Mark seamlines along pin marks.

2) Remove muslin. True seamlines, using straightedge. Fold muslin in half to check that piece is symmetrical; make any necessary adjustments. Add ½" (1.3 cm) seam allowances. Cut cushion top and bottom from slipcover fabric. Cut zipper and boxing strips, opposite. Mark wrong side of fabric pieces, using chalk.

How to Sew a Slipcover for a Boxed Cushion

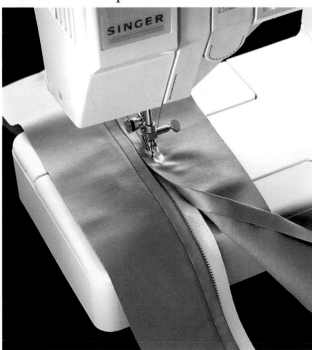

1) Press under ½" (1.3 cm) seam allowance on one long edge of each zipper strip. Position folded edges of strips along center of zipper teeth, right sides up. Using zipper foot, topstitch ⅜" (1 cm) from folds.

2) Press under 2" (5 cm) on one short end of the boxing strip. Lap the boxing strip over the zipper strip to cover zipper tab. Stitch through all layers 1½" (3.8 cm) from folded edge of boxing strip.

(Continued on next page)

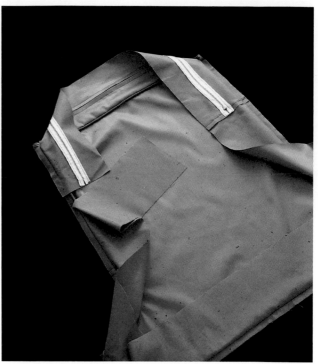

3) Make and apply plain welting as on pages 40 and 145; shirred cording as on page 147; or twisted welting as on pages 148 and 149, steps 1 to 5. Stitch welting to right side of top and bottom pieces.

4) Place boxing strip on slipcover top, right sides together; center zipper on back edge. Start stitching 2" (5 cm) from zipper end, crowding cording. Clip corners as you come to them; stop stitching 4" (10 cm) from starting point.

5) Clip to mark seam allowances at ends of boxing strip. Stitch boxing strip ends together. Trim excess fabric; finger-press seam open. Finish stitching boxing strip to slipcover top.

6) Fold boxing strip, and clip seam allowance to mark lower corners; be sure all four corners are aligned with corners on slipcover top. Open zipper.

7) **Place** boxing strip and slipcover bottom right sides together. Match clips of boxing strip to corners of slipcover bottom; stitch. Turn right side out.

8) **Fold** cushion to insert it into slipcover. If necessary, wrap cushion with plastic to help slide it into slipcover, then remove plastic.

9) **Stretch** cover from front to back. Close zipper. Smooth cushion from center to edges. Stretch welting taut from corner to corner to square the cushion.

Alternative zipper placement. Install zipper across the back of the slipcover, without extending it around the sides, if slipcover will be exposed on three sides.

Boxed Cushions with Welting

To update any room in the house, make new covers for loose cushions on chairs, benches, or window seats. Boxed cushions may be firm or soft, depending on the foam used. Foam is available in several thicknesses and densities. Use firm or medium density foam for seat cushions; select soft density foam for back cushions. Wrap the foam with bonded polyester batting to keep the cover from shifting and to soften the look of boxed cushions.

Install a zipper as for slipcovers for cushions (pages 268 and 269). Or install a zipper across only the back side for cushions that will be exposed on three sides (page 271).

✄ Cutting Directions

Cut top and bottom pieces 1" (2.5 cm) larger than finished cushion size to allow for seam allowances. Cut foam same size as top and bottom pieces for a firm, tight fit. Cut two zipper strips, each the length of the zipper tape; each zipper strip is half the thickness of finished cushion plus 1" (2.5 cm) for seam allowances. Cut boxing strip the length of cushion front plus twice the length of cushion side. Cut welting strips 1½" (3.8 cm) wide, with length 2 times the circumference of the cushion plus seam allowances.

YOU WILL NEED

Decorator fabric for top, bottom, boxing strips, and welting.

Upholstery bonded polyester batting to wrap all sides of cushion.

Foam in desired density and thickness.

Upholstery zipper, about 8" (20.5 cm) longer than back width measurement of cushion.

5/32" cording, 2 times the circumference of the cushion plus seam allowances.

How to Measure for and Cut a Boxed Cushion

1) Measure width and depth of cushion area to determine the size of finished cushion. Determine thickness of foam.

2) Cut fabric and foam. Mark the wrong side of fabric pieces with chalk.

How to Match Patterns on a Boxed Cushion

1) Cut cushion top, boxing strip, and bottom to match pattern at front seamlines. For reversible cushion, match pattern from cushion top, down boxing strip, and continue to the back.

2) Notch corners of boxing strip. Join boxing strip to cushion top and bottom, stitching front edge first. Then stitch along other sides of cushion.

Slip Seats

Upholstered seats on dining room or kitchen chairs are often referred to as slip seats. Because they are so easy to remove and reupholster, slip seats are a good choice for a beginning project. Whether the seat is worn or soiled, or if you simply want to change the fabric to coordinate with the room, a set of four chairs can easily be reupholstered in a day.

Most slip seats are made of a thin board, usually padded with foam and polyester batting. Another style of slip seat consists of an open wooden framework with a webbed top. The webbing is covered with burlap, and the seat may be padded with either horsehair and cotton batting or foam and polyester batting. If the padding is in good condition and the webbing is still taut, the chair seats can be reupholstered simply by removing the outer cover and attaching new fabric, as on page 276, steps 4 to 10. If the webbing is slack, the padding must be removed and the seat rewebbed. New foam and polyester batting can be attached, as on page 276, steps 2 and 3.

The slip seats of some chair styles drop into a recess in the chair seat. Other styles rest directly on the surface of the seat and may have welting attached around the lower edge. All styles are held in place by screws attached from the underside of the seat. Regardless of the style, if more than one chair in a set is being reupholstered, it is important to return seats to their original chairs, assuring proper fit and alignment of screw holes.

✂ Cutting Directions

Cut the fabric 6" (15 cm) larger than the length and width of the chair seat. If new padding is needed, cut the foam 1" (2.5 cm) larger than the length and width of the chair seat. Cut the batting roughly 4" (10 cm) larger than the length and width of the chair seat. Cut the cambric 2" (5 cm) larger than the chair seat.

For the welting at the bottom of the chair seat, cut fabric strips 1½" (3.8 cm) wide on either the bias or crosswise grain; the combined length of the strips is equal to the distance around the chair seat plus extra for seam allowances and butt joint.

YOU WILL NEED

Screwdriver; tack lifter or staple remover.

Foam, 1" (2.5 cm) thick.

Foam adhesive.

Polyester upholstery batting, 27" (68.5 cm) wide; 3 yd. (2.75 m) is sufficient for four chair seats.

Webbing and webbing stretcher, to replace webbing on webbed slip seat, optional.

Upholstery fabric.

Staple gun and ⅜" (1 cm) **staples.**

Welt cording, 5/32" (3.8 mm) diameter, for welting, optional.

Cambric, for underside of chair seat, optional; 2 yd. (1.85 m) is sufficient for four chair seats.

How to Upholster a Slip Seat

1) Remove screws on underside of seat; remove seat. Strip off existing outer fabric, using staple remover or tack lifter. If the foundation is intact, omit steps 2 and 3.

2) Apply spray adhesive to one side of foam; affix foam to top of seat.

3) Place upholstery batting on table; place seat, foam side down, over batting. Wrap batting around top and sides of seat. Trim excesss batting even with the bottom edge of seat.

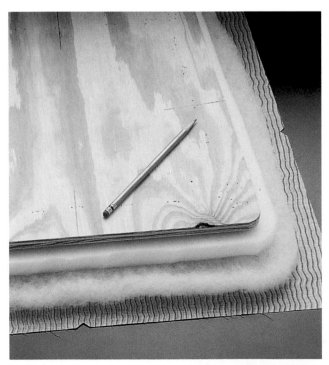

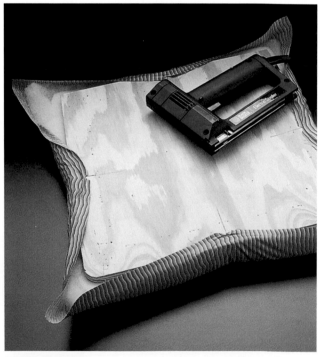

4) Mark center of each side on bottom of seat. Notch center of each side of fabric. Place fabric on table, wrong side up. Center the seat upside down over the fabric.

5) Staple fabric to bottom of seat at center back, matching center marks. Stretch fabric from back to front; staple at center front, matching the center marks. Repeat at center of each side.

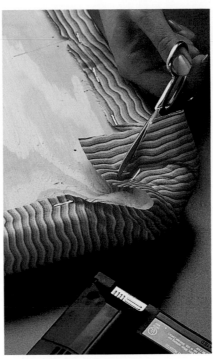

6) Apply staples to back of seat at 1½" (3.8 cm) intervals, working from center toward sides, to within 3" (7.5 cm) of corners. Pull fabric taut toward front of seat; staple. Repeat for sides.

7) Fold fabric diagonally at corner; stretch the fabric taut, and staple between screw hole and corner. Trim excess fabric diagonally across the corner.

8) Miter fabric at corner by folding in each side up to corner; staple in place. Repeat for remaining corners. Trim excess fabric, exposing screw holes. If welting is not desired, omit step 9. If cambric is not desired, omit step 10.

9) Make welting (page 40). Staple welting around seat at ¾" (2 cm) intervals, starting at back of seat; align stitching to edge of seat. Stretch welting slightly while stapling, and clip welting at corners and curves to help it lie flat.

10) Fold under raw edges of cambric; staple to bottom of seat at 1" (2.5 cm) intervals. Puncture cambric at screw holes in the chair seat. Screw upholstered seat to chair.

Carved-wood Footstools

Among the great finds at antique stores are footstools with lovely carved-wood frames. If the frame is still in good condition, the footstool can be restored to like-new condition by replacing the upholstery. Covered with a traditional fabric, such as tapestry or hand-stitched needlepoint, and trimmed with contrasting gimp or decorative nails, the footstool becomes a handsome room accessory.

The style shown here has a webbed base, originally covered with padding: possibly hair, cotton, or even straw. Footstools that originally had a spring foundation, with the webbing attached to the underside of the frame, may be reupholstered most easily by attaching new webbing to the upper side of the frame and padding the top with foam and batting.

YOU WILL NEED

Decorator fabric, such as tapestry fabric, or hand-stitched needlepoint.

Webbing and webbing stretcher.

Foam in 1" (2.5 cm) thickness; aerosol foam adhesive.

Polyester upholstery batting.

Burlap, for support under the foam.

Cambric, for dustcover on bottom of footstool.

Gimp trim; use gimp that matches fabric if decorative upholstery nails are being applied over the gimp, or use matching or contrasting color if gimp is used alone as a decorative edging.

Decorative upholstery nails, optional; upholstery hammer for inserting decorative nails.

Staple gun; 3/8" or 1/2" (1 or 1.3 cm) staples.

Hot glue gun and glue sticks.

How to Upholster a Footstool

1) Strip all layers of old fabric, padding, burlap, and webbing from the stool; remove all decorative nails and tacks. Refinish wood frame, if necessary.

2) Interweave webbing strips and secure folded ends to upper side of frame, using webbing nails (see page 290). Cut burlap 3" (7.5 cm) larger than the frame. Fold under edges of burlap; staple it to the top of the frame, over the webbing, at 1½" (3.8 cm) intervals, stretching burlap taut.

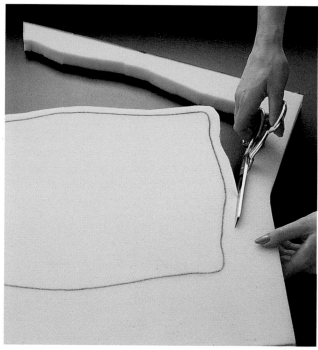

3) Place the footstool upside down on foam; draw outline of frame on foam, using pencil. Cut foam ½" (1.3 cm) beyond the marked lines, using scissors.

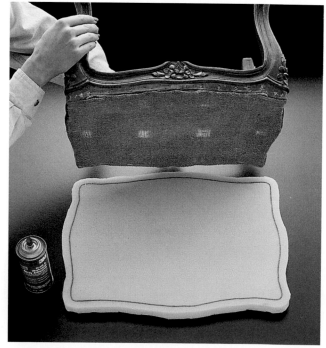

4) Apply aerosol adhesive to marked side of foam and to the burlap. Place the footstool upside down on foam, pressing down so foam adheres to the burlap. Stand footstool right side up; press down on foam.

5) Place a layer of upholstery batting over the foam, wrapping it around the sides of footstool; trim excess batting above the decorative wood.

6) Measure footstool length and width from decorative wood on one side, over foam and batting, to decorative wood on opposite side. Add 5" (12.5 cm) to these measurements; cut decorator fabric to this size.

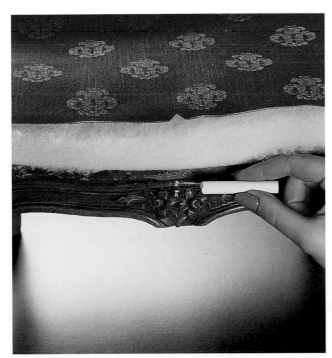

7) Notch the center of each side of the fabric; mark decorative wood on center of each side of footstool frame, using chalk.

8) Place fabric, right side up, over batting. Staple-baste center of fabric at center on front of frame, just above decorative wood, then at center on back of frame, stretching fabric slightly. Repeat in other direction, staple-basting fabric at center of each side.

(Continued on next page)

9) Remove the center staple from front of frame; stretch the fabric taut, and staple again at center. Working from center toward one side, apply staples at 1" (2.5 cm) intervals, stretching fabric taut; stop 3" (7.5 cm) from corner. Repeat, working from center toward opposite side.

10) Repeat step 9 on back of the footstool, stretching fabric taut; then repeat for sides of stool.

11) Stretch fabric at corner, dividing excess fullness equally on each side of corner; insert one staple, centered above the leg, just above decorative wood.

12) Fold fabric as shown, forming an inverted pleat, or "V," at the corner, folding out all excess fabric. Staple in place. Repeat at remaining corners.

13) Finish stapling each side at 1" (2.5 cm) intervals, up to corners, stretching the fabric taut. Trim excess fabric on all sides of the footstool, just above the decorative wood.

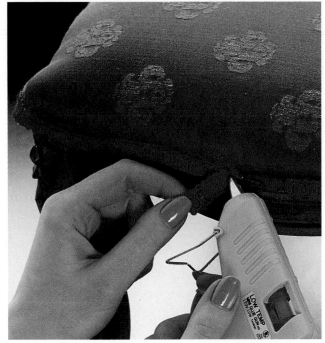

14) Glue gimp above the decorative wood, using hot glue gun, starting at center of one side; make sure that the raw edges and staples are covered. Fold under ½" (1.3 cm) at ends of gimp, and butt folded ends together. Omit step 15 if decorative nails are not being used.

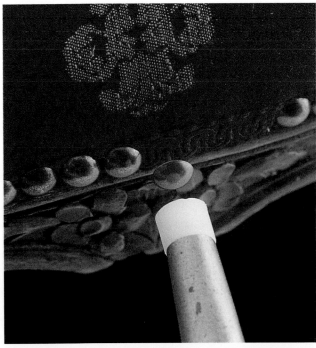

15) Tap the decorative nails into the wood, using upholstery hammer; center nails over gimp. Check the position of each nail before driving it in; if necessary, adjust vertical or horizontal position by tapping side of nail head slightly. Insert the nails head-to-head all around footstool.

16) Cut cambric 2" (5 cm) larger than the bottom of footstool. Fold under the edges of cambric; staple to the bottom of the footstool at 1" (2.5 cm) intervals.

Side chair has a decorative frame around the inset chair back and at the lower edge of the boxed seat. Double welting trims the seat, back, and arm posts.

Side Chairs

Small side chairs, often referred to as pull-up chairs, provide convenient extra seating when entertaining guests. The easy boxed-seat upholstery techniques on pages 286 to 291 can be used for a variety of side chair styles. These chairs may originally have padded boxed seats and inset backs, often framed with exposed decorative wood. Similar chairs may have pullover-style seats or loose boxed cushions. Chairs that originally had spring foundation seats can also be reupholstered using this easier method, if desired.

Before reupholstering, strip all layers of old fabric, padding, and burlap, and remove old webbing and any springs from the seat. Back webbing that is still in good condition and taut need not be replaced, unless the chair style has exposed wood with only a front tacking rail. Webbing must then be removed in order to replace the fabric that faces the back side of the chair. Refurbish the wood frame, if necessary.

✂ Cutting Directions

For the seat of the chair, cut a piece of burlap 3" (7.5 cm) larger than the chair frame. Cut cambric 2" (5 cm) larger than the bottom of the chair. Cut the fabric and the foam for the seat top as on page 286, step 2.

Cut the length of the boxing strip equal to the distance around the chair frame plus 2" (5 cm) overlap; if it is necessary to seam the boxing strip, add extra for seam allowances. For a chair with an exposed decorative seat frame, cut the width of the boxing strip equal to the foam thickness plus the distance from the top of the frame to the decorative wood plus 1½" (3.8 cm). For a chair without a decorative seat frame, cut the width of the boxing strip equal to the foam thickness plus the height of the frame plus 1½" (3.8 cm); the boxing strip wraps around to the bottom of the frame.

For the welting in the boxing seam, cut bias fabric strips (page 40), 1½" (3.8 cm) wide; the combined length of the strips is equal to the distance around the chair frame plus extra for seam allowances. For a chair with a decorative seat frame, also cut bias fabric strips, 3" (7.5 cm) wide, if double welting is to be used for the trim around the seat frame.

For the chair back, cut one rectangle of burlap, 5" (12.5 cm) larger than the frame opening. Cut two rectangles of fabric, 5" (12.5 cm) larger than

Side chair (above) is upholstered with a boxed seat that wraps under the chair frame. The inset chair back is trimmed with double welting.

the frame opening; these are to be used for the outside back and inside back pieces. Cut two or three layers of batting to the same size as the opening. If double welting is to be used, cut bias fabric strips, 3" (7.5 cm) wide.

For the chair arms, cut one rectangle of fabric, 4" (10 cm) larger than the area to be padded on the arm. Cut the batting to the size of the area to be padded. If double welting is to be used, cut bias fabric strips, 3" (7.5 cm) wide.

YOU WILL NEED

Decorator fabric; 2 yd. (1.85 m) is sufficient for most side chairs.

Welt cording, 5⁄32" (3.8 mm) diameter, for single welting and optional double welting.

Braid trim, such as gimp, if desired.

2 yd. (1.85 m) polyester or cotton upholstery batting, 27" (68.5 cm) wide.

Webbing and webbing stretcher.

Burlap, for reinforcing the seat and back.

1 yd. (0.95 m) cambric, for dustcover on bottom of chair.

Foam in 3" or 4" (7.5 or 10 cm) thickness, depending on style of chair; foam adhesive.

Hot glue gun and glue sticks, or white craft glue.

Staple gun; 3⁄8" or 1⁄2" (1 or 1.3 cm) staples.

How to Prepare the Chair and Sew the Boxed Seat

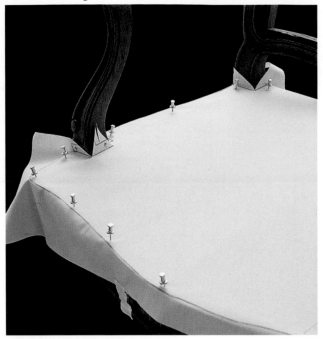

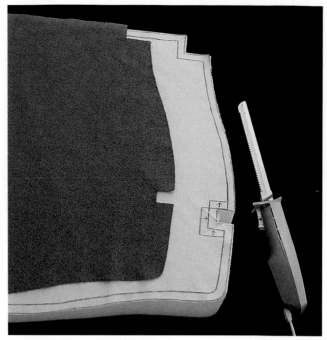

1) Make muslin pattern by placing muslin on frame, securing it with push pins. Mark muslin at edges of frame; draw around chair arms. For arms that slope out or back, redraw line ½" (1.3 cm) from original line so top of foam will fit around arm.

2) Remove muslin; add ½" (1.3 cm) seam allowances on all sides. Cut the fabric for seat top, following the pattern; cut the foam to same size for a firm, tight fit. Apply webbing and burlap to chair frame as on page 280, step 2. Affix foam over burlap, using spray adhesive.

3) Make welting; attach to right side of seat top (page 40). Clip welting seam allowances on rounded corner **(a)** or make one diagonal clip at square corner **(b).** Cut cord so ends butt; join ends, using tape. Stitch fabric strip ends so it lies flat.

4) Fold back 1" (2.5 cm) at end of boxing strip; place strip on seat top, right sides together, with fold at center back. Stitch seam, crowding the cording; clip the corners as in step 3. At end of seam, overlap ends of boxing strip.

5) Cover the top and sides of foam with upholstery batting, cutting the batting around the arm posts; trim away excess batting at corners. For chair with a decorative seat frame, trim batting above decorative wood.

How to Upholster the Seat of a Chair with Side Arm Posts

Chair with decorative frame. 1) Place seat cover over the batting; staple-baste the boxing strip to the frame at center front, just above the decorative wood. Repeat at the center back.

2) Smooth top of seat cover from side to side; fold back the boxing strip at arm post. Mark a line for a Y-cut from raw edge of boxing strip to within 2" (5 cm) of seam, aligning mark to center of arm post; cut on marked line.

3) Pull fabric down around the arm post. Repeat for opposite arm post.

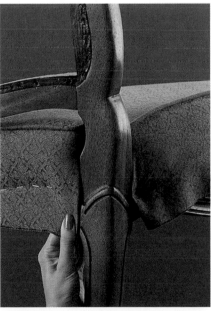

4) Remove staple at center back. At back corner, fold back boxing strip diagonally, as for chair with front arm posts on page 289, step 1. Mark line from raw edge to within 2" (5 cm) of seam, aligning mark to center of back post; cut on marked line. Repeat at opposite back post. Pull boxing strip down at back and side of chair frame.

5) Fold under fabric at side of chair, with fold along back post; staple boxing strip to chair frame at fold.

6) Repeat step 5 for opposite side of chair. On back of chair, staple boxing strip to frame, working from center toward sides. At back posts, fold under and staple fabric as in step 5.

(Continued on next page)

7) Pull fabric taut toward front of chair; staple boxing strip to front of frame, working from center toward sides of chair.

8) Fold under fabric along the front of the arm post as in step 5; staple boxing strip in front of arm post to frame.

9) Fold under fabric on the side of chair along back of arm post; staple boxing strip to side of the frame. Repeat for opposite side of chair.

10) Trim excess fabric on all sides of chair, just above decorative wood. Glue double welting (page 41) or gimp above the decorative wood, using hot glue or craft glue, making sure that raw edges and staples are covered. Butt the raw edges of double welting; or remove cording at ends and fold under edges. For gimp, fold under ends.

11) Fold under the edges of cambric; staple to the bottom of the chair at 1" (2.5 cm) intervals.

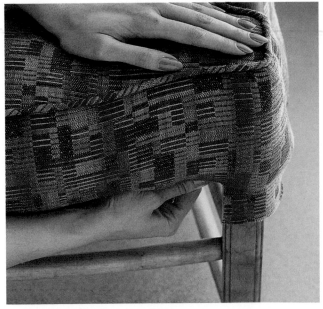

Chair without decorative frame. 1) Follow steps 1 to 7 on pages 287 and 288, except pull lower edge of boxing strip under frame, and staple to bottom of frame. Cut fabric at the front leg, from lower edge up to point where the leg and the bottom of frame meet; finish stapling boxing strip on front of chair frame up to the leg.

2) Cut fabric at side of chair, from lower edge up to point where leg and bottom of frame meet. At corner, trim excess fabric, allowing ¾" (2 cm) to fold under. Fold under fabric at front leg. Complete boxed seat as in steps 8 and 9, stapling lower edge to bottom of frame. Apply cambric as in step 11.

How to Upholster the Seat of a Chair with Front Arm Posts

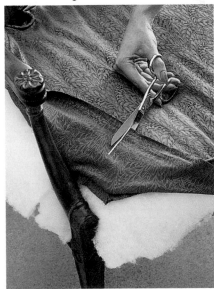

Chair with decorative frame. 1) Follow step 1 on page 287. Smooth the top of the seat cover from side to side; align welting seams around the front arm posts. Fold back the boxing strip diagonally at the arm post. Mark a line from raw edge to within 2" (5 cm) of seam, aligning mark to center of arm post; cut on marked line.

2) Pull the fabric down around the arm post. Repeat for opposite arm post. Follow steps 4 to 7 on pages 287 and 288. On front of chair, fold under and staple the fabric at the arm post as in step 5. Complete seat as in steps 9 to 11, opposite.

Chair without decorative frame. Follow steps 1 and 2, left, except pull lower edge of boxing strip around to bottom of chair frame, and staple to bottom of frame.

How to Upholster the Chair Back

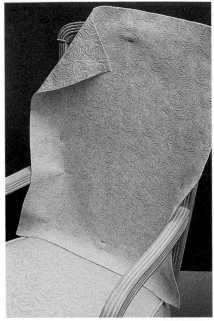

Tacking rail on inside back. 1) Apply fabric rectangle for outside back, with right side toward back of chair, staple-basting fabric at the center top to tacking rail on inside back of frame, 1/4" (6 mm) from molding. Repeat at center bottom and center of each side.

2) Staple the fabric from the center bottom, up to the beginning of curve at rounded corners or up to 3" (7.5 cm) from square corners. Staple fabric at top, stretching fabric taut; repeat at each side. Staple fabric at the corners. Trim excess fabric next to staples. Place one layer of batting over fabric.

3) Interweave webbing strips, folding ends under and stapling to tacking rail; webbing strips do not have to be folded over. Staple burlap over webbing; trim excess.

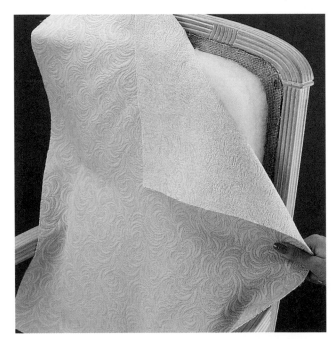

4) Place two layers of batting over the burlap. Place fabric rectangle for inside back, right side up, over batting: staple. Trim the excess fabric, and apply double welting or gimp as on page 288, step 10; butt ends of double welting, or fold under ends of gimp.

Tacking rails on inside and outside back. Follow steps 3 and 4, above and left. From back of chair, apply fabric rectangle for outside back, right side out, stapling into tacking rail on outside back of frame. Trim excess fabric, and apply double welting or gimp as on page 288, step 10.

How to Upholster the Chair Arms

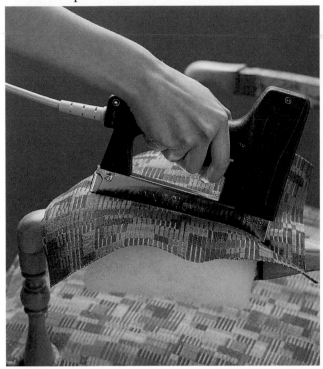

Wrapped arm pad. 1) Place two or three layers of batting on top of arm. Place fabric right side up over the batting; staple at back of arm.

2) Stretch to front of arm; staple. Pull fabric around arm; staple to bottom of arm. On opposite side, pull fabric around arm, folding under edge; staple.

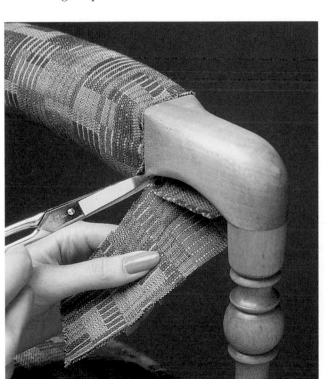

3) Finish stapling along back and front of arm. Trim excess fabric. Glue double welting or gimp as on page 288, step 10.

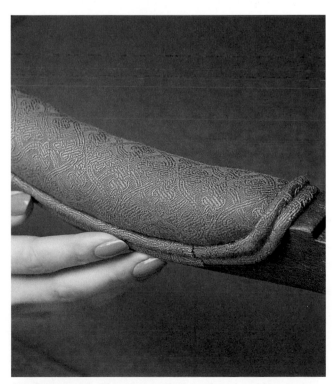

Oval arm pad. Place two or three layers of batting on top of arm. Place fabric right side up over the batting. Secure fabric as for chair back, steps 1 and 2, opposite. Trim excess fabric, and apply double welting or gimp as on page 288, step 10; butt ends of double welting, or fold under ends of gimp.

Accent with Trimming

The addition of a trim may be all that is needed to create a decorator look or embellish a special treatment. Fringe, tassels, braid, silk cord, lace, ribbons, and bows are custom trimmings that add fancy finishing touches throughout the home. Use them on window treatments, valances, and tiebacks as well as on pillows, cushions, and duvets.

Trimmings should be compatible with the mood of the room as well as the weight and care of the fabric. Silky braids and tassels are perfect partners with elegant high-gloss fabrics. Eyelet and lace edgings are essential to a romantic, feminine look. Be sure that washable trimmings are used on washable items.

To mark placement lines for trimmings, use a water-soluble marking pen or a marking pen with lines that evaporate. If pins distort the trim when it is temporarily positioned for stitching, use glue stick to hold the trim in place. If a project lacks interest after it is finished, an applied trim can save it.

Allow extra trim for mitering corners. To be sure that the miter is perfect, you may want to test the trim in place and then baste it in position before stitching, especially when a patterned braid or eyelet needs matching at the corners.

1) Edgings have one raw edge and one finished edge. Lace and eyelet edgings may be flat or preruffled and pregathered. The unfinished edge is stitched in a seam or under a hem. If used on the surface, the raw edge may be covered with a ribbon or braid.

2) Twisted cords are available with an attached woven banding that can be stitched in a seam allowance.

3) Loop fringe has continuous, uncut loops attached to a band heading. The heading may be stitched or glued onto a hem.

4) Tasseled tiebacks are decorative twisted cords with tassels for holding draperies or curtains open.

5) Tasseled fringe has small tufts or tassels attached to a heading. The heading may be stitched or glued onto a hem.

6) Fringe is made of loose strands knotted through a finished heading. The heading may be stitched or glued onto a hem.

7) Ribbons are available in a wide range of colors and widths for every decorative application. Grosgrain is a fine, narrow corded weave. Satin is a smooth weave with sheen. Velvet has dense pile weave on one side. Taffeta is crisp, shiny ribbon with plain, plaid, or moiré finish. Ribbons are stitched, glued, or fused onto the surface.

8) Gimp is a narrow decorative braid with a loop or scroll design in one or two colors, used to cover seams and raw edges. It may be glued or stitched in place.

9) Braid has several strands or cords braided together to form a flat surface trim. It is applied on the surface of an item, not in a seam, and is either stitched, glued, or fused in place.

10) Band trims have two finished edges. They are applied the same way as braid.

Trimming Ideas

Tie a wide ribbon and a narrow ribbon of contrasting colors in large bow for tieback or ties on chair seats.

Sew or fuse braid or banding along drapery edges. Use purchased trim, or cut stripes or strips from fabric.

Use flat braid down the sides or along the bottom edge of roller shades.

Use narrow ribbon as bows to tie quilts and comforters.

Apply silky cord on edges of pillows.

Use straight and looped fringe as traditional trims on edges of valances.

Apply lace on ruffled edges for quick hem on duvets, dust ruffles, and tablecloths.

Sew flat lace or eyelet on edges of pillow shams over solid colors.

Glue or sew braid or banding on edges of lampshades.

Sew six tucks down center of duvet cover; press three each way. Sew a row of lace edging down outside edges of tucks. Repeat on pillow shams.

Drape narrow decorative cord along the upper edge of a scalloped curtain (page 85), echoing the arc of the scallops. Hand-tack cord at the base of each tab or ring.

Cords & Tassels

Decorative cord gives a window treatment the look of elegance and high style. It can be draped in creative ways to emphasize design lines of the treatment or used for opulent tiebacks. Tassels are the perfect accompaniments for cord embellishments, since they are designed to look like beautifully ravelled cord ends. By themselves, tassels can be used for decorative accents in various ways.

Decorative cords and tassels are available in a variety of colors and sizes as well as fiber contents. Some cords are made of decorative threads wrapped around a plain cotton core and then twisted into a rope. Other twisted rope styles are made entirely of decorative threads.

Purchased cord and tassel tiebacks, while impressive, can also be very expensive. Decorative cord can be purchased in precut lengths, called *chair ties*, with

attached tassels at the ends; however, the length is not adjustable. As an attractive alternative, cords that are made entirely of decorative threads can be successfully raveled and given self tassels. Cords that do not ravel attractively can be given fringe end caps.

YOU WILL NEED

For self tassel:

Decorative cord; about 12" (30.5 cm) extra cord is needed for each tassel.

Heavy thread.

Gimp or other narrow decorative braid in coordinating color; needle and thread to match gimp or braid.

For end cap:

Heavy thread.

Liquid fray preventer.

Fringe with decorative heading, in color and fiber content to coordinate with decorative cord.

How to Make Self Tassels

1) Bind cord with heavy thread 3" to 4" (7.5 to 10 cm) from end. Ravel ends of cord up to knot; steam press to straighten threads.

2) Cut a length of cord 6" to 8" (15 to 20.5 cm) long. Ravel cord, keeping sets of threads separate; steam press to straighten threads.

3) Layer sets of thread on flat surface. Place raveled cord end over layered threads, aligning ends.

4) Wrap layered threads evenly around the cord. Bind the wrapped cord with heavy thread just above first binding.

5) Fold upper threads down over lower threads and raveled cord end, forming tassel. Bind with heavy thread ¾" (2 cm) below top of tassel.

6) Wrap gimp or narrow braid over the binding. Turn under end of gimp; hand-stitch. Stitch several times straight through tassel to secure. Trim tassel end evenly.

How to Make Fringe End Caps

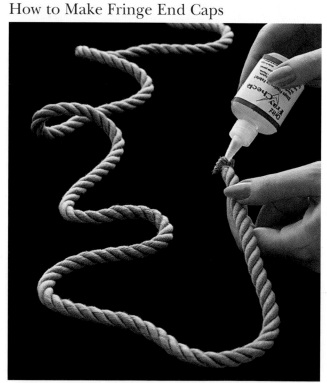

1) Bind cord with heavy thread ¼" (6 mm) from end. Apply liquid fray preventer to cord end. Allow to dry.

2) Wrap fringe twice around cord end, covering binding. Turn under heading; hand-stitch. Stitch several times straight through end cap to secure.

Fabric Rosettes

Use fabric rosettes as decorative accents at the corners of swags and on tiebacks, valances, and chair backs. They need a fairly crisp fabric such as chintz or moiré to stand up; in a soft fabric they take on a draped look. Rosettes may be cut on either the crosswise grain or on the bias; they have a softer effect when cut on the bias.

The directions that follow are for a 7" (18 cm) rosette. For a smaller rosette, reduce cutting measurements proportionately. The finished rosette is as wide as the original cut strip.

✀ Cutting Directions

Cut fabric strip 7" (18 cm) wide and 72" (183 cm) long for 7" (18 cm) rosette.

How to Sew a Fabric Rosette

1) Fold strip in half lengthwise, *wrong* sides together; gather raw edges; stitch across short ends to round the corners. Trim excess fabric at ends.

2) Roll one of the rounded ends tightly toward center to make center of rosette.

3) Continue rolling loosely toward opposite end, tacking gathers together with needle and thread.

4) Shape "petals" with your hands. Hand-tack rosette in place.

Tie chair seat cushions in place with bows.

Use bows on curtain tiebacks.

Use bows to accent table toppers or swags.

Bows & Knots

How to Sew a One-piece Bow or Knot

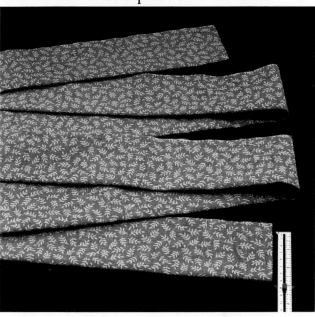

One of the easiest ways to accent a decorating scheme or give a new look is with large, soft bows or knots. At the window, use bows or knots to trim the corners of swags, to shape drapery or curtain panels into pouffed tiers, and to tie valances into draped scallops for a swag or cloud effect. Streamers, 16" to 20" (40.5 to 51 cm) long, give a luxurious effect.

In addition, bows or knots are a quick alternative to more tailored curtain and drapery tiebacks. To use as tiebacks on ruffled curtains, slit the panel next to the ruffle and seal the cut edges with liquid fray preventer; tie a bow through the slit, so the ruffle is not crushed. Sew a small plastic ring to the center of the bow, or knot the section to use as a tieback. You can also use bows or knots to trim lampshades and to anchor seat cushions on chairs.

The speediest bows or knots can be sewn from one continuous tube of fabric. Cut the tube into appropriate sections as needed. For best results, use lightweight fabric with a crisp finish. To add body to limp fabrics, apply soft fusible interfacing to the wrong side of the fabric before cutting and sewing.

1) Cut strips 7" (18 cm) wide for 3" (7.5 cm) wide bows or knots, and 9" (23 cm) wide for 4" (10 cm) wide bows or knots. Cut strips as long as possible, so multiple bows or knots can be cut from each strip. Fold strip in half lengthwise, right sides together. Sew seam on one long edge. Turn right side out, and press.

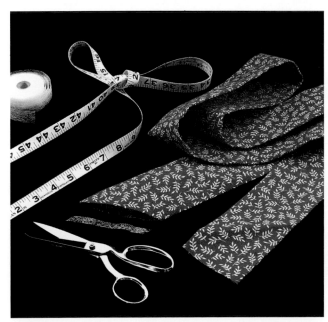

2) Cut strip into bow-length or knot-length sections. Determine length of sections by tying tape measure into bow or knot for desired effect. Cut ends of sections at an angle. Fold raw edges into tube, and press. Fuse or glue openings closed.

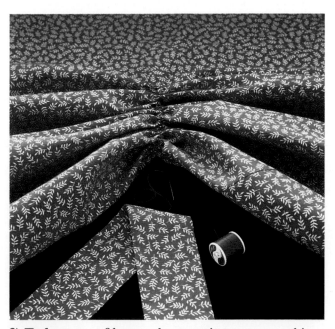

3) Tack center of bow or knot section to seat cushions and tie. Or, for tiebacks or swags, tie bow before attaching.

Bow
Picture Hangers

These attractive bows are used to accent a painting or portrait. They add interest to the wall at a higher level than most room furnishings, and they draw the eye upward, visually adding height to a room. Originally used to support the weight of pictures, bow picture hangers are now used as decorative, nonfunctional accessories.

Bow picture hangers are an excellent use for the long, narrow side cuts of fabric that are frequently left over after sewing other projects. For best results, use a fabric that has body, so the bow will hold its shape. Chintz and moiré are frequently used for crisp bows.

Bow picture hangers can be made to any size. The instructions that follow are for a picture hanger about 50" (127 cm) long.

✂ Cutting Directions

Cut one 11" × 34" (28 × 86.5 cm) piece of decorator fabric for bow, two 7" × 54" (18 × 137 cm) pieces for tails, and two 3" × 5" (7.5 × 12.5 cm) pieces for ties. These measurements include ½" (1.3 cm) seam allowances.

YOU WILL NEED

Decorator fabric.

Small plastic curtain ring.

How to Sew a Bow Picture Hanger

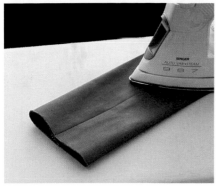

1) Fold bow piece in half lengthwise, right sides together; stitch long edges. Press seam open. Turn right side out. Press, centering seam on back of bow.

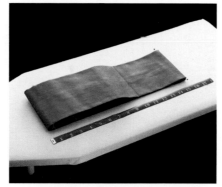

2) Stitch short ends, right sides together. Turn right side out. Fold in half, with seam at one end; pin-mark foldline. Stitch across the width of the bow, through all layers, 10" (25.5 cm) from seam.

3) Flatten bow, with stitching lines and marked foldline in the middle of the bow. Stitch through all layers at middle.

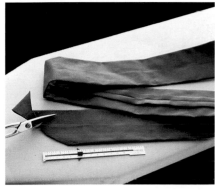

4) Stitch long edges of each tail, right sides together; press seam open. Center seam on back; mark points 2" (5 cm) up from lower edge at sides. Draw lines from marks to ½" (1.3 cm) from raw edge at the center. Stitch on marked lines; trim excess fabric.

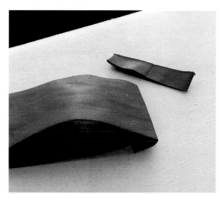

5) Turn tails right side out; press, centering seams on back. Press under ¾" (2 cm) at upper edge of one tail; trim ¾" (2 cm) from remaining tail. With right sides up, place tails together as shown.

6) Fold both tails over 4" (10 cm) from fold at upper edge. Stitch through all layers ¼" (6 mm) from first fold.

7) Fold in raw edges of tie pieces to make ties 1¼" × 5" (3.2 × 12.5 cm); press. Pinch bow at center. Hand-stitch one tie over center of bow, turning under raw edge.

8) Pull remaining tie through the previous tie. Pinch tails 4" (10 cm) from upper edge. Hand-stitch tie around tails, turning under raw edge.

9) Stitch curtain ring on back of bow for hanging on wall.

Decorating
with Lace

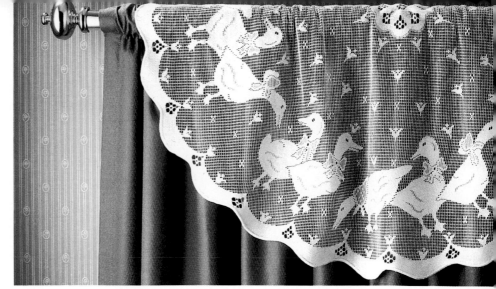

Valances. Drape circular lace panel over decorative pole rod for a timesaving valance. Use purchased round tablecloth, or cut circle from allover lace. No hems are necessary.

Tieback curtains. Stitch rod pocket heading on lace panel. Insert rod, and hang panel. Tie bow or tieback around lace. To make a bishop's sleeve curtain, use lace panel that is about 24" (61 cm) longer than measurement from rod to floor. Attach one or two tiebacks, and puff up lace panel to create bishop's sleeve effect. Allow lower edge to puddle gracefully onto floor.

Pillows. Slipcover pillows with tie-on lace cases to refresh a solid-color pillow. Cut lace sections to size of pillow plus ½" (1.3 cm) for seams. Stitch lace square on three sides. Use ribbon to tie fourth side closed.

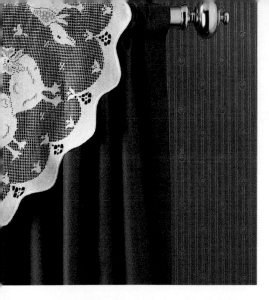

Tied panels. Thread satin or grosgrain ribbon through tops of lace panels. To hang panels, tie bows or knots over decorative curtain or shower rod.

Lampshades and shutters. Gather lace over lampshade frame. Staple lace panels behind shutter openings or to the frame of a folding screen.

Table toppers. Cut a lace circle, or purchase a round lace tablecloth. Trim edge with ruffled wide-lace trim, or divide edge into 6 to 8 sections and gather into swags. To show off lace pattern most effectively, layer lace over solid-color or printed floor-length cloth.

Transparent Appliqués

One or more layers of sheer fabric can be used to make an elegant transparent appliqué which can be added to sheer curtains or table linens. The sheer fabric is placed on the wrong side of the background fabric; the layers are stitched together along the design lines, and the background fabric is trimmed away from the right side to create sheer openings.

How to Apply a Transparent Appliqué

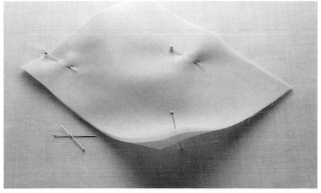

1) Mark placement of appliqué. Place background fabric right side down. Pin one or more layers of sheer fabric to background fabric, right side down, inserting pins at placement points of design. Remove pins from right side of fabric.

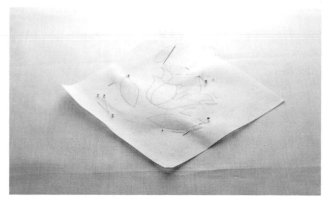

2) Cut tear-away stabilizer at least 2" (5 cm) larger than area to be appliquéd. Trace design onto stabilizer; if using an asymmetrical design, trace the mirror image. Position stabilizer over sheer fabric layers, matching placement points of design; pin in place. Baste stabilizer to garment through all layers. Remove pins.

3) Stitch three rows of straight stitches on outer design lines from wrong side, using short stitch length. Trim background fabric within design areas close to stitching. Insert a pin into background fabric layer; lift and clip a few threads, making an opening that allows for easier trimming without cutting sheer fabric.

4) Stitch three rows of straight stitches on remaining design lines, from wrong side. Trim away one or more sheer layers from right side of fabric, within design areas, using a pin to separate sheer layers for easier trimming.

5) Set machine for closely spaced zigzag stitches; set stitch width, as desired. Loosen needle thread tension, if necessary, so bobbin thread will not show on right side. Satin stitch around appliqué, as for cutwork (pages 310 and 311).

6) Remove tear-away stabilizer. Trim excess sheer fabric outside design area, from wrong side, close to the stitching.

Cutwork

Cutwork detailing has open, cutout design areas that are outlined with satin stitching. Cutwork is often used on fine linens.

Cutwork designs are available, but stencil designs may also be used for cutwork. Both cutwork and stencil designs include bars or bridges, which connect the cutout areas of the cutwork and add stability. If you design your own cutwork, be sure to place bars at frequent intervals. In selecting or planning a cutwork design, keep in mind that it is easier to stitch around large shapes than to follow intricate designs. Select a

closely woven fabric that does not ravel easily, such as batiste, chambray, or lightweight linen. All-purpose thread may be used to stitch along the design lines and reinforce the cutout areas; however, for the satin stitching, cotton or rayon machine embroidery thread is recommended. Use a size 70/9 or 80/11 needle.

Stitch the cutwork on the fabric before cutting out the garment section whenever possible. To prevent puckering, place water-soluble stabilizer under the fabric and place the fabric in an embroidery hoop.

How to Sew Cutwork

1) Trace mirror image of design on water-soluble stabilizer that is cut larger than embroidery hoop. Baste stabilizer to wrong side of fabric. Position fabric in hoop; place stabilizer side up.

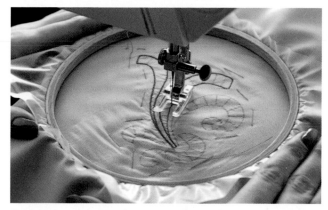

2) Remove presser foot to position hoop under the needle; attach open-toe presser foot. Reinforce outline of design by stitching three rows of straight stitches on design lines, using short stitch length; do not stitch bars.

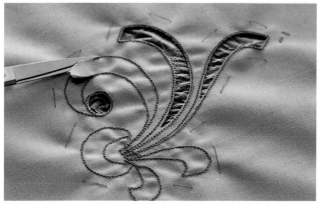

3) Remove fabric from hoop. Cut away fabric in open areas of design ¹⁄₁₆" (1.5 mm) from reinforcement stitches, using embroidery or appliqué scissors; do not cut through the stabilizer. Place fabric, stabilizer side up, in hoop.

4) Stitch three rows of straight stitches on design lines for bars, stitching bars to outer edge of previous rows of outline stitching; second row of stitching can be stitched using reverse setting. Clip threads carried from one design area to another.

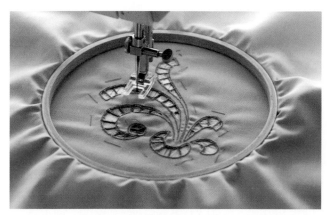

5) Place fabric in hoop right side up. Set machine for zigzag stitching, with stitch width just wide enough to cover straight stitches of bars. Satin stitch over bars.

6) Adjust stitch width so it is wide enough to cover straight stitches and raw edges. Satin stitch cutwork openings so needle stitches just over edge of fabric (pages 310 and 311); work from center of design out, stitching small details first. Remove stabilizer; press, wrong side up, on padded surface.

How to Satin Stitch Corners and Curves of Cutwork

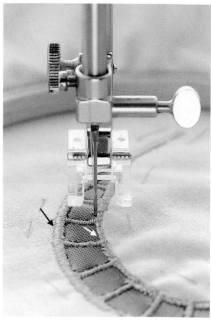

Inside corners. Stitch one stitch past edge of opening, stopping with needle down in stabilizer at inner edge of satin stitching; raise presser foot. Pivot and satin stitch next side of opening, covering previous stitches at corner.

Outside corners. Stitch past corner a distance equal to width of satin stitch, stopping with needle down at outer edge of satin stitching; raise presser foot. Pivot and satin stitch next side of opening, covering previous stitches at corner.

Curves. Raise presser foot and pivot fabric frequently, pivoting with needle down at longest edge of satin stitching (arrows).

How to Satin Stitch Inside Points of Cutwork

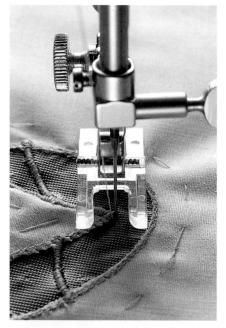

1) Stitch one stitch past the edge of opening, stopping with needle down in stabilizer at inner edge of satin stitching; raise presser foot.

2) Pivot fabric to an angle slightly less than 90°. Stitch two to four stitches, stopping when stitches just cover previous stitches; stop with needle down on inner edge of satin stitching. Raise presser foot.

3) Pivot fabric; continue satin stitching next side of opening.

How to Satin Stitch Outside Points of Cutwork

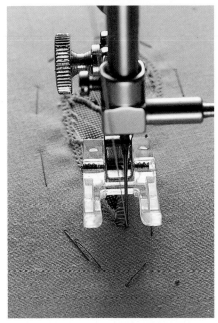

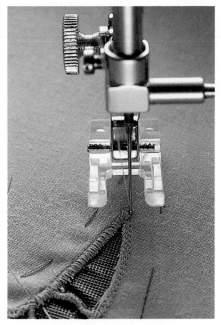

1) Stitch past point a distance equal to width of satin stitch, stopping with needle down at outer edge of satin stitching; raise presser foot.

2) Pivot fabric to an angle slightly less than 90°. Stitch two to four stitches, stopping when stitches just cover previous stitches; stop with needle down on outer edge of satin stitching. Raise presser foot.

3) Pivot fabric; continue satin stitching next side of opening.

How to Satin Stitch Tapered Outside Points

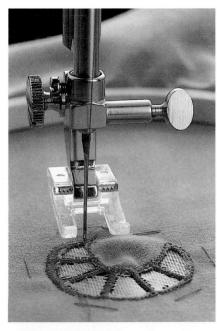

1) Stitch past point a distance equal to width of satin stitch, stopping with needle down at inner edge of satin stitching; raise presser foot.

2) Pivot fabric slightly. Continue stitching, gradually narrowing stitch width to 0 and stopping directly in front of point.

3) Turn fabric; stitch over previous stitches, gradually widening stitch width to original width and stopping at inner edge of satin stitching when stitches meet the finished side of opening. Pivot fabric slightly. Satin stitch next side of opening.

Monograms

Although the automatic monogram stitch patterns on computerized sewing machines are convenient and easy to stitch, you may want to create different sizes or styles of monograms, using free-motion machine embroidery.

Monograms can either be drawn directly onto the fabric or onto a piece of water-soluble stabilizer. If you are monogramming a bath towel or sweater, it is easier to draw the monogram on water-soluble stabilizer than it is to draw it on the textured fabric; the stabilizer is then placed over the fabric to use as a guide for stitching. Draw a horizon line under each letter and keep it horizontal as you stitch so the stitching will automatically taper in the right places.

Use a narrow, wooden hoop or a spring hoop for monogramming. Wooden hoops with fixing screws hold the fabric more tightly, but spring hoops are available in the small sizes needed for areas such as pockets, cuffs, and collars. It is helpful to place tear-away stabilizer under the hoop to prevent the fabric from puckering.

You can use either 30-weight or 40-weight machine embroidery thread for monogramming; the 30-weight thread is a little heavier and fills in faster than 40-weight thread.

Practice stitching the upper case "M" and lower case "e", because these two letters include all the techniques required for the other letters in the alphabet. When you monogram, think of the sewing machine needle as a pencil. Start to stitch each letter at the same place you would start writing it with a pencil.

The size of the letter determines the stitch width; the larger the letter, the wider the stitch width. The widest stitch width setting on the sewing machine works well for 2" (5 cm) letters, but a medium stitch width should be used for smaller letters.

How to Stitch an Upper Case "M" Monogram

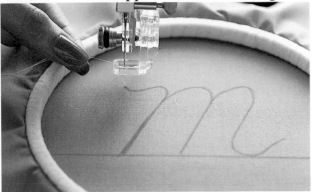

1) Draw an upper case "M" about 2" (5 cm) high on fabric; draw horizon line under letter. Place fabric in embroidery hoop. Set stitch width to 0. Draw up bobbin thread at top of "M"; stitch in place a few times to secure stitches. Set stitch width to the widest setting.

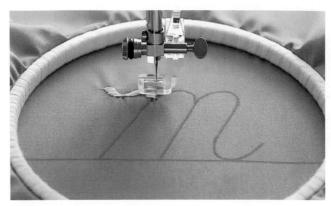

2) Satin stitch up to the first stem of the letter, using short zigzag stitches; keep horizon line horizontal as you sew.

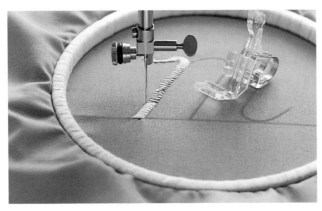

3) Stitch down the first stem of the letter, using longer zigzag stitches, to prevent a buildup of stitches on the stem. Satin stitch back over the stem, using short, closely spaced zigzag stitches. (Darning foot was removed to show detail.)

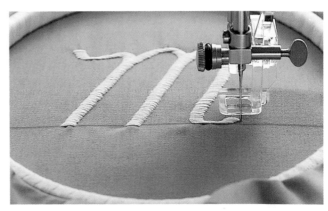

4) Continue satin stitching to second stem of letter; repeat step 3 for second stem. Satin stitch remainder of letter. Set stitch width to 0 and secure stitches.

How to Stitch a Lower Case "e" Monogram

1) Draw lower case "e" about 1" (2.5 cm) high on fabric; draw horizon line under letter. Place fabric in embroidery hoop. Set stitch width to 0. Draw up bobbin thread at left side of "e"; secure stitches. Set stitch width to a medium setting.

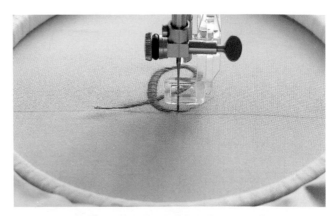

2) Satin stitch, using short, closely spaced zigzag stitches; stitch on the outside of loop so center of loop does not become too small. Keep the horizon line horizontal as you sew. Set the stitch width to 0 and secure stitches.

Tips for Monogramming

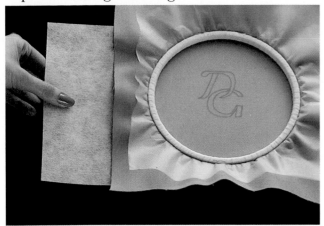

Trace letters on water-soluble stabilizer. Place the stabilizer on right side of fabric; position in hoop. Place tear-away stabilizer under hoop during stitching. Remove both stabilizers after stitching.

Change direction of the horizon line, such as placing it on the diagonal, so tapering of letter changes position for a different look.

Change direction of the horizon line within a letter for added emphasis.

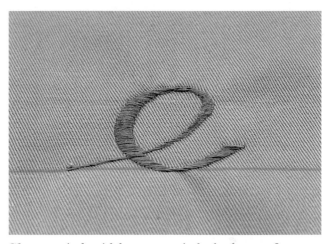

Change stitch width as you stitch the letters for an interesting effect. Change the width when sewing side stitch or at top of letter so width change is less noticeable and flows with the letter.

Stitch larger letters first with narrower stitches; then repeat stitching with wider stitches if raised or padded effect is desired.

Use wide stitch width for large letters and a narrower stitch width for small letters.

Floral Monograms

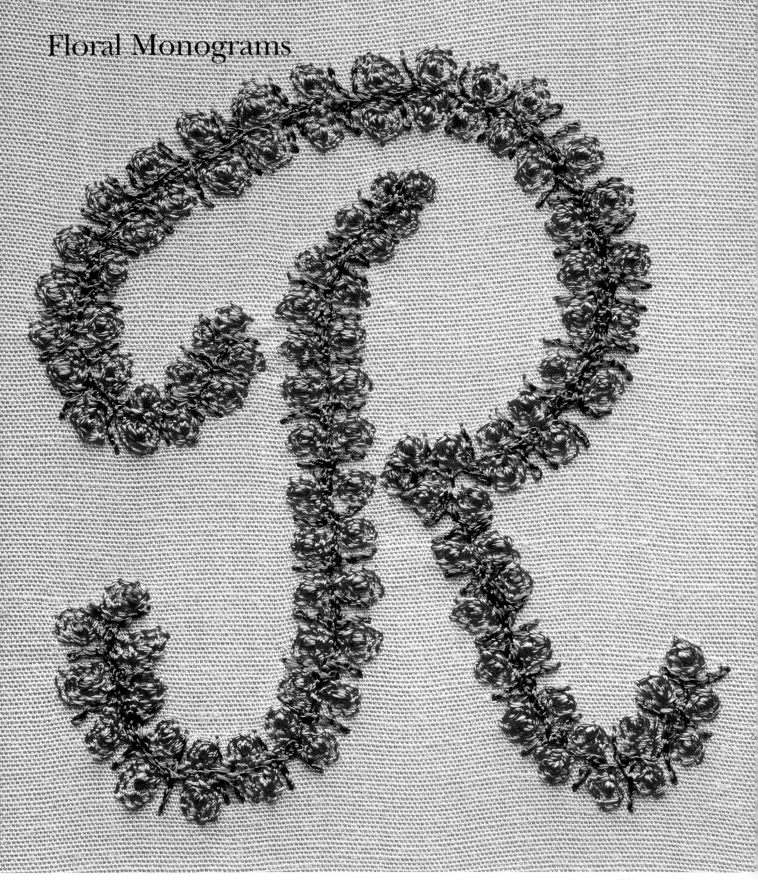

The floral monogram is made up of small flowers and leaves, and is sewn using free-motion embroidery techniques. This monogram can be added to bed linens or towels for a personal touch.

Letter styles that have smooth, curved lines are more appropriate for floral monograms than block styles. Select dark and light colors of thread to stitch the flowers and a green thread for the leaves.

How to Make Free-motion Floral Monograms

1) Draw 2" or 2½" (5 or 6.5 cm) letter on fabric with water-soluble marking pen. Draw small dots on each side of letter about ¼" (6 mm) apart; dots may be placed closer together on curves. Place fabric in the embroidery hoop.

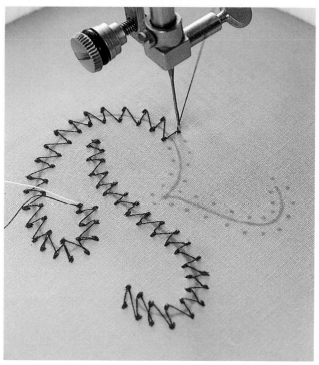

2) Set zigzag stitch to narrow width. Stitch in place on dot five or six times, using a dark-colored thread. Move across marked line to next dot; stitch in place. Continue until all dots are stitched, to make centers of flowers. Clip thread tails, but do not clip threads between dots.

3) Set machine for straight stitch; change to lighter-colored thread. Stitch around center of one flower; continue until all flowers are stitched. Clip thread tails, but do not clip threads between flowers.

4) Change to green thread. Using the straight stitch setting on machine, stitch leaves in curved motion, stitching in and out between the flowers.

Index

Creative Publishing international, Inc.
offers a variety of how-to books. For
information write:
   Creative Publishing international, Inc.
   Subscriber Books
   18705 Lake Drive East
   Chanhassen, MN 55317